THE COMPLETE BOOK OF
DECORATING

THE COMPLETE BOOK OF
DECORATING

Edited by Corinne Benicka

Exeter Books

NEW YORK

in association with Phoebus

This edition © Phoebus
Publishing Company/BPC Publishing Limited,
52 Poland Street, London W1A 2JX

First published in USA by
Exeter Books
Distributed by Bookthrift,
New York, NY 10018

This material first appeared in
Das grosse praktische Einrichtungsbuch
© 1976 Mosaik Verlag GmbH,
Verlagsgruppe Bertelsmann, München,
West Germany

Filmset by Tradespools Limited, Frome, Somerset
Made and printed in Great Britain by
Redwood Burn Limited, Trowbridge, Wilts.

ISBN 0 89673 048 4
Library of Congress Number 79-57471

CONTENTS

Consultants

John Crowther trained as an interior and furniture designer at the Central School of Art and Design, London, and has extensive experience in design practice. He became managing director of a specialist company designing and manufacturing furniture with a retail outlet covering all aspects of interior design.

During the latter part of his career, he was appointed to the staff of the Design Council where he worked for a number of years as a senior design adviser to the furniture industry.

Roger Daniels is an enthusiastic cabinet maker and has just finished compiling a major book on woodworking tools in conjunction with Record Tools, Sheffield and Garrett Wade in New York. He has also spent many a long weekend restoring an Edwardian house, and has first-hand experience of the do-it-yourself problems which are likely to be encountered.

Translated by Idiom Translation Services

Please note: When constructing the do-it-yourself items in this book, please keep to either the imperial or the metric measurements. Of necessity, the conversions cannot be exact, e.g. 1½ inches is given in metric measurements as 35 millimetres, whereas the exact conversion is 38.

INTRODUCTION

Here is a book packed with exciting, imaginative ideas for the design and decoration of your home. It will show you how to enhance your surroundings and go some way to achieving your ideal in home design. Even quite small adjustments, such as changing the way a room is lit, makes a major change to how it looks.

The Complete Book of Decorating concentrates on making the most of the good features of your home. You need not spend much money to make significant improvements to your home. It is all a matter of understanding good interior design and how it is best applied. For instance, the use of furniture with storage facilities, like beds and chairs which incorporate drawers, can help if you lack storage space. Sofas which convert into beds are invaluable if you have no spare bedroom.

Many other ideas to help in every part of your home are included, e.g., living rooms, kitchens, bathrooms, children's rooms, halls and bedrooms. For those prepared to invest some time in do-it-yourself there are projects ranging from simple coffee tables for the beginner to a four-poster bed for the experienced handyman. Instructions for the wallpapering, painting, tiling and various repairs are also included.

HOUSE AND HOME

Where would you rather live? In a modern, labour-saving apartment with all the modern appliances, or in a more spacious house where you can be your own master? In an older-style house with a wide range of rooms and correspondingly grander and more expensive style of furnishing? Or perhaps in a modernized period country cottage outside the town in the heart of the country?

Every kind of home has advantages and disadvantages. In an apartment you may be disturbed by noisy neighbours and you may find it necessary to restrict your own activities. A house, on the other hand, will prove more expensive than an apartment and you will have to shoulder some additional responsibilities. A period country cottage will involve high initial modernization and maintenance costs, and if too remote will lose its initial charm when you need to travel to work through snow and ice!

You will also have to bear in mind that your circumstances and style of living may change, so to save yourself the trouble of having to move several times, it is worthwhile seeking a home that will be adaptable to your future needs. An extra room, if you can afford it, can always be put to some use, if only as a spare bedroom to put up relatives and friends, and if you are starting a family it can always be converted from the study or spare bedroom into a nursery. As the family gets older and larger, you will probably have to move into a bigger home, but the time lapse may mean that you can at least afford it better. Later in life, when the family has grown up and left home, you will probably find your family home too large, and it may be more convenient to move into a smaller home.

Generally when buying a home it would seem to be worthwhile spending as much money as you can afford, not only because of its selling value, but also because moving is costly and time-consuming.

The main feature of this room is, of course, the beautiful, large window which shows off a marvellous view. A desk has been placed on the upper storey to make good use of the natural light.

Interlübke

8

Living in a one-roomed apartment

One-roomed apartments are very compact homes. All the objects that would be spread over several rooms in a larger home must be brought together into one room, and this must be done without clutter and overcrowding. The apartment will usually be occupied by only one person so it will need only a single bed, less storage space, a smaller table and fewer chairs than would be necessary for a family. Even so, this one room has to fulfil many functions. The occupant will need somewhere to sleep and sit, to eat and work, and much more besides.

All this makes special demands on the furnishings, therefore furniture which has more than one function will prove useful and practical. Typical examples include a bed which folds into a sofa or a wall cupboard; a wall storage system which includes shelves and a writing surface; seating which has storage drawers below (as illustrated opposite). As circumstances alter, it would be wise to choose furniture which at some later date can take its place in a larger home.

Now that we can buy multi-purpose furniture, it is much easier to furnish a one-roomed home. Whereas at one time many items of furniture had to stand side by side in the room, one item of furniture can now combine many functions.

A drop-down writing surface in a wall unit will be ample for any household writing tasks. All important papers and writing equipment can be stored in pigeon-holes provided behind the flap.

Drawers are very necessary, for in the course of time you will accumulate more small objects than you would imagine. Open shelves are not the best place to store these odds and ends. In a closed drawer you can organize them better and the room will remain neater.

It is advisable to choose the colour scheme for a one-roomed apartment with special care. One predominant colour may perhaps be combined with one contrasting colour, with very small amounts of a third colour. This should make the room look larger. A mixture of many bright colours would make it look smaller and more cluttered.

It will be easier to add to the furniture later if you choose coloured furniture. This is not the case with wood, as it is more difficult to match additional items.

This room has been furnished with a main central area (as seen from the plan below). It is made up of low seating and storage units, combined with one tall, narrow unit, and around this an aisle has been left free.

The distinguishing features of this room are the space-saving shelf units and seating which provides useful storage space below.

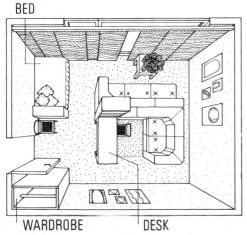

BED

WARDROBE   DESK

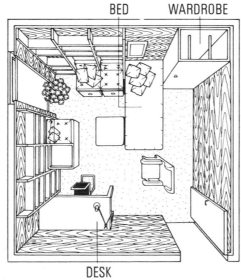

BED   WARDROBE

DESK

Living in an older house

Some people hunting for a new home may be looking for a larger or better equipped house, and one which is a little more expensive than their present home. In this case, an older house, perhaps one which is in need of modernization, may be suitable. Many of them were built at a time when not every house had a bathroom. The general sanitation, electrical wiring, heating and kitchen facilities will probably have to be improved to suit modern habits. Many have large rooms with very high ceilings, for when they were built people preferred to live in spacious surroundings at the cost of heating standards demanded today.

What can be done to make an old house more habitable? In most cases the first job will be to modernize the heating system and to replace the electrical wiring to modern standards and install new sanitary fittings.

Old floorboards can be ugly or damaged. If very uneven floors are to be carpeted, it will usually be necessary to cover the existing floorboards, after levelling and fixing loose boards as much as possible, with a layer of chipboard to provide a level surface on which fitted carpets or carpet tiles can be laid. (The latter have the advantage of being transportable when you move.) An intervening layer of cork or underfelt will improve sound and heat insulation.

If the ceilings are excessively high, and you would prefer them to be lower, a false ceiling can be installed. As a rule a wooden frame is hung below the old ceiling, to which sheets or planks of wood are attached. Instructions for putting in a false ceiling are given on page 66.

However, older houses are still popular, despite the various problems of dry rot, wet rot, woodworm and damp which may be encountered.

Set against these disadvantages are the appearance and atmosphere of an older property, features which frequently encourage the belief that whatever the cost of modernization, it is money well spent.

Of course, there are many older houses which have already been modernized, and where this has been done well, the character will have been preserved.

Modern furniture can look good in an older-type house, as shown here. The living room illustrated is from a house built in 1912, and original features, such as the mouldings on the ceiling, have been retained. The classically modern seating by the Danish designer Bernt form a charming contrast with this architectural detail, so that the room as a whole gives an impression of light, serenity and space.

Living in a country or holiday home

A country house out of town, imaginatively modernized and furnished, is the dream of many city dwellers. In theory this dream can be fairly easily realized. Old farmhouses, cottages, coach houses, stables and barns, generally with some land, can be bought comparatively cheaply. However, in practice, people tend to be over-optimistic about the modernization costs. One should neither buy nor plan the modernization of such property without professional advice. Anyone who has experienced the problems of modernizing such 'dream homes' is all too familiar with damp walls, rotting beams, supporting walls which are out of true, leaking roofs, crumbling chimneys, and so on.

Those who buy long neglected farmhouses and get builders to modernize them will often discover too late that modernization costs can work out considerably more than the original purchase price. So if you are making such plans you should attempt to do as much as possible yourself, and will probably have to give up a few holidays to work on it.

It can be less expensive actually to build a new holiday or weekend house in the country (depending of course on the state of the old property, and the size of the new). The first problem in achieving this dream is to find the plot of land.

ICI Paints Division

Opposite: This farmhouse-style kitchen is one that anybody would be happy to work in. It contains a beautiful blend of simplicity and functionality, reflecting the way of life for which it was designed. Many people who turn to living in the country do so as an alternative to high-speed city living, and because they prefer a more relaxed atmosphere.

Left: A coach house is a fashionable term for an elongated shed, in which carts and other agricultural tools were once kept. The illustration on the left shows a converted coach house. This is the comfortable living room, which has large gable windows.

Below: All the furniture here is made of solid wood, making it tough and resilient. Also most of it can be folded up or dismantled, which means that it is easily transported.

Assess the qualities of the house

What should you look for when choosing a new house? First you should have a good look at the neighbourhood, and then at the house itself.

You should not even consider any place that has a living room which measures less than 170 square feet (16 square metres). A room of 270 square feet (25 square metres) or more will offer the best possibilities for furnishing, providing the shape of the room is satisfactory. The best shape for a living room is rectangular, as it makes it easier to divide the room into separate areas. Two factors, size and shape, determine whether or not all the furniture from your previous living room will fit into the new one or whether one or more pieces will have to be sacrificed. You should therefore measure any large pieces of furniture (e.g., wall units, seating units) and check whether they will fit.

In addition, the living room should open off the hall; it should not be a so-called 'imprisoned room' to which you can gain access only through another room. It is of course also desirable that this room, in which much of your daily life will be spent, should have as much light as possible. The windows should therefore be south- or west-facing.

Light in the hall

If your house has an entrance hall, it should occupy no more than 10% of the living area, any more would be a waste of space. Look for a small hall, though not too narrow, which has not only enough room to hang hats and coats comfortably, but also receives sufficient light (usually through glass-panelled interior doors) to make it a cheerful reception area, even in daytime. If the hall is large, on the other hand, it can be used as a dining area or a play area for children. Possibly wardrobes from the bedroom could be used as hall cupboards, allowing the bedroom to be refurnished more spaciously.

Children need space

The following sizes are recommended for a child's bedroom: 160 square feet (15 square metres) for one child and 270

square feet (25 square metres) for a room shared by two children. If the children can have a large playroom near their bedrooms, which are used only for sleeping, then 110 square feet (10 square metres) will be a large enough size bedroom. This room needs daylight just as much as the living room and a west-facing bedroom is ideal here. For a playroom, on the other hand, it is important that little noise should penetrate beyond it, so that the children can at least make a noise in their own room without having to living in fear of angry neighbours. Similarly, the children's bedroom must be sheltered from outside noise so that their sleep is undisturbed during the day and night.

Bedrooms should be quiet

If you have bulky bedroom furniture and you want it to stand together in one room in the new house, you will have to measure the room in question thoroughly in advance, especially if your wardrobes were bought specifically to fit your old bedroom.

You should also bear in mind that here, as with the nursery, the room should be sheltered from night noise (traffic, neighbours, bathrooms).

Will your kitchen units fit?

With kitchens it is difficult to offer specific guidelines on size and layout, for a working person who is rarely at home will set less store by the kitchen than a person who spends every day cooking for a family of four. They will want the distance between the kitchen and the dining area to be as short as possible (if it cannot be in the kitchen itself). If in your old home you invested in a fitted kitchen, you should find out if it will fit into the new kitchen without necessitating extensive alterations.

A cooker and sink are the most important fittings in the kitchen, as most of the preparation and clearing away of meals are centred around these areas.

Refrigerators, freezers, washing machines and dishwashers also form a part of the modern kitchen. But frequently the necessary connections are not

present. In an old house, especially, it is advisable to find out whether the wiring is suitable for such high loads.

Kitchen windows are not as good for ventilation purposes as an extractor fan with an external outlet, but if there are windows they should open outwards so that when open they cannot obstruct the work surfaces.

The ideal bathroom

If the bathroom has to withstand the assault of a large family every morning it will have to be large and sensibly laid out: in a family bathroom a separate shower cubicle would be an advantage. A further shower over the bath should also be included. If there is room, two wash-basins would also save time in the morning. If you have a bidet too, your ideal bathroom is complete.

Separate W.C.

If there is only one W.C., and this is in the bathroom, it can really only serve a family of two. In a larger family, the W.C. should be in a different room. If possible, the separate W.C. should also have a small wash-basin.

If there is enough room and the size of the family requires it, you could install a large basin here to provide an alternative place for children to wash. This would ease the demands on the bathroom.

Balconies and patios

Balconies and patios need not serve only as external decoration, they can also be useful. That means that you should be able to bring out a table and chairs and still have room to move. It also means that they should not overlook a busy road.

If possible these outside areas should be on the sunny side of the building and out of view of the neighbours. If covered, you can also use these areas on rainy days, and by building solid or glass walls you will gain an extra living room for the summer.

Left: The rustic atmosphere is accentuated by natural colours.

Below: This beautiful fireplace has been emphasized by painting it white.

Bottom: The dark wood used in this country kitchen adds sophistication.

Plan your furnishings to scale on paper

As soon as you have decided on a new home, the next important question to consider is where your main items of furniture will go. If you have carefully measured both your existing furniture and the rooms of your new home, you should avoid any nasty surprises – such as not finding out until you move in that the large wall unit is too tall, or realizing too late that it will not be possible to stand the refrigerator by the kitchen door, because it would prevent the door opening and closing.

You can avoid difficulties of this kind if in advance you make a precise plan on paper to scale of the rooms of the house or apartment. You can also make cutout pieces of thin cardboard to represent your pieces of furniture to the same scale, so that you can experiment with different layouts.

The ground plan
A ground plan shows the layout of the rooms in any building seen from above with no distortions of perspective. Although it can only represent areas which are in fact three-dimensional (length, width and height) in two dimensions (length and width) it remains an essential requirement in all building, modernizing or furnishing undertakings. It is therefore important to know how to draw and interpret a plan.

In a single-storey building, there will be only one plan, and in a house of two or more storeys, there will be a plan for each floor. While the architect may produce drawings to smaller scales for planning permission purposes depending on the size of the overall development, the one which will be seen by the individual purchaser will probably be to the scale ¼ inch to 12 inches (or 1 to 50 millimetres) on the ground. This plan will show the general layout of the buildings, including the thicknesses of external and internal walls (these will be heavily lined-in so that they stand out quite clearly), the position of fireplace openings, windows and doors, and the direction in which they open. Although the plan is drawn to scale, it should also have the main dimensions marked on it. It may also have

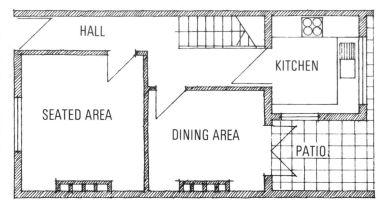

This is the simple ground plan drawing. All the walls are shaded so that window and door openings stand out clearly. The direction in which the doors open are marked clearly. The stairs are shown leading upstairs.

certain vertical heights indicated, like the overall room height, height of window-sills and door openings. In any case, these are very important and should be measured by you if you don't know what they are. In fact, you should check all the measurements as there may be variations between the drawings and the building.

This plan will be adequate for getting a complete picture of the layout and will do for preliminary planning, but for more detailed and accurate planning you should draw plans of the individual rooms to the scale ½ inch to 12 inches (or 1 to 20 millimetres) on the ground. You can buy squared graph paper which will represent the different scales and will also help you draw your lines at right angles.

Onto your large-scale drawing you will have plenty of space to include those details missing from the small plan, such as the heights already mentioned. Sill heights, for example, are particularly important in the kitchen, where there are fitted units. A sill lower than the height of your base units would obviously present a problem which you will need to solve now, and should not be left until everything has been delivered and is about to be installed. It is also a good idea to include the powerpoints and water supply positions. Now you are ready to begin planning your furniture. The idea of cutting out pieces of cardboard to represent the main items of furniture has already been mentioned. Another useful method is to lay a sheet of tracing paper over your plan on which you can experiment with different layouts until you find the one that works best.

Always stick precisely to the measurements, because there is a temptation to make something a little smaller so that you can just squeeze it in where you particularly want to put it. Remember too that storage cupboards are really bigger than your measurements, as you have to allow for doors and drawers to open. If you show chairs close around a table, remember that there has to be room to move then back when the occupant gets up. And you cannot place a piece of storage furniture too near a door in a corner, as it would prevent you opening the door fully.

Despite all your efforts a furniture plan can only provide a flat representation of a room. If you can draw well you might be able to do a perspective drawing (an example of this is illustrated right), which gives a better idea of the effect of the room.

A cardboard model is even more precise. You must start from the dimensions and sizes shown in the plan. Floors, walls (with doors and windows cut out), stairs and furniture must all be carefully drawn, cut out and stuck together. You can cut the furniture out of polystyrene or even construct it from cardboard.

Cardboard models should be built to the scale of at least ½ inch to the 12 inches (1 to 20 millimetres), otherwise it becomes a very difficult job. For added realism, you can even represent the position of the sun in the model by shining a torch at varying angles to gain some idea of how the light will affect your arrangement.

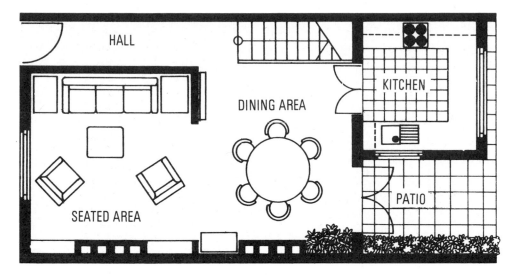

This is the same ground plan as shown in the left-hand diagram, with the furniture added. The walls between the living and dining areas and between the dining area and the hall have been removed. The kitchen fittings have been changed. Units have been built in the living room (lower edge of diagram) and there is also a conventional sofa and matching chairs with a coffee table and other tables to the left and right of the sofa.

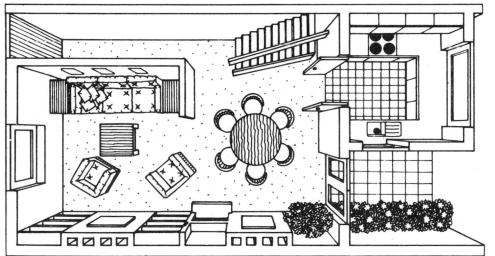

This type of perspective view introduces a third dimension, the height of the room. Many details can now be recognized more clearly. The units at the lower edge of the diagram can be seen as shelf units. The open fireplace on the left near the right-hand flues serves no useful purpose. The plants on the patio continue into the living area.

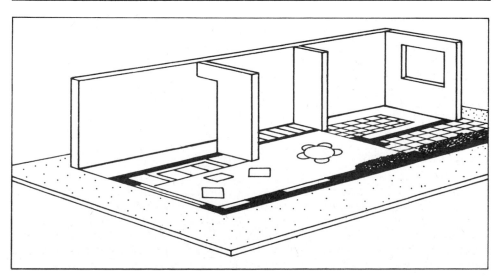

Clearest of all is a cardboard model of the house or flat. You start with the ground plan which gives all the lengths and widths. In addition heights are included, but you will have to measure these yourself – not only the ceiling height but also the heights of doors, windows, windowsills, etc. It is best to make the model on a wooden base. You can also build scale models of your pieces of furniture.

COLOUR AND LIGHT

Without light there would be no colours. Sunlight is white and is made-up of electromagnetic waves of varying wavelengths. By use of a prism it can be split up into its constituent parts to produce the whole colour range, the spectrum – as in a rainbow. Each wavelength produces a particular colour effect.

When light of varying wavelengths enters the eye, a uniform colour effect is created and is interpreted by the brain. Most of the things around us emit no light themselves. Their colours are produced when light falls on them (sunlight, candlelight, electric light, etc.) which is partly reflected and partly absorbed. For example, a carpet which is red reflects only red light and absorbs light of all other wavelengths.

In physical terms reflected and absorbed light are complementary, following the principle that complementary colours when combined always produce white (in terms of light). For example, if yellow is absorbed, we see its opposite purple. Likewise the colour combinations red and green, blue and orange are complementary.

Since colours affect our moods and feelings we should be concerned about the colours around us and try to improve our awareness of colour tones and combinations. Even in olden times, it was recognized that red has a warm, stimulating effect; blue on the other hand is cool and soothing. In the Middle Ages many doctors attributed healing powers to colours. Smallpox victims, for example, were put into rooms with red walls, furniture and bed linen. Epileptics were placed on a purple carpet and quack doctors gave assurances that yellow had a favourable influence upon diseases of the stomach.

Today scientists are investigating the psychological effect of colours and industry has found it beneficial to make use of their findings. Salerooms are decorated in colours that will encourage spending and offices and factories in colours which encourage production.

We should also have the right colours in the home. 'Laymen often make the mistake of thinking that the choice of grey will avoid any colour problems and satisfy every taste', writes the colour psychologist Max Lüscher. 'One might just as well say that all food should be unsalted and unspiced to satisfy every taste.'

Light is almost as important as colour in a room. These two creative elements can be used to create a mood, to make rooms appear larger or smaller and to disguise any unpleasant features. When we speak of light we mean more the tone of light created than the lamps used to produce it. Together with the use of light and shade, the choice of the right type and colour of light is most important. In a living room, a warm, yellowish light is usually preferred.

The colour wheel, showing the three primary colours in the centre. The complementaries of every colour in the wheel are shown directly opposite each other. Complementary colours provide the strongest contrast of all.

The photograph (right) shows a living room whose main features (carpets, walls, sofa frame, tables) are all the same colour.

Colour in the home

These next two pages will help you to understand how colour schemes are created. This will be useful if you are planning new curtains, wallpaper or carpets to go with the colours of the furniture already present in the room or, alternatively, if you are completely refurnishing a room or apartment and you want to achieve a pleasant and interesting effect.

When you put two colours together, you will get a contrast and this contrast must be a harmonious one. Colours can harmonize – like music – but only if certain rules are observed.

There are three basic colours – the primary colours – red, yellow and blue. These can be combined to make secondary colours – i.e. red and yellow make orange; blue and yellow make green; red and blue make violet or purple (depending on how much of each colour you use). There is an unlimited number of colour combinations, in theory at least. Added to this is the possibility of lightening every colour by adding white, or darkening it by adding black. In this way, you get lighter or darker shades of the same basic colour. The soft contrast which this produces is here called tone-on-tone harmony.

A second possibility is to combine one of the main colours with its neighbouring colour. This will give a fairly strong contrast and is quite popular in furnishing schemes.

Here are some combinations and the effect they generally produce: green/yellow can give a very sunny feel to a room, as does yellow/orange; purple/red and purple/blue can look very grand as they are traditionally regal colours. The latter can look particularly pleasant if used in pastel shades; green/blue is restful and fresh-looking, while red/orange would be very warm and enervating and particularly suitable for a room which does not receive much sunlight and would therefore have a fairly cold atmosphere.

However, if you combine complementary colours (e.g. red/green, yellow/purple, orange/blue) you will normally get too strong a contrast depending on how bright the colours are.

Yellow as the main colour in a room makes it look bright and sunny. If we combine a rich yellow with lighter or darker shades of yellow, the result is tone-on-tone harmony. This produces a very soft colour contrast. The effect will be more exciting if we combine it with its neighbouring colours for this brings together completely different colour values. The strongest contrast is produced by combining yellow and purple. The purple must be used sparingly or the constrast between these complementary colours would make the room feel uncomfortable.

Red is an active colour, and combining it with different colours can produce many different effects. With the tone-on-tone contrast the red is tinted by the lighter shades. When combined with neighbouring colours, on the other hand, it is intensified. For example, red stands out vividly against brown, and orange intensifies the impression of heat. The contrasting of its complementary colour, green, can give a very sophisticated effect if you use slightly darker shades of the basic colours.

Green as the main colour in a room: some very pretty shades of green can be seen by using tone-on-tone harmony. In the middle illustration we have chosen yellow as a neighbouring colour. Both here and with the contrasting of complementary colours, it is important to choose the right shade of green. The one chosen here (left) is neither too loud nor too vivid, so that it combines well with other colours to give a pleasant, harmonious effect, and also goes well with many types of wood.

Blue is the darkest and also the most peaceful colour of the colours used in these examples. It should therefore generally be used with lighter colours. You can use it with lighter shades of the same colour (tone-on-tone), right through to white, or with lighter, more exciting neighbouring colours (like pale green or lilac). Constrasting it with complementary colours is more difficult, and you would have to be very careful with the exact shades that you want to use.

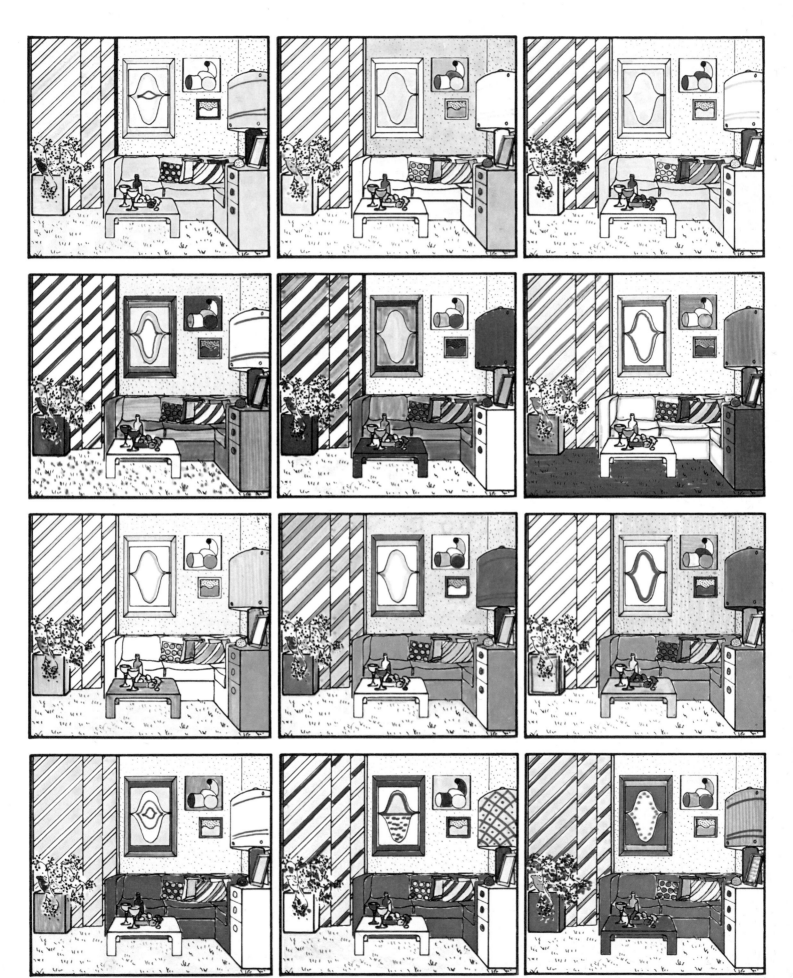

Camouflage

Colour can do many things. It can make rooms look bigger or smaller. Colour can give a room a warm or cold atmosphere. It can also camouflage. It can change things that you don't like or things that irritate you to such an extent that you will hardly notice them.

To have this effect, colour need not always be applied in the form of paint. The same effects can be achieved with wallpaper or fabrics.

Individual features of a room can be given a lively or even dramatic effect if accentuated by colour. It is purely a matter of personal taste which features to disguise and which to emphasize. The photographs show in each case the same room and the same furniture. Only the colours of the walls, ceiling, floor and window frames have been changed.

Where should you begin when deciding on the colour scheme for a room? First of all you should consider the light, because without light there is no colour at all. This means that you will only be able to decide about the colours if you know the amount of light which each room gets and for how long. Very light rooms can be decorated in cool colours (with shades of blue or green), rooms which do not get much sun need warm colours (shades of yellow and red). It is also very important to consider at what time of day the room will mainly be used. Morning light produces a different effect from afternoon light – and, often, if the colours in a room are suited to sunlight there will be a complete change of effect in the evening with artificial light.

If you already have some of the furniture you will have to use their colours as a basis and the rest of the fittings will have to tone or contrast with them. It will probably be only rarely that you decide on more than two basic colours.

Usually you will have to decide on your colours by comparing small colour or pattern samples. For example you can compare wood, curtain and carpet samples (against a white background!) to see how they match. Take these samples with you when you go to buy materials because they will help you to explain what you want.

Left: Both the walls and panelling are painted in a sandy colour so that you scarcely notice the wooden panelling. The stuccoed frieze has disappeared behind a wooden screen. The period characteristics of this room have been disguised. *Below left:* In contrast, the period characteristics have been emphasized. Their light stone colour contrasts with the walls which have been painted an earthy, dark brown colour.

Two treatments for an attic (illustrated below): In the left-hand photograph the window has the same paper as the walls. The raffia blind is the same colour tone as the paper. This camouflage gives a snug atmosphere. In the right-hand photograph the emphasis given to the window alcove by the white border makes the same attic richer in contrast.

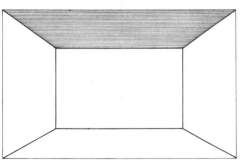

1. Bold ceiling colour: The room may look lower than it actually is.

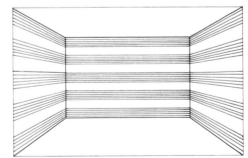

2. Horizontal stripes: The room may look bigger but lower.

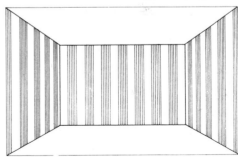

3. Vertical stripes: The room may look higher but smaller.

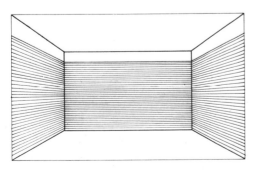

4. Frieze: The room may look lower; not generally recommended.

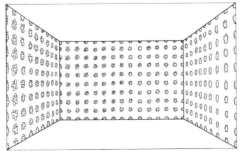

5. Small patterned paper: The room may look bigger than it is.

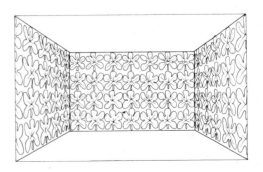

6. Large patterned paper: The room may look smaller that it actually is.

Using wood in the home

Wood is a natural product like wool or leather. All these natural products can be combined with almost any colour. Nevertheless you should restrict yourself to one type of wood in a room as far as you possibly can – or choose two woods with similar characteristics. For in addition to different tones, woods also have different characteristics. There are rustic woods and elegant woods. When you are furnishing a room you should decide first on the type of wood you want for the furniture. The particular colour of the wood you choose will provide a basic colour for the room. It is then easy to build on this with further shades.

Oak: A hard, very resistant wood with a clearly marked grain. It gives a strong, powerful effect. Because of its cream colour, oak can be combined with practically any colour and shade in the living room, but it will go best with earthy colours. Also it is often stained brown.

Pine: A soft, clearly marked coniferous wood. Its warm colour is most attractive and this becomes gradually deeper with age to be more beautiful still. It goes well with strong, bright colours like yellow.

Mahogany: A traditional furniture wood, the best coming from America. Many varied grains and colours of red are found. As with oak, it is sometimes stained to give a richer shade. Its warm colour can be used in a delicate colour scheme, with contrasting cool colours.

Rosewood: Usually deep reddish-brown to purplish-black, dense, hard and beautifully figured. This elegant wood should be combined with restrained colours.

Teak: A light to deep golden-brown wood with a darker brown grain. It goes well with bright, expressive colours. Greens go with it admirably, as do many shades of orange.

Sapele: A reddish-brown wood with a striped grain from West Africa. Pastel colours go best with it but it can also be used with bright, strong colours.

Earthy colours go well with dark-stained oak (far left) since they emphasize its slightly coarse, rustic effect.

Pine is a light, simple wood (below), which will fit into any colour scheme.

Mahogany is the traditional wood for fine furniture (bottom). Its warm colour gives a room a feeling of elegance.

Creating a mood

Once people were satisfied with hanging a single light fitting in the middle of the living room and maybe placing a floor lamp for reading or working. Today's interior decorators no longer think that this is the best way of lighting a room.

'Planned lighting' can make a room friendlier, more comfortable and more homely. Electric lighting is no substitute for daylight, but it is an important element in creating a mood. Just like colour, light can emphasize or disguise certain features in your room. It can divide one area from another, give shape to surfaces, accentuate or repress colours. It can be either static or flexible. Good lighting is not always cheap but the running costs can usually be kept within reasonable limits.

Light intensity

The intensity of light at one particular point in the room depends on the type and wattage of the fittings used, on the amount of light produced (fluorescent light produces on average about four times as much light as tungsten lights), and on the distance and direction of the light source. The prevailing intensity of light, taking all these factors (and others) into account, is measured in lux (abbreviated lx). A scientifically precise measurement of light intensity (for example, used by lighting engineers in planning lighting equipment for a factory or office) is given as a nominal value of lux. Then types of lights and wattage, positioning, direction, colour, etc. are determined.

The same lux value can be achieved in quite different ways. To achieve 250 lux a direct light would only require a 75-watt bulb. The frosted glass of a globe lamp reduces efficiency to such an extent that a 200-watt bulb would be required to achieve the same 250 lux. When planning the lighting for your home there is no need to buy a light meter, the eye alone should be able to tell you when you need a weak or a strong light:

Weaker lamps: Lights near the surface to be illuminated; direct lights; no screening off of the direction of the beam; light-coloured walls.

Stronger lamps: Shaded lights or those which are quite far away from the surface to be illuminated; semi-direct or indirect positioning; dark walls.

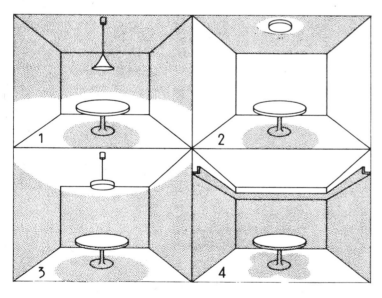

You should be familiar with the four basic types of lighting if you want to use planned lighting as a means of creating atmosphere in your home. (1) A low direct light usually casts deep shadows. (2) Direct light from the ceiling illuminates the room evenly. (3) Semi-indirect light is provided by lamps where all the light is directed upwards. (4) Indirect light, supplied here by strip lighting, illuminates the ceiling. It will usually be accompanied by other sources of light.

Four ways of arranging lights: (1) An overhead light illuminating a narrowly defined area, here the dining table. (2) A row of lights, here pendent lights, used above a sofa. (3) A floor lamp providing background lighting with a wall lamp shining directly onto the sofa for reading. (4) Ceiling light and wall light in a bedroom complement each other well. The ceiling light should be fairly bright.

Above: Here all the light is concentrated on the dining area. The dining table, adjoining walls and ceiling are lit by five spotlights.

Left: Eight spotlights are here directed onto the ceiling, so that the room has indirect lighting. This gives a soft, cosy light to set an intimate mood.

Below: The collection of pictures behind the sofa, collector's items contained in the wall units and one individual picture near the dining table are here directly lit to emphasize the most attractive items in the room.

Flexible lighting systems

Although it is impossible to change the position of the connection of your light source without undertaking expensive conversion work, modern lighting systems are so versatile that it may not be necessary. A good mobile system is for several spotlights to be mounted on a track which can be positioned on the wall or the ceiling (depending on where the connections are). Spotlights give a very flexible light because you can direct it in whatever direction you wish. It is also possible to buy spotlights which have adjustable arms for mounting on the wall.

Spotlights

Spotlights consist of a metal shade containing a tungsten light. The fitting can be swivelled on its mounting clamp. There are spotlights with simple spring clamps or with screw-clamps. Lights of this kind can be fixed to a shelf, for example, or to a headboard of a bed or table top.

Spotlights make it possible to change the lighting in a room many times; sometimes very bright, sometimes lowered. The three photographs on page 29 demonstrate how you can dispense with the usual pendent, table and floor lamps in a room: all the light is provided by spotlights, none of which have a fixed place.

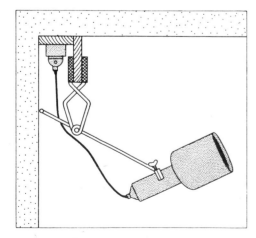

Spotlights need not be fixed in one place, but can be moved from one place to another. If you use a pelmet this will also conceal the point of supply.

They can be fixed in different positions in the room, so that they can be used for background lighting, the intensity of which can be regulated by switching on only one lamp – or four or five at the same time.

So the lighting has become mobile. The lamps are not all fixed and the direction of the light can be easily changed. The spotlights can be directed upwards to give a splendid, bright indirect light, or you can have a group of lamps over the dining table with only one other light, perhaps shining over a picture. You can have a row of spotlights over your wall of pictures or your shelf units. You can fix them to a low shelf, windowsill or table top to create a magical light effect which illuminates from below.

A low-level modern light fitting doesn't look out of place in this country-style dining area. It is positioned so that the whole table area is well lit, but the light won't dazzle those sitting down.

You can use a few lights to create a uniform light and then shine spotlights onto a bright area of colour, a beautiful picture or particular items in a collection which you feel proud of. The possibilities are endless.

Mobile lighting of this kind need not be expensive. In general, spotlights will always give a lot of light in relation to their cost. Nevertheless, you may find that you need additional light fittings. If you do, it is best to call in the electrician to fit extra light sources, because doing it yourself can be very dangerous.

Light tracks

When you are in a shop or gallery look not only at the goods on display but also at how the counters or walls are lit, and in many cases you will find light fittings like the one illustrated below: lights fitted onto a track. These lights can be moved along the track, and, as we mentioned before, they can also be turned and angled. You can either use them to light a room or to pick out certain objects in a room.

Track lighting can be used, for example, to give effective, non-dazzle lighting for a wall of pictures; to pick out individual objects in a wall unit or display cabinet; to emphasize certain areas of a room without the light itself getting in the way; to light a ceiling from a wall track (in old rooms, for example, where there is a particularly fine ceiling) to give the room a strong or, perhaps, subtle, indirect lighting.

The most practical aspect of these systems is that since the lights are fixed to the ceiling or just below it, the lights themselves are never in the way. Another practical aspect lies in the fact that you can build up the system and have more than one track, joined either to make a longer track, or at right angles.

Rctraflex Homelighting

Some different models of spotlights are shown below: (1) Cylindrical (2) Spherical (3) Narrow-beam reflector (4) Moulded glass reflector (5) Metal reflector for normal or reflector bulbs (6) Contour spotlight.

Here is a light track system which is fixed in a right angle, such that all parts of the spacious room are well lit. This kind of system is ideal because you can turn the spotlights to wherever you want, e.g. the seating area.

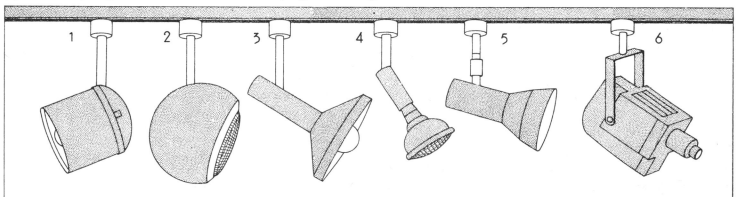

Lighting ideas to make yourself

What can you do to improve the lighting in your home or to make it more original? The easiest way is to use lamp or lampshade kits available from large stores, hardware and do-it-yourself shops. There are, for example, kits for wooden lamps or wire frames for shades for pendent and table lamps. The wooden lights have only to be glued together, the frames are covered with fabric, paper or even plastic sheets. The following suggestions are a bit more complicated.

False ceiling with lighting
The diagram on the right shows how a false ceiling, made from planks for a hall that is too high, should look.

The ceiling is made up of U-shaped boxes, their length is determined by the size of the room, and they are about 16 inches (400 millimetres) wide and 3 inches (80 millimetres) deep and placed at intervals of about 10 inches (250 millimetres). The planks used are of 1-inch (25-millimetre) pine. You could also use chipboard of a corresponding thickness.

The under and side pieces are glued and screwed together. These will be fixed to the wall by means of 14-inch (350-millimetre) battens with a cross-section 2 by 1 inches (50 by 30 millimetres). The battens are fixed to the wall using wood screws and wall plugs – exact measurements are most important. The pine boxes are screwed to the battens with wood screws.

If the pine boxes have been neatly made they can be stained and given a matt finish. If the screwheads are to remain visible use raised-head screws. Flat-headed screws should be countersunk 1/16 inch (2 millimetres) deep and covered with plastic wood. Chipboard boxes should be primed, filled, sanded and painted. They could also be covered with fabric or have plastic sheeting stuck or nailed to them.

Each box contains a fluorescent tube, which does not necessarily need to be screwed down – it is sufficient merely to place them in the boxes. The connections for each tube, which should be able to be switched on and off from the hall light

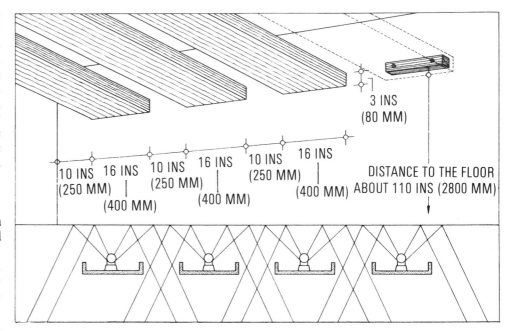

10 INS (250 MM) 16 INS (400 MM) 10 INS (250 MM) 16 INS (400 MM) 10 INS (250 MM) 16 INS (400 MM)

3 INS (80 MM)

DISTANCE TO THE FLOOR ABOUT 110 INS (2800 MM)

This example of a beamed ceiling with indirect lighting is especially suitable for dark halls. U-shaped box units are glued and screwed together and fitted from wall to wall, being fixed to battens which are nailed or screwed to the wall. The boxes contain fluorescent tubes which need only be placed in the centre of each box.

switch, should be installed by an electrician and preferably plastered in. In place of the fluorescent tubes you can use less expensive light bulbs. Each box will need at least two, depending on the width of the hall. The bulbholders are screwed to the inside of the box.

Pelmet with indirect lighting
Curtain pelmets and fluorescent tubes can be used together. Thus, when the lights are on, the window wall with its curtains or blind will be emphasized. Lighting of this kind is mainly used for decorative effect rather than as a light source. Only in exceptional circumstances would you use the combination of pelmet and fluorescent light as the sole light source.

The simplest method is to combine a normal curtain rail with a pelmet in front

of it behind which the light is housed. The tube-holder is either screwed to the curtain fittings (with a wall mounting) or to the pelmet. Of course it can also be fixed to the wall or ceiling. It is best to try out the light effect before fitting the tube, as this will prevent any surprises afterwards. There are several possibilities:

Narrow downwards beam (top right): the curtain pelmet is positioned immediately below the ceiling. The fluorescent tube-holder sits on the curtain fixture. No light can go upwards. The light falls on the curtains which are strongly illuminated at the top and more weakly lower down.

Narrow beam upwards and downwards (right): the curtain pelmet is positioned just above the window and the curtain fitting is correspondingly lower. The fluorescent tube, which is placed on the curtain fitting, illuminates the curtains and part of the ceiling also.

Wide beam upwards: the curtain fittings and pelmet are positioned as in the second example. The fluorescent tube-holder is fastened to the pelmet so that light goes only upwards.

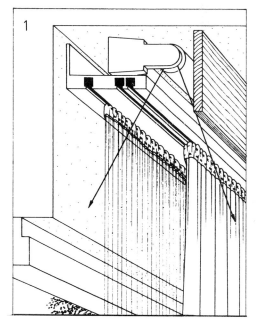

Ceiling light

Another possible way of installing ceiling lighting in a hall or other dark corner is with a fabric-covered frame. In contrast to the beamed ceiling described above, the frames are set close together and so form an uninterruped mass.

The frame is made from 3 by 1 inch (80 by 30 millimetre) battening, nailed or screwed together (you can also strengthen the corners with steel corner plates). The length of the frame depends on the width of the hall, from which you will have to deduct 2½ inches (60 millimetres) to allow for the hanging fixtures. The frame should be between 20 and 30 inches (500 and 800 millimetres) wide.

The whole frame is covered with muslin or cheap lining material. The material is held in place by upholstery tacks (short nails with flat, wide heads). It is important that the material should be well and evenly tensioned to prevent it sagging later. When the frame has been covered, 1 by 1 inch (25 by 25 millimetre) battens are nailed to both narrow sides of the frame flush with the top edge.

The frame is supported by 1½ by 1½ inch (30 by 30 millimetre) battens screwed to the long walls of the hall at the right height. The small battens on the frame rest on these supports. In this way you will find that the frame itself will conceal the supports.

Tungsten lights hang above the frame providing a soft, non-dazzle lighting. You will have to experiment to see how many lights you need. When a bulb needs replacing you can take down one or more of the frames and replace them without difficulty.

You can emphasize the window wall by using this curtain rail above which is a fluorescent tube. Here only the curtains are illuminated.

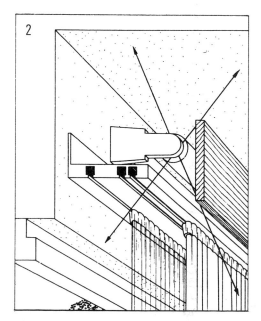

With this arrangement, both the curtains and ceilings are illuminated. You can also position the tube so that only the ceiling is illuminated.

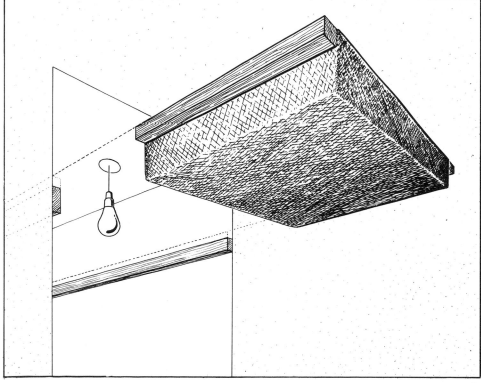

Diffused lighting in a hallway can be achieved by constructing a wooden frame covered with a suitable material like muslin. A batten is fixed to the sides of the frame which rest upon two battens attached to the side walls. This allows for easy removal of the frame for cleaning and replacement of light bulbs.

Better lighting for all your rooms

The choice of the right light fitting is not always easy, but you need only follow a few rules. It is important to start with the function of the room or area and to choose your lighting accordingly. It is important to have non-dazzle lighting – by either screening the light source, directing the beam of light or increasing the light surface. It is equally important to allow for an amount of variation when choosing the type and intensity of your lights, and to avoid letting the room take on a boring atmosphere in the evening. Here are some tips for better lighting in some of the most important parts of the house.

Light for the dining table

At the dining table the source of light should be directly in front of you, so when choosing your light the style is not too important. What is important is that the light works effectively and does not dazzle, so choose a light in which all – or almost all – the light is directed downwards, and there is only weak sideways illumination. Your eyes should not look directly into the light, so lights with a metal shade are ideal. Domed lights of coloured glass and thick fabric shades are also recommended. Plain glass domes and light, translucent textiles are not recommended for these will dazzle. The whole table top should be evenly lit, so the shade should not be too small nor the cone of light too narrow. Otherwise only the centre of the table will be well lit and the plates will be in semi-darkness.

It is also particularly important to hang the light at the right height: just above eye level or at least high enough to avoid the eyes being dazzled by the bright inside surface of the shade.

Adjustable rise and fall lamps have become fashionable again, because they make it easy to get the correct height. If the light bulb is to be visible, use a crown silvered bulb which only emits reflected light.

Directed light

Light for reading, knitting or doing crossword puzzles should be directed light which shines only on the object which you are handling and not into your eyes. Here you should choose lights which emit a directed beam, since the light source will be surrounded by an opaque shade. To get the best light for everything you may want to do in your 'reading chair', choose an adjustable light. If you can raise and also angle the light you can control the direction and intensity of the light. Floor lights are generally better here than table lights. You won't need a table to stand it on, so the table is left free for other things. In addition the light can stand behind the chair so that you will not be dazzled.

The position of the light can also be important for watching television, otherwise you may find that the light is being reflected onto the screen, preventing you from getting a good picture. Many armchair lamps are on a stand. A flat base supports a rod of varying thickness along which the lamp and its shade can be moved up and down, turned and angled.

Overhanging curved lamps are also used over armchairs and can look very elegant. They can be placed slightly away from the chair or sofa, but the light can still be directed. With many lamps of this kind you can adjust the height of the arc. Spotlights too can usually be swivelled.

Bedside lights

If you find the usual light in the centre of the ceiling too boring, you can use pelmet lighting with the light directed downwards and upwards (onto the ceiling) to provide indirect light. Instructions for this can be found on page 33.

Just as important as the general lighting is the choice of bedside light. You need good light so that you can read in bed without straining your eyes. But on the other hand bedside lights should not illuminate too wide an area, or your partner in the double bed, who might have finished reading, won't be able to get to sleep. Well designed bedside lights give directed light with a narrow cone of light. They should be able to swivel or have an adjustable shade so that you can regulate the amount of light or angle it in a particular direction.

Many lights can be fixed to the wall. This has the advantage of removing them from your field of vision when you are lying in bed or leaning against the wall. You will not be dazzled and you will be able to read longer than with a lamp which makes you read with your eyes half closed. These models also leave more room on the bedside table.

You will need a separate, directed, adjustable light if you have a sewing or writing table, make-up or manicure area in the bedroom.

Even light for a work table

Even if a writing desk in the home is used less often than one in an office, it is still important to have the correct light. As a rule it will be used mainly in the evening under artificial light. The light should be adjustable and the table surface should be evenly lit.

For a long time such lights have always had metal or opaque plastic shades, and even now it is difficult to buy anything else. If you choose a less functional light make sure that the shade does not allow too much sideways light. You can adjust a narrow cone of light if the lamp is variable. Lights which clamp onto the table are ideal, for they occupy no surface area. Wall lights with an adjustable arm are also very good. If the table stands against a wall you may want to direct the light onto the wall. The light is then reflected off it so that it is softer and will light a larger area. You should only use wall lights when the adjoining wall is to the left of the table – that is if you are right-handed.

Light in the bathroom

A 60-watt bulb in a glass dome on the bathroom ceiling serves its purpose of overall lighting, but more important are lights near the mirror over the washbasin – in small bathrooms these can replace overall lighting.

Generally a fluorescent tube the same length as the mirror is fitted over it. If you want more sophisticated light fittings you can fit a tube either side of the mirror. This ensures shadow-free, bright light. If you want to use domed lights you will need at least two, one either side of

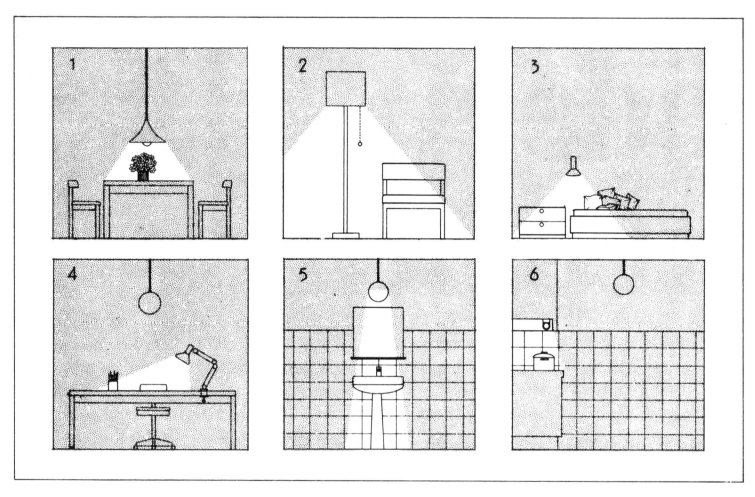

the mirror, and they should be installed just above head height. This is the best height to give a good light for shaving, brushing your hair or putting on make-up. For safety reasons, bathroom lights must be waterproof.

A light for kitchen work surfaces

Like the bathroom, the kitchen is often not very well lit. The ceiling light should only be used to give overall background lighting. It is more important to have lights under the wall units or on the wall. Only in this way can you ensure that the work surfaces will be free from shadow.

Fluorescent tubes are ideal for they light a wide area and can be fixed fairly low: they can also be screened by a narrow wooden pelmet.

It is worth having separate (or additional) powerpoints for your lights for you never have enough powerpoints over the work surfaces in these days of electrical kitchen gadgets. Individual lights generally have their own switches so that they need be switched on only when the adjoining work surface is being used. This is better than having all the wall lights operated by the switch for the ceiling light.

Hall lighting

Since halls generally receive little light at any time of day, you should not economize on lighting here. The ideal is soft background lighting, as provided, for instance, by built-in, concealed fluorescent tubes or a lighted ceiling (see page 32). Any hall cupboards can have extra lights, possibly spotlights. If you have a wardrobe in the hall, you could fix a fluorescent tube light above it.

Directed light for all parts of the house: (1) The lamp over the dining table should light the whole table without dazzling. (2) A floor lamp provides a good, clear light to read by. (3) Bedside lights should not give too wide a beam and should be able to swivel or turn in any direction. (4) A work table needs a particularly even light. (5) The bathroom mirror should be lit to avoid shadows. (6) In the kitchen, each work surface should have its own light. You will need a background light too.

FLOOR AND STAIR COVERINGS

There are two different types of floors found in houses today:

Suspended floors: These will be found in most older houses at ground level, and in both old and new houses at other levels: at ground level they consist of wooden floorboards laid on wooden joists, which in turn rest on wooden plates on 'sleeper' walls. At other levels the floorboards are supported on joists spanning between structural walls.

Floorboards have a tendency to warp so that the joints between the boards will show through thin flooring materials. In the case of linoleum, some form of underlay is sufficient to overcome this, but with thin vinyl tiles or sheets, it is necessary to cover the floor first with hardboard or even thin chipboard. In fact, in new houses where suspended floors are found, sheet materials are used initially rather than the traditional floorboards.

Solid floors: At ground level the suspended wooden floor has been superseded by concrete sub-floors in all types of buildings. In small-scale domestic properties upper floors may still be of the suspended type, but in flats, etc., solid floors of various types will be employed at all levels.

At ground level the sub-floor will consist of some 6 inches (150 millimetres) of concrete laid on hardcore with a damp-proof membrane such as polythene in between. At other levels the concrete will be reinforced with steel mesh or supported on concrete joists spanning the distance between structural walls. Reinforced hollow-pot floors are an alternative – these also lighten the structure.

A solid floor will in general give greater insulation against noise and so the heavier the floor construction the better in this context. However, impact noise can be greatly diminished by means of a 'floating floor' which is produced by laying a screed on top of a fibreglass pad, thus isolating it from the sub-floor.

Solid floors are suitable for all types of flooring, although certain precautions must be taken. For example, you should not lay thin tiles or sheet flooring directly onto the site concrete for it has too rough a surface and must first be covered with a sand and cement screed to smoothen it out. Decorative wood floors, wood block and parquet, may be laid on an asphalt base, though wooden strip flooring can rest on battens fixed directly to the structural floor.

Choosing a floor covering is more difficult than you might at first think – a good covering must answer several requirements. It should be durable and resistant to indentation, but also resilient and firm underfoot. It should also be warm to the touch, should muffle sound, be water-resistant and, above all, easy to care for. Of course, it should also be attractive and not too expensive. No floor covering can fulfil all these demands, so you will have to compromise and choose the best suited to the circumstances.

Fitted carpets are generally the most popular floor covering. During the last ten years they have come to be used in every room in the home, even the kitchen. Today it is one of the main ways of making your home look more comfortable, warm and elegant. The basic atmosphere in a room is often set by the colour and pattern of the carpet and other items in the room are determined by it. This is demonstrated in the bedroom illustrated.

Carpets

Fitted carpeting is not cheap, but nevertheless, laid either in widths or tiles, it is the most popular floor covering nowadays. It is warmer, more comfortable, quieter and safer than other floor coverings. Often the colour of the carpet determines the colour scheme of the whole room, so choose it carefully. Since you can't change your mind about a carpet a few months after you've bought it, it is important to choose not only the right colour and pattern, but also the right grade.

Furnishing is fun but not always easy. You may be looking for curtaining in the same bluey-green shade as the paint on the wardrobes, and you will want the colour of the carpet to match.

Often the search for matching carpets and fabric develops into an obstacle race leading you from one shop to another to another – and finally to the conclusion that you can buy fabric in a multitude of colours with the exception of the one colour you are looking for.

Because of the striking black and white wall covering, this bedroom (right) has most of its furnishings in plain colours. The carpet echoes the geometric pattern of the walls, but because of its neutral colour, it doesn't distract the eye too much.

Here the walls, sofa and roller blind have the same pattern in toning colours (below). The carpet also tones well and its light colour prevents the room from being too dark.

A podium replaces sofa and chairs

'There are few pieces of furniture that I like, and those that I like are too expensive'. From this not uncommon viewpoint, a young commerical artist decided to take an unusual step in furnishing his apartment – he simply limited his furniture to as few pieces as possible. To achieve this he simply turned his living and dining room into one single (inhabitable) piece of furniture by fitting a platform around it surrounding a lower level where you can walk about, and including an upholstered step as a substitute for chairs. The photograph on this page shows how he did it. The fact that he and his wife made it all themselves shows their aptitude for do-it-yourself.

The idea proved so effective that four friends have already copied it. This is their unanimous opinion: 'Very comfortable. You couldn't live more easily or more comfortably anywhere else.'

The lowered seating area is 'roofed over' with an additional pine ceiling which was lightly stained and varnished. The platform was made from chipboard and covered with brown Berber carpet, which is soft and comfortable to sit on. The upholstered seats with backrests lie on the platform and thus have no base of their own. The colour of the covers tones with the carpet. The wall alcoves were panelled and converted into shelf units. This provided a lot of space for ornaments and built-in hi-fi equipment.

The sack chair is a great favourite. It stands besides an old cupboard which was found in a friend's barn and carefully restored.

Another possible way of building a lower-level seating area is shown in the photograph on the right-hand page. Here the low-level floor was planned and contracted in advance, but it can be built afterwards – using floorboards as here, or chipboard which would then be carpeted. The first method is easier and cheaper and the natural colour of the sealed floorboards tones excellently with the unusual patterned cotton-covered foam-filled cushions which are 26 by 26 inches (650 by 650 millimetres) in size and 6 inches (150 millimetres) thick.

The cushions can be used in several ways. If you want to sit high up they are placed on the edge of the platform. You can sit closer together if you place them around the edge of the lower level (as illustrated). The shape of the lower level is so suited to the shape of the cushions that the whole area can be completely filled with cushions (so that the sides are just under 6 feet [2 metres] long). This provides a bed on which you can stretch out comfortably, or which can be used as a guest bed – with room for three people to sleep side by side if necessary. A lot of smaller cushions make the seating area more interesting and replace backrests or even pillows.

This can be ideal for a first apartment. If you decide to live like this you will need to be bold and sacrifice conventional living room furniture. You will be rewarded by the pleasure of having a thoroughly relaxed life style.

A less controversial possibility, recommended for a smaller room, is to build a platform along one wall (or several walls), and then cover it with carpet and large cushions. The height of the platform will depend on the seating height that you want and the thickness of the cushions. If you want your seats at a height of 16 inches (400 millimetres) and your cushions are 6 inches (150 millimetres) thick, you will need to build a platform about 12 inches (300 millimetres) high. It is easiest to use chipboard to construct the platform. The cushions can be filled with pieces of foam. Cushions with a down filling are much softer but are considerably more expensive.

Cushions filling a low-level floor on a home-made platform replace conventional seating in this living room (right). When the floor is completely covered with cushions it can be used as an extra bed for friends or relatives.

The platform here is an extension of the floor and provides a lower seating area (left). Chipboard is used for the platform and is covered with brown Berber carpet which tones with the upholstery very well.

40

Floor tiles

The main use of floor tiles is for rooms which need a waterproof surface: for kitchens, bathrooms, W.C.s, and utility rooms. Secondly, there are similar tiles for areas which have to withstand more wear and tear: for halls, porches and cloakrooms, for staircases and of course for outside areas.

Floor tiles can be broadly divided into two types: hard, i.e. ceramic, stone, etc., and soft, i.e. rubber, linoleum, etc.

Ceramics: Clay tiles are pressed from refined natural clays and fired at high temperatures. Fully vitrified tiles have additives and are fired at higher temperatures, which makes them frostproof and able to be used externally. Clay tiles are made in a wide variety of colours, patterns, surface finishes (glazed or natural), textured (non-slip). Various shapes and sizes are available.

Quarries: These are similar to clay. The name comes from the French *carré*, meaning square, and is nothing to do with quarrying. They are extruded from unrefined clays and fired. The best quality tiles may be used externally as well as internally, and they are very hard-wearing. They tend to be in natural colours with a random quality and various sizes.

Mosaics: These are generally made the same way as clay tiles, though there are marble and glass types, but all are smaller in size, from about ¾ by ¾ inch (20 by 20 millimetres). They can be obtained mounted on paper in sheets.

Stone: These tiles, usually larger than other types of tiles, can be cut from stone, or they can be cast by mixing stone chippings with cement. The main stones used are sandstone, limestone, granite. Obviously such tiles are really more for external use and for fairly large areas.

Floor tiles can also be used on the wall (left), but the reverse process is not recommended. The yellow and white zig-zag pattern accentuates the functional practicality of the white kitchen units.

Marble: This has similar uses to stone, and is also cut in large sizes, though it is used much more internally especially in public areas. There is an immense range of colours available.

Terrazzo: Again similar to cast stone tiles, these are made from marble chippings mixed with cement. They are made in various sizes from 6 inches (150 millimetres) upwards.

Quartzite: This material has a riven finish, so that it is a non-slip tile. It is hard-wearing and is used internally or externally. Colours range from silver grey through yellows to olive green. They are cut square and rectangular in a few sizes.

Slate: This material also has a riven finish, but it can be sawn and polished to a smooth finish. Colours range from green through greys to blue. They are cut square or rectangular in a range of sizes.

The above is only a brief survey of the hard type of floor tiles available. There is an equal variety of soft tiles, of which the following is also a brief survey.

Linoleum: This is probably the oldest of this type of tile, but it is still widely used in kitchens and bathrooms etc., and in other parts of the home, though it has been superseded here by various types of carpet tile etc. Produced from linseed oil, resins, and cork with a hessian backing, and available in a wide range of colours, they are available in squares of various sizes, and also in sheet form.

Rubber: In appearance these tiles are not unlike linoleum. They are produced either from natural rubber or a mixture of natural and synthetic and sometimes with a fabric backing. There is a wide range of colours, and also inlaid patterns. They are available in squares of varying sizes and also in sheet form.

Thermoplastic: These are made from asbestos fibres, filler, pigments and a thermoplastic binder. There is a limited range of dark, flecked colours. Later types, known as vinylized thermoplastic tiles, have a vinyl content, providing more flexibility and a better colour range.

Vinyl asbestos: These tiles are a development of the above using PVC and asbestos fibres. More flexible and resistant to chemicals and oils, they are available in many clear colours with flecked effects.

Flexible PVC: There are the most versatile of the plastic type of tiles. They can be textured or embossed, to give the appearance of, for example, travertine marble, old tiles, mosaics or wooden flooring. There is an infinite number of colours.

You should have a cement base for all types of stone tiles, so they are not recommended for wood and similar floors. Just as when you lay plastic or carpet tiles (page 45) the room should first be measured exactly and divided up to correspond with the size of the tiles. It is best to take the main wall in the room as a starting point, as this is the wall which will lie in your line of vision and be fully illuminated.

When clay or quarry tiles are laid professionally the cement mortar bed process is used. For this the concrete floor is covered with mortar mixed with damp sand, using one part cement to five parts medium grade sand to a thickness of about ¾ inch (20 millimetres). The mortar base is smoothed over to give an even, flat surface. It is sprinkled with dry cement (for better adhesion) and the tiles laid on it. Spaces of about ¹⁄₁₆ inch (2 millimetres) are left between the tiles which are filled with grouting. If the mortar base has been carefully prepared, the tiles will only need tapping gently into position.

If you are going to lay the tiles yourself, it is best to use an adhesive, and you will require a smooth, even surface to lay them on. Don't use wall-tile adhesive but a special adhesive consisting essentially of a mixture of cement and plastic. When grouting, you can again use the fluid cement mortar or a prepared filler of your choice. Before grouting you must allow the adhesive to set firmly.

Plastic tiles and flooring

At first glance the choice is extremely large. Anyone who has never before used plastic tiles and flooring will soon be lost in the maze of trade and company names. In fact these floor coverings can be classified and described quite easily:

PVC floor covering: This is produced from polyvinylchloride. Almost all types are available in rolls or tiles. You should distinguish between homogenous PVC coverings and PVC coated or compounded coverings.

Vinyl-asbestos floor covering: This is produced from PVC mixed with synthetic resin, asbestos powder, filling and colouring agents. It is much harder than PVC and is sold only in tile form.

You can lay plastic tiles yourself with little previous experience, but rolls of floor covering are more difficult to handle. In both cases, the surface to be covered must be thoroughly inspected.

New houses: You can stick plastic materials to a smooth, thoroughly dried cement floor without great difficulty. A very porous floor will need to be coated with thinned adhesive first. Rough concrete floors are not a suitable surface. They must be covered (professionally) with a layer of cement.

Old houses: Wooden floorboards must be very firm and level with good joints if you are to stick directly onto them. You will have to nail down loose boards and even out any irregularities with filler. It is safer, but more complicated, to cover the floorboards with hardboard or chipboard. The board should be nailed or screwed down. You will have to fill and sand joints between the boards. It is best, especially in bathrooms, kitchens, etc., to use a water-resistant board.

Here the walls are covered with the same foam-backed plastic material as was used on the floor.

How to lay plastic tiles

When you have prepared the surface, you can start dividing up the floor surface. First mark the centre line parallel to the longest wall, then mark the centre point. From this point you can then mark a second guide line at right angles. The two diagrams below make this clear.

Always begin laying in the centre of the room. Depending on the adhesive used, coat either the floor or both the floor and the tiles with adhesive. Lay the tiles side by side leaving no gaps. You can lay lines of tiles either parallel with the wall or diagonally. From the middle, work outwards towards the wall on each side. The tiles which adjoin the wall are laid last.

You can cut PVC tiles with a sharp knife or scissors; it is best to use a linoleum knife. This has a hook-shaped blade which will make your work easier. Before cutting vinyl-asbestos tiles, they should generally be warmed to 50° to 60°C. You can use the oven (with care!) or a hairdryer for this. If they are not warmed they will probably break easily when you cut them.

In rooms with skirting boards, place the tiles right up to the end of the board and cover with triangular beading or a PVC edging strip. In rooms without skirting boards stick a PVC edge strip to the wall and the tiles when the floor is completed, using the same adhesive as for the floor. There are also self-adhesive base strips. You can of course use a wooden skirting board and in this case it should be fixed to the wall with wall plugs.

Flexible PVC sheeting

This sheet material can be laid without adhesive, although the use of a suitable adhesive will result in a more permanent floor, but it is a difficult process. If the material is laid loose, the joints must be fixed with an adhesive tape. The joints should be overlapped, and when the rolls are correctly positioned, cut through both layers against a metal straight edge to produce a good tight joint. To make the sheet fully flexible while laying it is a good idea to store it in a warm room overnight before use.

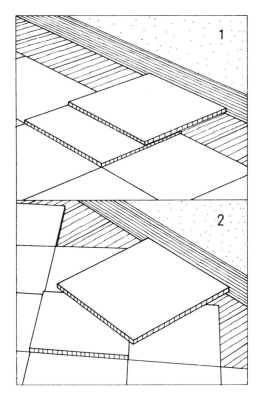

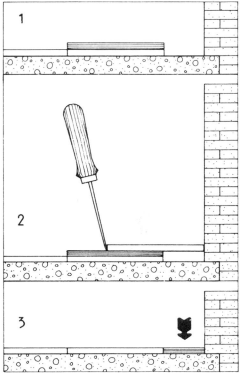

Above left: **Marking the end tiles for parallel lines (1) and diagonal lines (2). Each end tile must be marked to show how much to cut off.**

Above: **Here the marking process is shown again in side view.**

Below: **Lay plastic tiles from the centre of the room. The centre line must run parallel to the wall. The numbers denote the order of laying the first tile for parallel lines (1) and lines diagonal to the wall (2).**

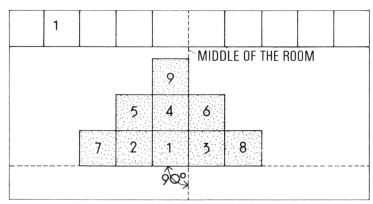

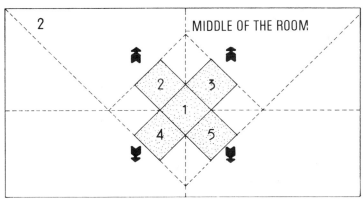

Laying carpet and carpet tiles

If you decide to lay carpet yourself you have two choices: carpet tiles or carpet in a roll. Tiles are easier to fit, and can be changed when they become damaged or worn, and you can take them with you when you move. You can also leave carpet loose, at least in small rooms, in order to be able to take them with you too, thought it is not usually recommended.

Carpet tiles

When buying tiles (once you have carefully calculated how many you will need), find out precisely what method of laying the manufacturer recommends. There are several possibilities.

You can get felt and other types of tiles where the fibres from adjacent tiles work together so that they can be laid loose with no other method of joining. With others you are recommended to fix the outside tiles with double-sided adhesive tape. With other makes all the tiles have to be held in place with double-sided adhesive tape. Self-adhesive tiles present no problems and these too can usually be changed or taken up. Lastly there are those tiles which the manufacturer recommends to be fixed by an all-over (permanent) application of a light synthetic resin adhesive.

It depends, therefore, on the type of tile. Self-adhesive tiles cause the least problems. If you choose ordinary carpet tiles you should at least stick all the joins and edges with double-sided adhesive tape, otherwise they will move whenever a chair is moved.

The floor on which the tiles are to be laid must be even, dry and clean. You cannot lay tiles over floorboards with wide gaps between them. You will have to cover it first with ½ to ⅝ inch (12 to 16 millimetre) chipboard or hardboard. Parquet, vinyl or linoleum floors present no problem.

Like all floor coverings, carpet tiles should not be laid as soon as you have bought them. They need time to adapt to the room temperature, and humidity can cause changes in size. Unpack the tiles and spread them on the floor, leaving them for at least 24 hours. If you don't do this, gaps will appear between the tiles.

In contrast to the method of laying plastic tiles (page 45), you don't begin in the centre of the room with carpet tiles, but along the window wall. Lay the first row without gluing it, to find out whether the end tiles will need cutting, which is generally the case, unless you are lucky. Arrange your first row of tiles so that the tiles that need cutting will be along a wall that has a lot of furniture (cupboards, bookshelves etc.).

When laying tiles make sure that they all go in the same direction. You will be able to see this by looking at the tile surface and it is usually marked by a line

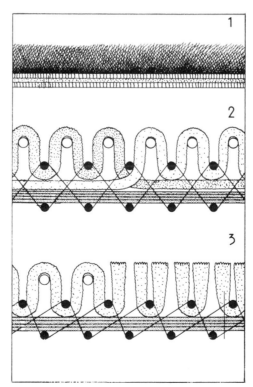

Carpet theory in brief: With non-woven carpet (1), the tufts are inserted into a jute backing and then secured on the underside with a coat of latex. Carpets can also be woven (traditional method) or tufted (woven base with pile inserted and secured on the underside with a coating of latex). If the resulting loops are left intact this is twist pile or bouclé carpet (2), if they are cut this gives smooth pile or velours (3).

on the underside. Either arrange all the tiles in this direction, or turn every other tile through 90° to get a sort of chessboard effect.

Don't cut tiles with scissors but use a sharp knife. Cut along the underside following the edge of a steel ruler. Rest the tile on a piece of wood or an offcut of chipboard or blockboard.

When you finally lay the tiles, push them firmly together but don't use too much pressure or tension as this causes individual tiles to 'stick up' eventually. When using adhesive, press each tile down well. You can use a rolling pin or wine bottle.

It is possible to use an insulating underlay of cork felt or similar material which has definite advantages on slightly uneven surfaces. This can be stuck to the floor and then the tiles are either fixed around the edges only with adhesive tape, or completely coated with adhesive and stuck down. You can also leave the underlay loose (fixing the seams to the floor with tape) but then the tiles should be stuck with double-sided adhesive tape along every join and around the edge. This precaution is unnecessary with self-adhesive tiles.

Laying widths of carpet

An expert will not generally lay a good carpet loose or stick it down, but will tension it. For this, he uses lengths of carpet grippers (metal strips with teeth that hold the carpet firmly in position round the walls). The grippers hold the carpet in place along one wall while the carpet-layer, using a special tool, stretches the carpet to the opposite wall and fixes it to the grippers. This is the most effective way of laying a carpet but it is too difficult for the non-professional, and in any case the tools used are not worth buying for only occasional usage. If you have some aptitude for do-it-yourself you can try other methods: using double-sided adhesive tape; laying carpet loose over an underlay (with the seams firmly joined); sticking it down by covering the whole underside with adhesive.

As with all similar processes, you must first find out if the floor is suitable for covering. Flat floors (vinyl, linoleum, parquet, cement) will be suitable as long as they are in good condition. Old floorboards will have to be covered with chipboard, otherwise the gaps between the boards would soon show through the carpet, and these areas would soon wear.

Carpet is usually 9 feet (2.7 metres) or 12 feet (3.7 metres) wide (although other widths are available), and is difficult to handle on your own, so you should get someone to help you. It would be a good idea to ask a friend who has had some previous experience.

When you are cutting the carpet, remember the following points: seams show up least if they run towards the window; foam-backed carpet should always be cut on the right side, smooth and twist-pile carpets on the other hand should always be cut on the underside.

Do not fasten down the carpet until it fits the shape of the room exactly at all corners and edges, alcoves and chimney breasts. Foam-backed carpet can be fixed with double-sided adhesive tape which withstands ageing, and you need only stick the edges and any seams. The tape is stuck to the floor, fixed firmly in place and the protective paper removed from the top surface. Then the edge of the carpet is pressed firmly onto it. Alternatively, you could use carpet tacks.

If you want to lay the carpet over a soft underlay the process is slightly different. The underlay is fixed with adhesive tape and the carpet itself left loose. The carpet seams are held together using a woven tape stuck with latex adhesive; you will need to apply the adhesive to both the tape and the carpet.

These two methods allow for small inaccuracies, but they don't hold the carpet firmly in place. If you aren't worried about taking the carpet up when you move, and you don't want the expense of grippers, use a few tacks around the edges, as mentioned earlier.

For gluing down the edges, one side of the width (cut to size) is folded back, the adhesive is spread on the floor with a comb spreader and the carpet pressed firmly onto the adhesive. Repeat the process with the adjoining edge.

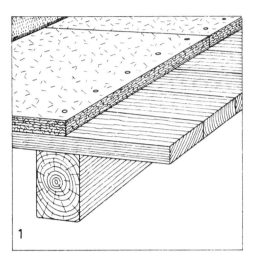

(1) Floorboards are not always suitable for carpeting, sometimes they have become warped or damaged in some way. To prevent this showing through the carpet, screw a layer of chipboard or hardboard over the floorboards.

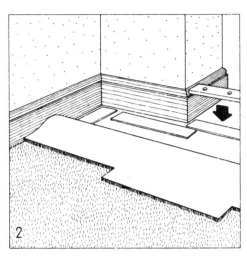

(2) To lay carpet with double-sided adhesive tape, you must first cut the carpet exactly. Fold back the carpet and stick the tape to the floor under the carpet edges. Then fold the carpet back onto the tape and press down firmly.

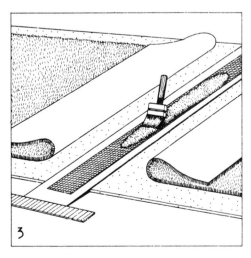

(3) The carpet can be left loose over a soft underlay. The underlay is stuck to the floor with double-sided adhesive tape. The strips of carpet are joined with fabric tape using latex adhesive (e.g. Copydex) applied to both the tape and the carpet edges. This will avoid dangerous loose edges.

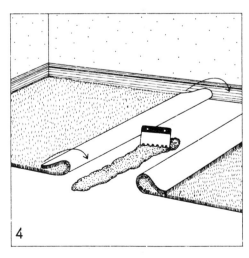

(4) If gluing down the edges, first cut the widths of carpet and lay them in position. Fold the edges back along the seams, apply adhesive to the floor and press the carpet onto it. Then repeat the process with the other half of the strip.

Wooden floors

Traditional wooden floorboards have not yet disappeared. Although you will seldom find them in new houses, they still survive in most old houses – often sanded to a clean surface with a varnished finish.

Parquet flooring, which, because it was a craftsman's job, was once favoured only by the rich, has become in the past few years an economic and practical form of flooring, because more mass production methods have been applied to it. Both types of wooden floor are of interest to the do-it-yourself enthusiast.

Laying a wood-strip floor

Perhaps you want to renew a worn wood-strip floor. This is not as difficult as it sounds – although there are other simpler ways of renovating an old floor. You could for example cover it with chipboard and then lay carpet or carpet tiles, or cover with chipboard then with linoleum or plastic tiles.

But maybe you want to convert a loft or (with the necessary insulation) a cellar to make an extra room, which will of course need a floor. Then you will need to know the main stages in constructing a wood-strip floor. It is made up from tongue and groove planks at least 7/8 inch (22 millimetres) thick, usually in pine or other softwood. The planks must be nailed down, invisibly, though the tongues. The floor is supported by wooden joists to which the planks are nailed.

Checking the joists

If the floor is to lie absolutely flat, the top edge of each joist must be level. So the first job is to check the existing joists precisely, using a spirit level. Since it is much too short to stretch across several joists, use a long, straight plank of wood.

To measure you lay the plank on edge across several joists and place the spirit level on top of it. If the spirit level shows up any discrepancies in height, they will have to be made level (with pieces of wood, wedges, bits of plywood, etc.).

Joists that you fit yourself should have a cross-section of 1½ by 3 inches (40 by 80 millimetres) if they are to be placed on a concrete surface. Before positioning the floor joists must be thoroughly treated with wood preservative. The distance between one joist and the next should be 18 inches (600 millimetres). If they are too far apart the floor will be springy, so the weaker the planks, the closer the joists. The floor planks should be bought the same length (or width) as the room if possible, so that they will stretch from one wall to another without any unsightly joins. If you are unable to get them long enough you should at least make sure that the joins are staggered. This means that the first plank is joined at the centre of the third joist, the second plank on the seventh joist, the third plank on the third joist, and so on.

You should leave a gap of ½ inch (12 millimetres) between the floor and the wall (to allow for play). The gap is eventually filled with some insulation material and covered by the skirting board.

Laying begins

Now if you just nail down the planks one after another, after a few weeks you will usually find that the cracks between the planks have become wider. The wood is still settling – and it usually contracts slightly after laying, hence the widening cracks. Ugly cracks may also be due to the fact that every plank is not quite straight and some are slightly twisted.

To prevent both these faults you should wedge the planks together before nailing them down. This is how you do it: Begin by nailing the first plank in position along one side of the room, which is at right angles to the joists. Position it about ½ inch (12 millimetres) from the wall. Choose the first plank very carefully, it must not be warped.

The nails should not be knocked straight in through the top of the plank as they will be visible. They should be knocked at a slight angle into the tongue which runs down the side of each plank. You will have to be careful not to split the wood as it is quite thin here. When the first plank is nailed down push the second one up to it. The groove on this plank slides into the tongue on the first one thus concealing the nails. Hit the second plank several times with a hammer (placing a spare bit of wood between plank and hammer) to push it into the first.

This is where you use the wedges. Cut a few wedge-shaped pieces from a spare piece of wood. They should be about 12 inches (300 millimetres) long and taper from 2 to ¾ inch (50 to 20 millimetres). Knock a peg into two or three of the joists about 1½ inches (40 millimetres) from the last plank and push a wedge between each peg and the plank. Knock in each wedge in turn so that the plank is held under pressure and no gap is visible. Now it can be nailed.

Lastly take the pegs out and place the next plank in position. If you are nailing into the top of the plank you can wedge several planks at once – this will speed up the process. Finally the skirting board should be fitted.

Parquet flooring

Parquet flooring is suitable for use throughout the house with the possible exception of the bathroom. It is produced in various forms and sizes from either solid hardwoods – oak, teak, etc., or plywood with a hardwood veneer, which has the advantage of being less likely to split or warp, but is less hard-wearing.

Block parquet: Individual pieces of hardwood of varying sizes, but generally about 10 inches (250 millimetres) by 3 inches (80 millimetres) and about ¾ inch (22 millimetres) thick which can be laid in parallel lines (when longer lengths are also used) usually to form a border to either a basket or herring-bone pattern. This type of parquet is laid on smooth floorboards starting with the border and working towards the centre. This is really not a process to be undertaken by an amateur.

Mosaic parquet: Smaller pieces of hardwood jointed together into square tiles of varying sizes but generally 6 to 10 inches (150 to 250 millimetres) square, and usually laid in a basket pattern. They can be laid either on flat floorboards or a

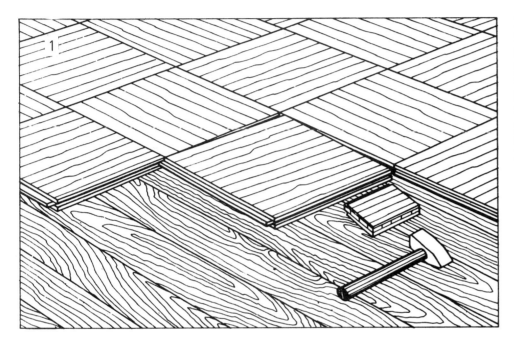

Laying parquet tiles on smooth floorboards. This block parquet doesn't need to be glued, as the tongue and groove joints should fit exactly. Place a piece of wood between the hammer and the tile when fixing them, so that the tiles don't get damaged. If the surface you are covering isn't completely smooth, you will have to nail down a layer of ply or hardboard.

It is best to stick mosaic parquet. When coating with an adhesive, only cover an area which you can tile within a few minutes (3). Position the parquet carefully and press down well. You must leave a gap between the tiles and the wall to allow for expansion (2). This will be filled with insulating material and covered by beading (it is nailed to the edge of the parquet). The width of the gap should be about ½ inch (10 millimetres).

LEAVE A SMALL GAP

really level cement screed. Various forms of these made-up tiles can be bought and the laying of them is a job which can be undertaken by the do-it-yourself enthusiast. In this case they are laid in a similar way to plastic tiles (see page 45), i.e. beginning in the centre of the room and working towards the walls, leaving a space of ½ inch (10 millimetres) between the tiles and the wall to allow for expansion. The tiles are stuck down using the adhesive advised by the makers of the tiles.

Plywood parquet: In effect this is similar to the mosaic type and consists of plywood tiles onto which strips of thick veneer are glued. These are laid in the same way as was described above.

Ideas for stairs

Most people have stairs of some kind in their house, and even though they take up a lot of valuable space, we have to try and make the best of them. In some cases, as with spiral staircases, you may want to make them a particular feature.

An ideal staircase
As well as looking at the amount of light the living room gets and the modern kitchen fittings when you go to look at a new house or flat, have a good look at the stairs as well. People forget that they are used many times every day.

Stairs in a new house should be 32 to 36 inches (800 to 900 millimetres) wide. But more important than this is the gradient. It should be suitable for the average stride, about 24 or 25 inches (620 or 630 millimetres). Whith an ideal staircase the sum of a tread depth and the height of two steps should give this number. For example: tread depth 11 inches (280 millimetres), step height 6½ inches (170 millimetres) = gradient 6½/11 (170/280): 11 (280) + 2 × 6½ (170) = 24 (620).

If there is insufficient space stairs are often steeper and more difficult to climb, for example 7/10½ (180/270) or 7/10 (180/260). Although there is only ½ inch (10 millimetres) difference this has a pronounced effect if you have to use the stairs regularly. With staircases in new buildings, the architect will often remedy a difficult gradient by having the tread projecting slightly (or even designing stairs consisting only of treads). This does not alter the gradient, but the tread width is improved so that you can use the stairs quite comfortably and safely.

The simplest staircase is a straight, direct link between two storeys; these are called 'single-barrelled stairs'. Double-barrelled stairs have a landing in the middle. There are also stairs with a few turning steps at the bottom, stairs which turn a corner and those which go up in a semi-circle. Spiral stairs (see right-hand page) are nowadays almost always built round a spindle. These are unsuitable for the main staircase in a house or apartment in which there are children.

Carpet for stairs
All types of stone stairs, as well as wooden or vinyl-covered stairs are often constructed in such a way that the noise of footsteps goes right through the house, unless you are wearing slippers or rubber-soled shoes. In addition if the stairs are polished with a wax polish, the household will have to cope with stairs which are as smooth as a mirror.

Stair carpet is a good method of dealing with both problems. You can cut pieces to fit the stair treads and stick them on with the recommended adhesive. There are special edge strips to secure the front edges which are also stuck on. They prevent the edges of the carpet fraying. It might look better if you stick pieces of carpet onto the risers as well. If you want to do this begin with the risers and cover the treads last.

The traditional method of covering the whole staircase with a runner (diagram below) is still quite popular today. A removable stair-rod holds the runner in the angle between the riser and the tread.

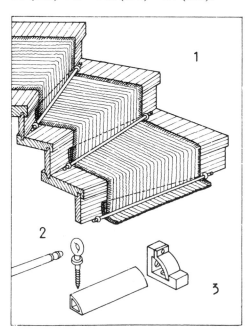

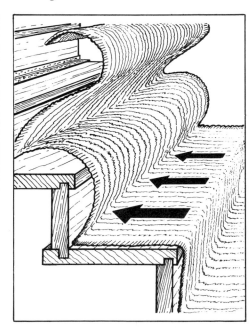

It is important to have stair rods (2,3) which hold the carpet firm but can be easily removed. If the stairs turn (1) you will have to make folds which must be held firmly in place behind the carpet.

The disadvantage of stair rods is that some of the wood on either side of the carpet will be visible. By using tackless fittings the carpet can be made to fit the full width of the stairs. This fitting

consists of a metal 'L'-shaped strip with teeth that grip the carpet. Work up the stairs pulling the carpet over the nosings and pressing it into the angled strip.

There are a number of systems for holding the stair-rods in place. Choose one which does not damage the stairs too much and which, while holding the rods absolutely firmly, allows the carpet to be removed easily for cleaning. The rods must not be able to move at all when the stairs are used.

With wooden stairs you should be able simply to screw in the rod brackets, drilling screw holes where required in advance. Artificial and natural stone stairs will require wall plugs.

You can only cover stairs that turn with a runner if you take the trouble to lay it with neat folds (see diagram). The folds should be turned under the carpet covering the riser. These wedge-shaped folds should be secured at the side with a few stitches, so that they can't come loose.

Finally you can have fitted carpet on the stairs. Like ordinary floors it is best to leave the tension method to an expert (page 46) who will nail grippers into the angle between the riser and the tread, stick down felt or rubber underlay and then with one piece of carpet cover the stairs, starting from the bottom and pressing the carpet into the grippers.

Stairs in old houses

You can only use carpet or other coverings (vinyl or linoleum) on stairs which are firm, with level treads and undamaged edges. Badly worn stairs must be repaired before you can cover them – and this can be a long job.

With wooden stairs, you can even out broken edges with hardwood battens. These must be cut carefully to size, glued and screwed on. Any depressions in the tread can be filled and then thoroughly sanded. Squeaking wooden stairs present special problems. The squeaking and creaking is usually due to the wood contracting over the years. A wooden staircase usually consists of treads joined to perpendicular risers. The treads and risers are mounted at the sides on supporting planks. If one of these joints becomes loose through the wood drying out you get squeaking and other similar noises.

Sometimes it helps if you screw the

tread to the riser from above and possibly from under the stairs too with countersunk screws. The screwheads should be countersunk slightly, then cover with plastic wood or wood filler and carpet or paint the stairs.

A more complicated process is to place wedges under the tread to lift it off the place where it is squeaking. It is held in place in this position by strips of wood screwed to the riser on the front, or better still, the underside of the stairs.

It is also possible to screw the tread to the riser on the front of the stairs using metal corner plates. The plates should be set into the tread and better still into the riser too. The stairs will have to be covered afterwards.

Solid stairs such as stone should be evened out with filler before covering. You can also repair worn or broken front edges with a special filler. To get a clean edge fix a batten across the edge of the step and remove it when the filler is dry.

PVC coverings for wood or stone stairs should be stuck to the prepared surface with the recommended adhesive. Use the appropriate PVC edge strip at the ends. There are also special edge strips for any outside edges (for stairs with no sides, e.g., spiral stairs).

Spiral stairs

You can get various types of ready-made spiral staircases with steps in all the main materials (wood, metal, concrete, marble, etc.). They should not, as mentioned before, be installed as a main staircase in a home in which there are children.

The only difficult part of the building process is the essential opening that has to be made in the ceiling. It is not worthwhile breaking through a steel and concrete ceiling. If you have ceilings like this you shouldn't consider installing a spiral staircase. Wood joist ceilings present fewer problems, but you will almost always find that one of the joists is situated where you want the hole. When having the hole cut (by a builder) you must therefore see that the load which the joist carried is transferred to the next joist by means of a short cross joist (relay).

Unfortunately this method is not always possible and you will have to test thoroughly in advance whether the load ratio will allow you to saw through the joist. The main disadvantage of spiral stairs is that they are difficult to negotiate, particularly for old people, and they are certainly unsuitable for carrying furniture up and down.

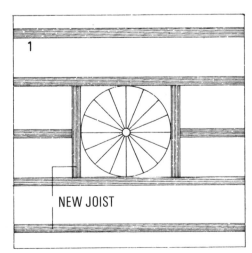

You can add a spiral staircase to your home if the upper storey has a wood-joist floor. 'Relay' joists take the strain where necessary, supporting the load of the joist which has been sawn through.

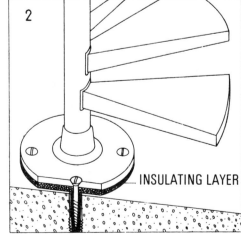

Spiral staircases are supported by a single central column. It must be securely anchored to the floor at the base. An insulating layer will help to reduce noise.

WALLS AND CEILINGS

If walls are to fulfil their function of supporting ceilings and roofs, they must be built from materials which are firm and capable of supporting the load. But the walls must also provide protection from cold and heat and it isn't easy to combine both sets of requirements. Statistics have shown that a wall built with conventional materials to the thickness demanded by its stability and load capacity will not usually be sufficiently thick to protect against cold and heat. If it were built to the thickness required for this protection, the excessive amount of building materials required would considerably increase costs.

So walls in modern houses are generally built from materials which by and large fulfil both sets of requirements. Since air trapped in cells or cavities effectively prevents heat loss and penetrating cold, perforated bricks (with air holes) are used. In addition, walls can be insulated with a variety of insulation board which helps to keep the temperature of the room reasonable, and often helps with the sound-proofing too.

Like ceilings, interior walls are generally plastered and then painted or papered. Woodchip or textured wallpapers can make smooth wall surfaces more interesting. After papering with either type of paper (and drying) they are painted. If you want to change the colour at a later date, all you need to do is to paint another colour over it.

In many cases you can repaper over existing wallpaper, but papers with two layers are more practical. If you want to change vinyl wallpaper, the top layer can simply be peeled off leaving a white under-layer (this remains on the wall to act as a lining paper for the new wallpaper). But it need not always be paint or wallpaper which gives the wall its texture or colour. Nowadays anyone can use fabric wall coverings because you can get tools to help you tension it evenly. Widths of felt, cork tiles and mirror foil, hessian (burlap) and tiles provide further variety. Although these can be expensive, they can be used by the do-it-yourself enthusiast.

This is also true of wood cladding for walls and ceilings. Panels up to the ceiling make the room comfortable and hard-wearing. Lattice board gives the room a lively atmosphere. Laminated wood can be used for converted cellars to give a rural atmosphere. False ceilings in wood make high rooms lower and can also improve sound-proofing. Windows and doors break up the walls. Windows and window coverings are dealt with in the next chapter. Interior doors are usually flat nowadays and covered in plywood which can be painted. Instead of painting it, you could have a veneered surface instead. Suitable woods for veneering are ash, cherry, elm, walnut, oak, teak and mahogany.

There are numerous ways to cover a wall – subdued or exciting, traditional or modern. If you are not in favour of young, avant-garde styles and if the walls are to emphasize the elegance of your furnishings, woven fabric papers are a good choice. This textured paper based on an old Japanese pattern provides a beautiful wall surface and gives the room a Far Eastern charm. However, they can be rather expensive.

Wallpapers

There are wallpapers to satisfy every taste, and they can be used very effectively to accentuate the style of furnishing in a room.

Woodchip paper is one of the most popular. It has a surface which resembles rough plaster and has to be painted (with emulsion paint). Embossed papers which you can also paint are more elegant.

Vinyl papers are recommended for all rooms which get a lot of wear and tear because they are longer lasting and more resilient. They consist of paper coated in PVC and, since they can be washed with soapy water, are extremely hygienic.

Another hard-wearing type is cork wallpaper, consisting of paper with a top layer of cork in varying colours and textures. In place of cork papers you can also use cork tiles, which are usually 12 by 12 inches (300 by 300 millimetres) in size. Both types are practical as well as beautiful, because they contribute to sound- and heat-proofing, and can be wiped.

Fabric papers are available in many colours and patterns and in a variety of fabric surfaces. These range from open weave to flock piles which are similar to velvet. The range of patterns includes bold stripes and flowers. There is also a large range of finely graduated plain colours especially in the linen-look papers. Fabric papers are easy to use with a special adhesive.

Papers with shiny metallic surfaces look particularly splendid and elegant, if rather cold. Shiny gloss papers are available in many different plain colours. They are usually backed with foam. Glass-fibre papers resemble fabric in texture and like woodchip papers must be painted.

To help you choose your wallpaper, stores have thick pattern books which contain samples about the size of a dishtowel. However, it is better to use the samples only to make a preliminary choice and then have two or three rolls of the papers you have chosen spread out.

Wallpapering is one of the most common do-it-yourself activities. You will find all you need to know about it on pages 244-5.

'Traditional' wallpaper (left and below) is still one of the simplest methods of decorating walls in an individual style. Since the advent of double-layer wallpapers, re-papering has become quite simple. The new paper is just pasted onto the old lining paper or onto a special wall coating.

Cork papers (below) are available in many textures. They consist of thin layers of cork with paper backing. Cork is a natural material with a soft, matt surface. You can of course also cover the walls with cork tiles. The cork surface helps with sound and heat insulation, is resistant to compression and can be wiped down, but the price is unfortunately rather high.

Making the most of your walls

In addition to wallpapers there are many other ways of giving a wall a new, unusual look. Try felt, mirror foil or wood. Such clever wall coverings will make even a simple room look special.

Mirror foil is so thin that it shouldn't be stuck straight onto the wall, because even tiny irregularities in the wall's surface would show through, so it must be stretched over hardboard. It is glued to the underside of the board or attached with double-sided adhesive tape. When sticking down the foil, place a soft cloth under it to avoid scratches.

The hardboard is stuck directly onto the wall using double-sided adhesive tape or with pieces of double-sided adhesive foam. The wall surface must be clean, dry and firm.

Felt papers can be stuck directly to the wall with special adhesive. The back of this paper is specially prepared for papering. They are no more difficult to handle than vinyl papers.

However, ordinary felt cannot be glued. It must be stretched over ¼-inch (8-millimetre) chipboard which should be cut about 18 inches (500 millimetres) wide and the same length as the height of the room excluding the skirting board. Smooth down the edges of the cut board and cover with a soft foam lining (about ⅛ inch (3 millimetres) thick). Both the lining and the felt are held in position on the back with upholstery tacks (short nails with wide, flat heads). Use the method described on page 61 (right-hand diagram, example 2) to fasten it to the wall. This allows the boards to be taken down whenever necessary.

A wood-fibre wall covering goes well in a room with bamboo or cane furniture. These wood-fibre papers, which come from Japan, are available in maple or mahogany tones and are sold in widths of 36 inches (900 millimetres), 48 inches (1200 millimetres) and 60 inches (1500 millimetres). They are stapled to the wall and the joins can be covered by toning painted beading. As well as wood-fibre matting you can also buy bamboo matting for which the same method is used. Among the unusual wall coverings which can be stuck onto the wall are real wood papers. These consist of wallpaper onto which a wafer-thin veneer is stuck. Real wood papers are easy to apply. When dry they are treated with furniture polish.

For a cheerful striped look, you can use felt for a wall covering (right). Decorating felt is available in many colours, but you must of course choose colours that go well together. It must first be stretched over chipboard which is fastened to wall battens.

Mirror foil (above) will make a room look bigger and bolder. It can't be stuck straight onto the wall, but must be stretched over hardboard which is fastened onto the wall.

If you like bamboo or cane furniture and prefer natural colours for furnishing, you can cover the wall with wood fibre paper (right). It is stapled to the wall and painted battens cover unavoidable joins.

Tiled walls

There is no hard and fast rule that tiles should be used only in the kitchen and in the bathroom. Today there are so many interesting and unusual shapes, patterns and colours that it is quite conceivable to cover a living room wall or the whole dining area with wall tiles. Not only because of their looks but also because plastic and ceramic tiles are easy to care for.

One disadvantage is that unlike wallpapers, tiles are difficult to change when you get tired of them, so patterns and colours should be chosen with special care so that you won't begin to dislike them after a fairly short time. You will find instructions on hanging tiles yourself on pages 182-3. Few difficulties will arise if you use tile adhesive, i.e. if you hang tiles with the 'thin-bed' technique. Hanging tiles on a cement mortar base should be left to the professional – it is too difficult for the amateur. The adhesive method is used for all kinds of plastic tiles, for hard PVC tiles and also for foam-filled cushioned vinyl coverings as illustrated right. Cushion vinyls also come in roll form which can be simply pressed onto the wall.

Steel tiles are usually used in public areas as their designs are quite bold. They are also rather clinical but if used with restraint they can be very effective. A framework of battening is used as a substructure, with divisions corresponding to the size of the tiles. The tiles have various shapes: pyramids, curves, angles, wafer, diamond or waves. Each side has two grooves for fastening. The first tile is screwed to the battening on the left and right. The next tile is pushed under one side of the tile which is in position, so only needs to be screwed down on the opposite side. With the second row the grooves on two adjacent sides can be pushed under adjacent tiles which are already in position.

Sheets of plastic laminate (e.g. Formica), made from resin-impregnated layers of paper, are sometimes used on walls in damp rooms. There is also hardboard or chipboard with a plastic coating which serves the same purpose. All of these should be fixed to battens first.

Ceramic tiles are available in so many patterns and colours that they can also be used in a living room (left). They are very easy to keep clean and are virtually indestructible. For reasons of cost, this type of wall covering can't be changed as often as wallpaper, for example. Therefore it is better to avoid colours and patterns which are very fashionable or loud.

Here the wall, floor and vanity unit have the same covering (below) – foam-filled vinyl in relief effect. The vinyl is stuck down. You can do this yourself but ensure that the surface is smooth and even.

Wood – the natural look

You can cover a wall with either wood panels or planks; both are equally suitable. Once made of solid oak, panels are now usually hardboard, chipboard or blockboard covered with wood veneer or some other facing material (e.g. plastic). Their surface can be rough or smooth or can have grooves cut into them to give the appearance of separate planks.

Wood cladding is more expensive than wallpaper, but is nevertheless worthwhile, because it is unnecessary to fill or sand down any irregularities in the wall. Damaged plaster disappears behind it. In addition a wood-clad wall will not get dirty like wallpaper. It is both hardwearing and good to look at.

Tongue-and-groove boarding is another type of wooden wall covering, usually made of cedar or pine. They interlock, and are fixed to battens on the wall.

Wooden planking (solid wood) comes from spruce, Brazilian pine, western red cedar, Oregon pine, pitch pine and red pine among others. All these are conifers and softwoods. More precious woods are too expensive to be used as solid wood. In these cases veneered boards are used, for example, panels with oak, teak, ash, walnut or rosewood veneer. The top layer of these panels is ready-prepared. If you are intending to varnish them this should be done as soon as they are in position. For outside use planks should also be treated with a protective agent on both sides. Veneered panels are not suitable for outside use.

Wooden wall coverings give the room a solid and secure look (top). Today, wood panels are available in several types of wood. They are cut to room height and are easy to put up (see right-hand page for examples).

A wall which is covered in overlapping strips of wood is used here in a converted cellar (right) in a room which can be used for parties or as a second living room. The angling of the planks to the wall gives it a bright, sculptured effect.

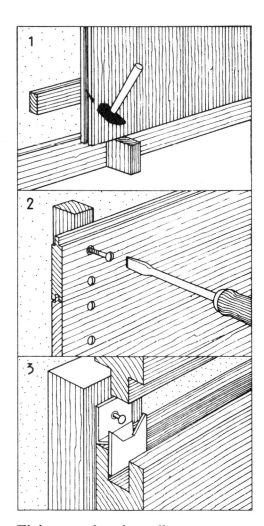

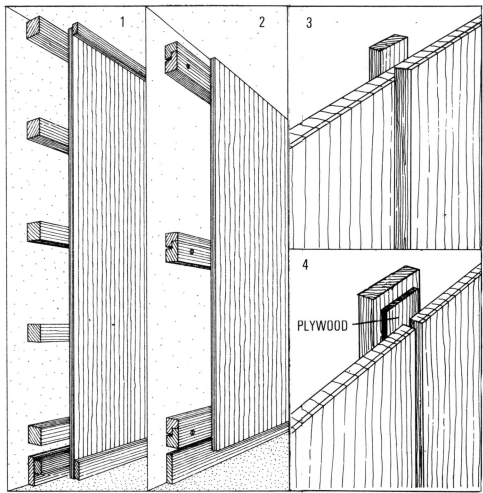

PLYWOOD

Fixing wood to the wall

A battening substructure is necessary if you want to fix planks or panels to a wall or ceiling.

If the planks or panels are to be perpendicular, the battens must run horizontally. They should be placed at intervals of about 30 inches (800 millimetres), therefore to cover the whole height of the wall you will need about four rows of battens. They are screwed to the wall with screws at 18-inch (500-millimetre) intervals. It is better to drill holes in the battening first and then drill the wall plug holes through them – this will ensure that they match.

To allow air to reach the back of the wood cladding, saw wedge-shaped pieces out of the battens at intervals of 18 inches

(500 millimetres). The cuts should be to the wall.

Correspondingly, horizontal planks require vertical battens.

There are now several possible ways of fixing up the wood cladding. Planks can be fixed using panel pins, round-head screws or retaining plates onto the battens. If you are leaving a gap between the planks you will have to cover the batten, preferably by sticking on a veneered strip of plywood.

Panels can be stuck to the horizontal battens if they are to be a permanent fixture (1), but you can also use grooved battens if you want them to be removable (2).

If you don't want a flat wall of wood but prefer the effect of shadows, put up

Wooden wall coverings should be firmly fixed to battening: (1) concealed nails (2) raised-head screws (3) retaining plates are nailed on.

Ceiling-height wall panels can be glued to battening (1) or be removable (2). For the latter, use grooved battens which fit into each other. Veneered or fabric-covered boards should be fixed onto a framework (3). Here veneered plywood is used to line joins (4).

the planks as illustrated in the right-hand diagram. The planks which lie on the wall are attached as before and the raised layer of planks is fixed to the first with panel pins or screws. In this case all the planks should be the same width.

Covering a wall with fabric

Normally walls are painted or papered and sometimes covered with wood. Fabric wall coverings are less common, possibly because they are considered to be difficult to use and keep clean. Yet there are easy methods of application which are suitable for beginners – and a few special tips that anyone can follow.

Fabric over insulation board

You can buy ceiling-height insulation or fibre boards. Cut them to fit the area to be covered and stretch fabric over them. The fabric is folded over at the back and held with drawing pins or staples which can be removed when the fabric needs cleaning. Another method is to make a fairly wide turning at the back and to cut the fabric close to the row of drawing pins with a razor blade for cleaning purposes. Afterwards it is fastened with a new row of pins closer to the edge of the board. To hang the board fix 2 by 1 inch (50 by 25 millimetre) horizontal battens to the wall at intervals of 30 inches (800 millimetres), making four rows of battens one above the other for a room of normal height. The fabric-covered boards are screwed to the battens with short screws at 18-inch (400-millimetre) intervals. Matching washers are placed between the screw and the fabric to prevent the screwhead from tearing it.

Instead of insulating board you can use hardboard. As this is pliable, you are recommended to fill the gaps between the battens and the board with expanded polystyrene. This additional insulating filling can also be used with insulation board.

Adhesives for small areas

Double-sided adhesive tape, such as is used for carpet-laying, is also suitable for use on small wall areas. Only in exceptional circumstances would you use this method for a complete wall.

In the example illustrated, the wall is divided into rectangles of about 4 by 12 inches (100 by 300 millimetres) by narrow, shallow battening. The battens can be fastened with masonry nails or screwed on with wall plugs.

The battens divide the wall surface

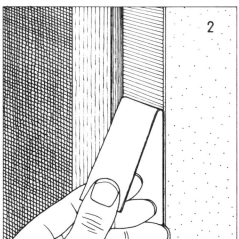

(1) One of the many ways of covering a wall with fabric is to use double-sided adhesive tape. Here the underside of the tape is stuck to the prepared wall surface.

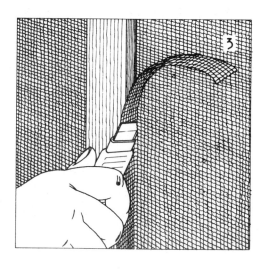

(2) When the tape is correctly positioned, the protective paper is removed from the top layer and the fabric, cut with an extra ¾ inch (20 millimetres) at each edge, is carefully pressed onto the tape.

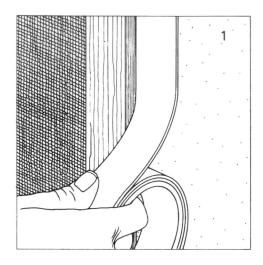

(3) The excess fabric (the allowance at the edges) is cut off with a sharp knife along the edge of the batten. With checked fabrics you will have to take the pattern into account.

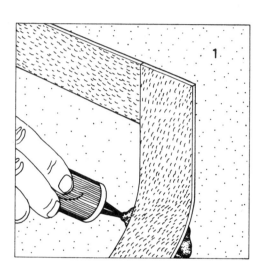

(1) A removable (and therefore washable) covering can be made using interlocking tape (Velcro) which is glued or nailed around the edge of the area to be covered.

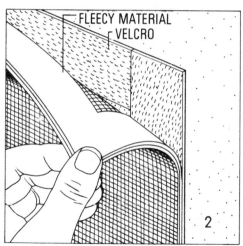

FLEECY MATERIAL
VELCRO

(2) The fabric is cut exactly to size and hemmed. A strip of fleecy material is sewn around the edge of the fabric. Now the covering can be positioned with one tape over the other.

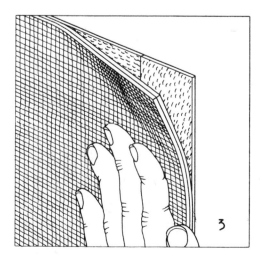

(3) The cover is easy to remove for washing, and the fleecy tape can be washed with it. This type of fabric wall covering is · particularly suitable for a nursery or hall.

into equal areas, each of which is covered separately. The covering fabric is cut ½ inch (15 millimetres) larger all round than the area to be covered. Instead of material you could also use adhesive plastic. Then the underside of the adhesive tape is stuck down around the inside of the battens. The wall must be clean, dry and firm where you are sticking or the tape will not hold. When you have removed the top layer of protective paper from the tape the material is spread evenly over the area and pressed onto the tape.

Excess fabric is cut off with a sharp knife exactly along the edge of the battens. You could on the other hand stick the material onto the wall using the same method and then fix the battens into position.

Arthur Sanderson and Sons Ltd

This oatmeal-coloured fabric wall covering completes the pleasant blue and cream colour scheme in this room. The attractive texture of the fabric adds interest to the decor.

Insulating walls

Noise consists of vibrations in the air which are registered not only by our ears but by the walls and ceilings around us which react according to their construction. Brick walls and concrete ceilings will deflect part of the sound, but on the other hand they themselves vibrate in absorbing the sound waves, and create noise which runs through the whole structure of the building, especially through the metal joists and water pipes.

Correct building techniques can limit the spread of noise but these techniques are omitted when many houses are built. Anything you may do once the house is complete can only be a makeshift solution.

Almost all methods of sound-proofing also help with heat-proofing, that is to say 'cold walls' become less apparent and less heating appliances are required. On the other hand, the simplest insulation methods such as covering walls with polystyrene have only a limited effect on sound-proofing. In the home therefore it is difficult to find really effective methods of sound-proofing. However, these two pages contain some suggestions that might be of some use.

Dry lining for a brick wall

First an important point: Sound-proofing walls should have as little direct contact with existing walls as possible. All points of contact between the insulating wall and the main structure of the building (e.g. ceilings, floors, walls) must be lined with strips of an elastic insulating material (e.g. foam). Otherwise you will get 'sound bridges' which make the whole purpose of the inner wall useless.

A dry lining which is nailed onto a brick or concrete wall (diagram below left) is one of the most common methods of sound-proofing. To form a substructure, 2 by 2 inch (50 by 50 millimetre) battening is fastened vertically to the wall at intervals of 24 inches (620 millimetres). If they are screwed to the wall you must again place strips of foam between the battens and the wall. The insulation is improved if the battening stands about 1 inch (20 millimetres). For this you will need a horizontal batten along the floor and ceiling to which the vertical battens can be nailed.

The spaces between the battens are lined with insulating material. For this you can use insulation board or rolls of insulating wadding. The insulating mate-

rial should touch the old wall without forming a sound bridge. As a top layer plasterboard is fastened to the side of the battens facing into the room. Instructions for using plasterboard are given right.

The wall is finally prepared. To make it as airtight as possible (important for sound-proofing!) the gaps where walls, ceiling and floor meet can be filled with rubber caulking before papering.

Sound-proofed partition wall

Simple partition walls are built with a batten framework, fixed between the floor and the ceiling with a facing on both sides of plasterboard. Walls like this have no sound-proofing effect at all. A sound-proofing partition wall must consist of two dry linings insulated from one another. You can of course build walls like this – but they are rather expensive.

The method illustrated on the left is simpler but less effective. Here a 3 by 2 inch (80 by 50 millimetre) framework is erected and plasterboard is nailed to one side of it.

Insulation board is nailed to the other 'insulated' side. Smaller 2 by 1 inch (50 by 30 millimetre) battens are then fitted horizontally to the supporting frame-

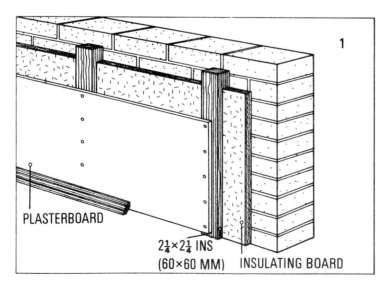

A dry lining for a brick wall has battens which are glued or screwed to the wall. The areas between are filled with insulating board. Plasterboard is nailed to the battens, which can be painted, papered or covered with fabric.

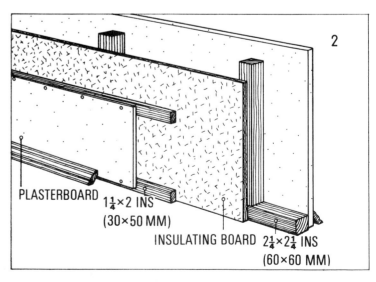

Here is an example of a sound-proofed and insulated partition wall. Insulation board is nailed to the batten framework and then thinner battens are fixed to this to support the top layer of plasterboard.

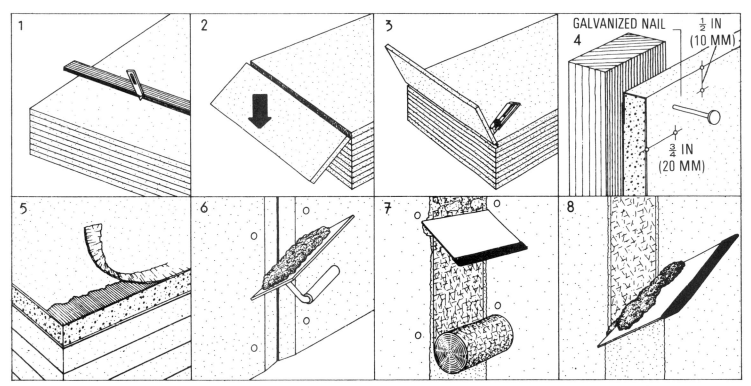

work. These support the plasterboard top layer, which can finally be papered.

Here too all parts of the dry lining which meet walls, ceiling or floor should be lined with an elastic insulating material. Naturally it is possible to insulate both sides of the partition wall using the method recommended.

To provide additional insulation, widths of insulating paper (glass or mineral fibre on bitumen paper) can be laid between the supporting battens. To prevent them crumpling up they can be held in place with roofing-felt nails. If the partition wall is to have a door you must make allowances for this in advance.

Tips for using plasterboard

These boards consist of plaster covered in a special paste-board. Board and plaster are joined together so firmly that a considerable bending strength and elasticity is produced. In the building industry, plasterboard is used among other things for dry lining of walls and ceilings, replacing plaster. Generally, for the dry plastering process the boards are attached to the unplastered walls with a special mortar. In contrast to ordinary plaster they do not need to be left to dry out, so the building is ready for occupation rather more quickly.

Plasterboard is grey on one side and ivory on the other. The grey side is used if you wish to finish it with a scim of plaster, or the ivory side as a surface ready for papering.

The second method of using plasterboard is better suited for do-it-yourself; nailing and screwing the boards to a batten framework. Plasterboard is usually sold in 96 by 48 inch (2400 by 1200 millimetres) sheets, ⅜ inch (10 millimetres) thick, but smaller sizes are available.

The span width (distance from one fastening to the next) should not be more than 16 inches (620 millimetres) when covering walls with board. For ceilings and sloping roofs the distance should be less. It should be fixed with galvanized screw nails, spaced at 6-inch (150-millimetre) intervals. Leave ⅛ inch (3 millimetres) space between the boards. The diagram (example 4) shows how far they should be from the edge of the board.

How to work with plasterboard: (1) Cut the cardboard on the side which is to be visible with a sharp knife. (2) The plaster centre can then be easily broken over a sharp edge. (3) Now the board is turned over so that the cardboard on the underside can be cut. (4) Nail at this distance from the edge of the board; countersink the nail-heads and fill. (5) Before filling the gaps, tear a narrow strip of cardboard from the edges. (6) Press filler into the gaps. (7) Press on the strip. (8) Fill over the gap. Sand down and paint or paper the wall.

Working with plasterboard requires, in addition to a hammer and pincers, only a sharp knife, preferably a gardener's knife with a curved blade and a flat trowel for filling gaps. If necessary you can use a scraper. You will also need special nails, filler and reinforcing strips.

To cut plasterboard, cut through the cardboard on the top surface along the edge of a metal rule, break the plaster centre over a hard edge, turn the board over and cut the cardboard on the underside.

How to make a false ceiling

Often when decorating a room, the appearance of the ceiling is not taken into account. It is painted white, with or without woodchip paper, and that is all.

There are many ways of emphasizing the ceiling. It could be painted in a colour or covered with coloured wallpaper – hints on doing this are to be found on pages 244–5. You could also make it warmer and more homely by covering it with wood, sticking on textured tiles, or even building an entire false ceiling which can also improve sound-proofing.

Covering ceilings with wood
Whatever material you choose, every ceiling that is to be covered with wood requires a sub- or supporting structure to support the planks, veneered board or strips. The choice of materials depends on how the room is to be furnished. Simple grained timbers free from knots generally go better with a modern, impressively furnished room. Knotty woods with rough structures and surfaces are better suited to country-style rooms. Light, high rooms can take dark woods and strongly marked, broken surfaces. Small low rooms look best with smooth ceilings of light timber.

You must also consider in what direction the wood markings and strong lines (e.g. the joins between the planks) should run. The room will appear elongated in the direction of lines and markings. Softwoods (e.g. pine, larch, Oregon pine) are usually worked as solid wood in the form of planks and tongues and grooves. Hardwoods supply veneers with which chipboard or plywood are covered. Expensive, exotic woods are also available in this form. The substructure for a plank or veneered board covering for the ceiling consists in its simplest form of a criss-cross framework of 2 by 1 inch (50 by 30 millimetre) roofing battens. The first layer will run in the same direction as that chosen for the ceiling planks, fastened to the underside of the ceiling at 18-inch (500-millimetre) intervals by means of wood screws and wall plugs, if you have a solid ceiling, or screwed into the ceiling joists. A second layer is nailed or screwed under the first at right angles (see diagram on this page). During this process, irregularities in the ceiling should be evened out with thin wooden wedges, strips of plywood etc. You can use a spirit level and a tensioned string to find out if the substructure is level.

At the wall edges fasten a planed, dark-painted batten around the wall so that the bottom is at exactly the same height as the bottom of the second layer of battens.

The planks are cut so that they are ½ inch (12 millimetres) from each wall. Tongue-and-groove planks are invisibly nailed through the tongue. With veneered board make sure that the second layer of battens are fixed at intervals which match the width of the boards. Veneered board can be glued into place or held by special hooks which will eventually be invisible.

Polystyrene ceiling
A ceiling covered with expanded polystyrene (diagram left) requires the same substructure as a wooden ceiling. Then ¼-inch (5-millimetre) hardboard or chipboard is nailed onto the batten frame. The boards should always meet at the centre of a batten and be very precisely nailed at this point. If you were not careful when using the string and spirit level when making the frame this will now become obvious.

The expanded polystyrene tiles are glued to the underside of the boards with a special adhesive. You should not begin in a corner, but preferably in the middle of the room: Mark the centre line of the ceiling using the string, and at right angles mark a line across the room through the centre point. Place the first tile in one of the corners of the cross and then work out from here in a star-fashion.

Hanging ceiling
A hanging ceiling differs from one fixed directly onto the ceiling only by the fact that it comes down into the room. You could choose this type if you want to make a very high room seem more intimate and cosy. Here again planks or veneered boards are used. Of course you can also use expanded polystyrene or acoustic tiles, or plasterboard.

Vertical supports are nailed to a framework of 2 by 2 inch (50 by 50 millimetre) battens fixed to the ceiling as before.

Sound-proofing ceilings is difficult to achieve. Most effective is a sprung construction the underside of which can be plastered or covered with plasterboard. Sound-proofing insulation board is inserted in between. This is a ceiling with a top layer of expanded polystyrene tiles fastened to a batten framework. The first row of battens is fixed to the concrete ceiling with wall plugs and wood screws. The second row can be nailed. Hardboard is fastened onto them again with nails. The expanded polystyrene tiles are glued on beginning at the centre of the room using a special adhesive.

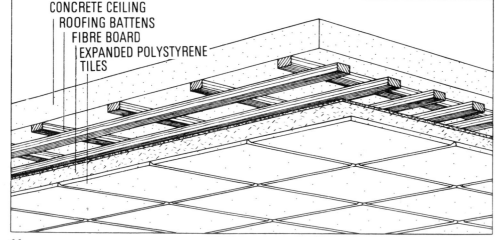

CONCRETE CEILING
ROOFING BATTENS
FIBRE BOARD
EXPANDED POLYSTYRENE TILES

Their length depends on the height of the ceiling required. Battens, to which the ceiling is attached, are screwed to the bottom of the vertical supports. The distance between the battens depends on the type of ceiling covering. Planks need supporting battens every 18 inches (500 millimetres). For veneered boards they may possibly have to be closer together. About every 6 feet (2 metres) the lower frame should be reinforced by a stabilizing batten. This is pushed between the ceiling and the supporting battens and nailed. Here again a clean wall join is provided by a dark-painted wall batten all the way around the edges. The ceiling planks are fixed with concealed nails, veneered sheets can be glued on or fixed with special hooks. Expanded polystyrene and acoustic tiles need a layer of hardboard onto which they can be glued.

Sound-proofed ceiling

If you have a lot of noise coming from above, effective solutions will be dear. Simply nailing or sticking sound-proofing tiles onto the ceiling scarcely helps at all. Even the batten-construction ceilings already described can only help slightly with sound-proofing.

Sound-proofing a ceiling from below to eliminate footstep noise from above is both complicated and expensive, for firstly the construction which you hang from the ceiling must be solid and heavy, and secondly you should sound-proof the walls as well if possible for noise passes mainly from the ceiling to the walls (and vice versa). In general there are two points to watch:

A sound-proofed ceiling should, where possible, be sprung so that there are no rigid joints (diagram above left). A plastered or plasterboard construction will be heavy enough to stop noise from above.

The ceiling should not touch the walls, but should be separated from them by strips of foam rubber (diagram above right). The illustrated extra timber ceiling can do nothing on its own to cut out noise effectively. Here sound-proofing material (mineral fibre) must be inserted between the concrete ceiling and

the timber. In addition acoustic board should be glued to the underside of the timber.

Other ways of covering the ceiling include expanded polystyrene tiles, acoustic planks (with a strongly jointed surface) and noise-absorbent reed matting. If the room above is part of your home, thicker carpet is still the most effective way of sound-proofing footsteps.

Fabric on the ceiling

One part of the room, the seating area, for example, could be 'roofed over' by a carpet hung from the ceiling.

How do you hang carpet on a ceiling? Firstly, you make a frame the size of the carpet using 4 by 1 inch (100 by 30 millimetre) timber (roofing battens can be used for a light carpet), reinforced at 39-inch (1000-millimetre) intervals by cross pieces. Nail a ¼-inch (6-millimetre) sheet of chipboard to the underside. The carpet is firmly tacked to the board.

Using strong screws, fasten chains to the four corners of the frame and screw four hooks into the ceiling using plugs which should be sufficiently long and strong. Now you can hang the carpet on the ceiling. It should be at least 8 inches (200 millimetres) below the ceiling. Firstly this will make it easier to work – secondly it is this that produces the cave-like atmosphere.

Another possibility is to put a canopy below the ceiling. It should be made from white muslin, or similar material and be held in place by wires.

Screw eyebolts at intervals of 18 to 24 inches (500 to 700 millimetres) into the walls of the room or part of the room that you want to cover at the required height. The bolts on the two side walls should be exactly opposite one another. Stretch wires across the room between the rings like rungs in a ladder.

Sew the material together to form a strip of the required width. The length should be half as long again as the length of the area to be covered so that it can hang down between the wires. The fabric is held in place on the wire at both sides with press studs.

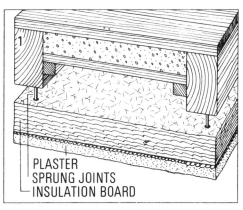

PLASTER
SPRUNG JOINTS
INSULATION BOARD

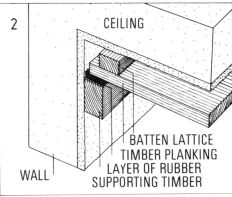

CEILING

BATTEN LATTICE
TIMBER PLANKING
LAYER OF RUBBER
SUPPORTING TIMBER

WALL

The ceiling should not touch the wall but should be separated from it by strips of foam rubber. Otherwise sound passes down the wall and back up to the ceiling. The most effective method is to combine a sound-proofed ceiling with sound-proofed walls.

WINDOWS AND CURTAINS

Old houses sometimes have small windows which are divided into small panes. This is mainly attributable to the materials used in their construction – wood and stone – both materials possessing rather limited spanning capacity. In addition glass was expensive; large panes cost a lot of money. Window openings were therefore divided up so that smaller and cheaper panes could be used.

We no longer have the same problem. In this age of ferro-concrete we can span window openings of any width. There is also no problem in manufacturing large panes of glass. Consequently windows have become increasingly larger in the last ten years and no longer need to be divided up.

Large windows allow the eye to see more of the outside of the house. They also, of course, let in more light, and make the room seem larger. These are the advantages. But large windows also let more cold into the room and are inevitably the weakest point in the wall and therefore are apt to let in noise to a varying degree.

Since nobody would consider changing a beautiful large window for a smaller one in order to save heating costs, the only alternative is to pay more attention to the quality of the window. Well fitting windows with thick glass keep out cold and noise better than windows where draughts blow through every crack and where traffic sets the panes vibrating. Some solutions to these problems are explained on pages 82–3.

For anyone furnishing a home the same problem crops up again and again – how the window, which breaks up the wall surface, can be incorporated into the furnishings of the room. Today the most popular window decoration is still net curtains and thicker fabric curtains. The basic rule here is that it is better to adopt a more lavish style of curtaining to link the window with the neighbouring walls than to under-emphasize the window. There are many possibilities for decorating a window. Apart from curtains, there are plastic or fabric roller blinds which not only need less material than a curtain, but can go better with a more functional style of furnishing and are more versatile. Curtains which draw up are suitable for individual windows, in a kitchen, nursery or bathroom, for example. Screens go well with oriental-type furniture. Vertical venetian blinds, which are widely used to protect display windows and glass-fronted office blocks from the light, are stylish and go well in lavishly furnished rooms.

Like all the main furnishing elements, window decorations must be carefully matched with the carpet, colour scheme and the furniture. If you choose your curtains in isolation this can spoil your whole furnishing scheme.

'Beautiful windows are the dimples on the face of your home', say the Japanese. Airy voiles billow beside coarse fabrics, or old-fashioned lace competes with bold geometric shapes.

Nets and curtains

Curtaining could be described as the decorative continuation of a wall using a different material. But it is more than that. It is an integral part of the furnishing, a protection from inquisitive eyes, and a screen against the rays of the sun. First here is an explanation of the terms:

Net curtains are transparent window coverings, usually made from artificial fibres, plain or with a pattern worked into them.

Curtains consist of non-transparent plain or patterned fabrics, which can be pushed back to occupy a narrow strip either side of the window when not in use.

Effective decoration of windows or glass doors depends firstly on the right choice of materials, the type of fabric, colour and pattern, and secondly on the choice of curtain style which must go with the room size. These two elements must be complementary if the room is to have the desired effect. The main rules are as follows: Window decoration forms part of interior design and must therefore fit into the general furnishing scheme. Functional windows require functional decorations. Bay and bow windows, romanesque windows, and windows which are sub-divided into small panes will need a more decorative style. One of the best ways to ensure that your curtains are integrated with the rest of the room is to have wall-to-wall curtaining, from ceiling to floor. Of course this is not always so, and the following pages give examples of many other possible ways.

Above: **The net curtain is here the dominant feature of this room. This modern window has no curtains, as the floor-length, boldly patterned nets cover the whole window wall, and in the evening roller blinds are used.**

Right: **A windowsill-length curtain leaves space under the window for low cupboard units. The wooden curtain pole and the pattern of the fabric have a comfortable, cosy effect. Nets are not needed. Here the dining chairs have been covered in the same material as the curtains.**

70

A wall-to-wall floor-length curtain
unifies the whole window wall. The
window looks larger and more tranquil
while at the same time the room
becomes more airy. A more
conventional method of curtaining
would overemphasize the shape of the
window and break up the fairly narrow
wall. The curtains give even more
feeling of space if the wall surfaces
around the window are the same colour
as the main colour of the curtains.

Using a roller blind and wallpaper with the same pattern (left) is an effective and stylish way of making even small rooms appear more spacious. When the blind is pulled down, the wall and window area become one continuous surface. You can also paint the window-frame and the radiator under the window in one of the colours in the fabric and wallpaper.

It is not easy to decorate a window with a glazed door alongside it in a unified, bold way. A curtain drawn to one side during the day would hide too much of the window. In this case it is better to use several roller blinds (below) which are all the same width. These give unity to the windows and door.

Roller blinds

Many windows are unsuitable for the usual 'nets and curtains' type of decoration – those in nurseries, for example, or old-fashioned windows whose shape and frame are too attractive to be continually covered, or above a work surface where they would always be in the way.

In cases like this, a fabric roller blind could be used. When it is rolled up it gets in the way neither visually nor practically, and when pulled down it shows off its pattern particularly clearly because of its flat surface. A further advantage of roller blinds is that they require less material than for curtains, and are therefore less expensive.

Blinds are therefore not only practical and original but also economical. Some wallpaper shops have patterns which have matching fabrics. The photograph at the top of the left-hand page shows one example of how effective this can be. The room looks bigger and more unified, especially if other objects in the room (e.g. window frames, radiators) are painted in a matching colour.

Depending on the depth of the lintel, blinds can be fitted into the window alcove or directly above it. Hints on putting up roller blinds can be found on page 80.

A draw-up curtain is related to the roller blind (see below right). Here again you only need a piece of material the size of the window (plus seam allowance). A draw-up curtain does not wrap around a pole, but is drawn up by cords. For this purpose, curtain rings are sewn to the back of the fabric and the cords run through them. The cords are tied together on one side of the curtain and they are used to draw the curtain up or let it down. Locking hooks are screwed into the frame within easy reach and the cords are wrapped round them to hold the curtain in position. Draw-up curtains are particularly recommended for windows which are difficult to get to (e.g., high windows over cupboard units), or for glazed doors leading to a balcony or patio where traditional curtains or even roller blinds would be unsuitable – the latter mainly because you would have to stoop low to reach the cord to release the blind. The buttoned curtain, illustrated below left, is also related to the roller blind. This consists of canvas with eyelets let in around the edges. These fit over toggles which are screwed to the window frame.

Canvas which can be unbuttoned is a good curtaining idea for a nursery. The canvas has wide hems and is about 1½ inches (40 millimetres) wider and longer than the windowpane. Twelve eyelets are let into the seam, four along the top and bottom and two on each side. Simple rotating toggles are screwed to the window-frame.

Normal curtains would get in the way on this balcony door, so a fabric draw-up curtain has been used instead. Curtain rings are sewn to the back of the fabric through which the cords run. These are used to draw up the curtain and let it down again. You can make draw-up curtains yourself (see page 81).

Other window coverings

There are two unusual methods of decoration which are particularly suited to large windows: sliding curtains and vertical venetian blinds.

Wall-to-wall windows and very large windows make a room lighter and give it a spacious, uncluttered feel. Covering them is difficult, as ordinary curtains are not recommended.

It is a better idea to make sliding curtains. They are fastened to sliding bars which fit into a metal runner fastened to the ceiling. Runners with up to six tracks can be used depending on the number of fabric widths and sliding bars you want to use. During the day the widths of fabric can be pushed one behind the other so that they cover only a small part of the window. A heavy rod is inserted into the bottom seam of the curtains so that the fabric hangs straight.

Perpendicular or vertical venetian blinds consist of narrow strips of material which can be pushed to and fro by means of small casters running along a rail. When the blinds are open and pushed to the side the slats condense into a very narrow area. The amount of light entering the room can be regulated very precisely. When the slats are at an angle you can look out but you can't see into the room from outside.

Sliding curtains which run along rails on the ceiling are particularly recommended for wall-to-wall windows. Ordinary curtains would take up too much valuable space when open.

Vertical venetian blinds (right) consist of narrow strips of material which can be pushed along a ceiling rail by means of small casters. They can also be placed at any angle.

Decorating difficult windows

One of the general rules when choosing curtains is that large patterns are suitable only for large rooms and that small and delicate patterns are better for smaller rooms. Also bold colours tend to shorten a room, while light pastel colours make it look deeper.

If you prefer traditional curtains they should be generously cut. The ideal width of curtain is two times the window width. When the curtains are drawn back they should not really overlap the window unless you want to make it look narrower. Otherwise it is better to choose roller blinds, draw-up curtains or sliding curtains.

A few tips for dealing with problem windows:

Two small windows lying close together should not be curtained separately for this emphasizes their smallness. It is better to curtain the whole window wall (see diagram above right). Roller blinds can be used in the evening if you choose transparent or semi-transparent fabric for the curtains.

A good way to give unity to a window and glazed door side by side is to use wall-to-wall curtains. The curtaining should not be too heavy or thick if there is a radiator under the window. You could use roller or venetian blinds with them.

A floor-length, wall-to-wall window would be better suited to sliding curtains of a fabric which lets through the light. Full length, old-fashioned arch windows are suitable for sliding curtains. If they are not directly side by side you can cover the walls to right and left and in-between the windows with fabric and make sliding curtains for the windows.

A window in the corner of the room is best accommodated by roller blinds. Traditional curtains drawn back during the day would cover too much of the window. You can buy fabric for the blind and wallpaper with the same pattern.

Windows let into the slope of the roof are particularly difficult to curtain. You could use a roller blind with rings attached left and right to the bottom edge which are held by hooks on the lower edge of the window. However, the idea

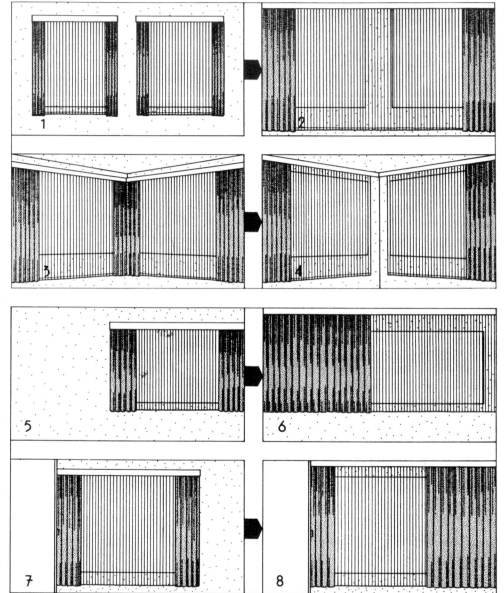

illustrated on the right-hand page is better. The fabric is cut to the size of the window, and is drawn up by rings on poles like a ship's sail. Each draw cord is fastened to the bottom ring and the cords are tied together to give a double cord.

Windows or doors between fitted shelves or wardrobes look best with a roller blind. You could also use a draw-up curtain.

With kitchen windows over units or work surfaces you simply use short nets with a fabric or plastic roller blind.

Curtaining two small windows on one wall separately doesn't work very well (1). It is better to curtain the whole wall (2). With corner windows the centre curtain gets in the way (3). The curtains should both be drawn to one side only (4). The curtains shown here (5) for the window in the corner of the room will look much better if the curtained area is widened (6). Economizing on curtaining (7) makes the wall look smaller. The room will look more spacious if the whole wall is curtained (8).

Two small living room windows that are close together should not be curtained separately, as this will emphasize their smallness. The semi-transparent curtain (right) used here makes the windows look unified.

Windows that are in a sloping roof often present problems. Here the fabric, which has been cut to the size of the window, is drawn up by means of rings on poles. Both draw-cords are fastened to the bottom ring and are tied together. A hook stops the cords dangling.

How to hang curtains

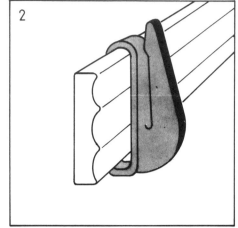

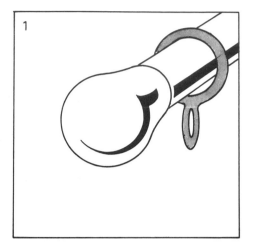

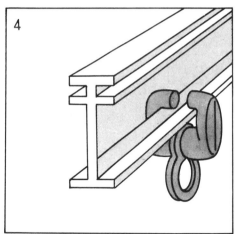

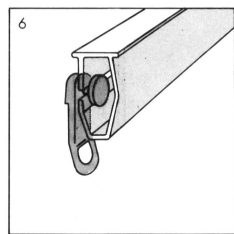

Once plastic and metal curtain rods replaced the former curtain poles along which rings were pushed back and forth, the method of hanging curtains improved considerably. Today there are devices for almost every type of curtain hanging with silent runners which control the pattern of pleats down to the last thread.

But poles and rings have not disappeared completely. There are wooden and brass fittings for country-style rooms which have their own individual charm.

Fitting curtain rods yourself
A very large selection of curtain rods are available. Plastic or metal rods with a double 'T' formation can be screwed to the pelmet quite easily. They can be bent into a curve (for a bay window) and at both ends to make the curtains turn in towards the wall, or where the curtains

overlap so that they close well together.

Wall mounting: The rod is fastened to a metal or plastic bracket which can be fixed with wood screws and wall plugs.

Ceiling mounting: Allow enough distance from the wall for both nets and curtains to hang free of the windowsill. For concrete ceilings fit a wall plug for every screw or use screws with brass plugs. On cavity ceilings, screw the joists or use cavity fixings. The screw holes should be covered with concealing caps.

Plaster mounting: The rod is fastened to the ceiling before plastering (with new houses) and plastered in so that it is flush with the plaster ceiling. The rod must be protected with a strip of tape until the room has been painted.

For period and country style rooms a pole with rings is suitable (1), however it can only be used on a straight run. The plastic rail (2) does not need a pelmet, but is not suitable for very heavy curtains. The double 'T' rail is usually made of brass (3) or clear plastic (4). On this type of rail the curtains hang below the runners, so a pelmet is required. A cord-pull mechanism can be used with an alloy rail (5) and it can be used with or without a pelmet. The steel rail (6) is specifically designed for a cord-pull mechanism and is strong enough for very heavy, lined curtains.

Sewing nets and curtains

Nets and curtains do not hang flat against the wall but are gathered. Curtain tape sewn into the curtains provides for even pleats. The curtain hooks are fitted to the tape. Measuring is easy once you have decided what area you are going to curtain and with what style of curtains.

For floor-length curtains measure from the lower edge of the curtain rod to the floor. Add on about 6 inches (150 millimetres) to allow for the heading and bottom hem. Also measure the width of the area you want to curtain. Modern synthetic fabric nets are sold in standard drops. They have ready-made bottom edges and so don't need hemming.

Always buy the next size up, so if your room is 94 inches (2400 millimetres) high, you should buy curtains with a drop of 96 inches (2500 millimetres). The excess length can be cut off, but remember to allow for the top hem. You can also fold the excess over and sew it.

When calculating the amount of fabric you need, the width measurement is usually multiplied by two. For a window 5 feet (1.6 metres) wide you would need 10 feet (3.2 metres) of net.

Curtaining on the other hand is not usually sold in standard drops. To calculate how much you need you have to work from (a) the amount of fabric required (two times the actual width), and (b) the width of the fabric, and try to average it out.

When sewing nets take care to use a thread which is suitable for the fabric. A fully synthetic thread is recommended for synthetic nets, and for cotton nets use a cotton thread.

The appropriate thread is also necessary for curtains. Sew the widths together and hem the outside edges. Baste the cut edges (with a zig-zag stitch) before sewing the widths together. Then sew on the rufflette or pleating tape, allowing for a heading.

Put in the curtain hooks, hang up the curtain and mark the required length at several points. Pin and then sew the hem. Close hem edges by hand. Ruffle up the curtains and nets to the right width, or alternatively pleat them, and hang.

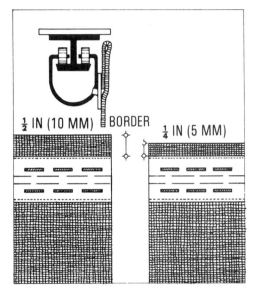

The rufflette tape should be sewn on in such a way that a border is left along the top edge. This covers the curtain runners and its top edge comes up against the underside of the wall, so a pelmet is not usually necessary.

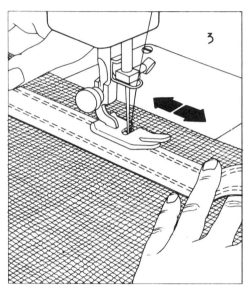

Sewing on the tape. The top raw edge of the curtain lies under the centre of the tape. The curtain and tape are tensioned under the needle.

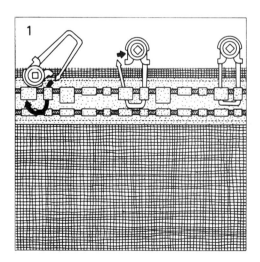

Here we show on a flat curtain how the runners are attached and closed. Finally the curtain is hung up so that the required length can be carefully marked.

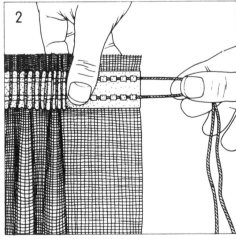

When the bottom hem has been sewn, you can ruffle up the curtain. Pull the threads in the tape while carefully pushing the curtain as far as is necessary.

Practical tips

Fabric roller blinds have already ousted traditional curtains in many homes, and are becoming increasingly popular. You can buy them ready-made or make them yourself. This is also true of other modern window coverings such as draw-up curtains or sliding curtains.

Putting up a roller blind

With roller blinds the curtain fabric hangs flat rather than in folds. It doesn't run along a rail but rolls around a spring-loaded rod. A roller blind has many advantages – you need less material, the pattern can be seen more clearly, and you can change the fabric more often. However, it takes more time to make than curtains do because you have to do more than just cutting and sewing the fabric.

It is not difficult to put up a roller blind. You can buy the spring-loaded rod, the main component, in many curtain, hardware or department stores complete with all the necessary fittings. The rods come in standard lengths but you can easily shorten them: Remove the cap from the left-hand end of the rod, saw down the rod and replace the cap. The right-hand end contains the spring mechanism, so don't saw from this end.

If the window is wider than the longest rod, you can use several and fix up two, three or even more blinds.

You can use most ordinary furnishing fabrics. Ideally the width of the fabric should be the same as the length of the rod (½ inch [10 millimetres] only should be left uncovered at both ends) and it should also have selvedged edges. Then the material will only need hemming top and bottom. If you have to make the material narrower you should only cut the edges with pinking shears or oversew them. The fabric should not be turned under at the sides, because the double layer of fabric would prevent the blind running smoothly. If absolutely necessary, you will have to use a foam lining (see below). If the window is wider than the fabric you have two alternatives: either put up two narrow blinds side by side – or turn the material through 90° and sew widths of the required length

80

together. Cross seams won't interfere with the rolling mechanism but you shouldn't have vertical seams in the blind.

The fabric should be 8 to 12 inches (200 to 300 millimetres) longer than the area you are covering, so that the blind is always wrapped a few times around the roller even when it is pulled down to the windowsill or floor. The fabric is fastened to the roller by drawing pins or staples which should not be longer than ¼ inch (4 millimetres) long. The easiest method is to fasten it with double-sided adhesive tape. This method is easiest too for removing the fabric for washing or cleaning.

If you have to hem the material up both sides you can stick a layer of foam, ¼ to ⅜ inch (5 to 10 millimetres) thick, onto the pole before you fasten on the fabric. The foam should be the same width as the width between the inside edges of the seams. This will prevent the fabric rolling up unevenly, which will always happen if the material is hemmed and fitted to the roller with no lining to even it out.

The bottom edge of the fabric requires a wide hem into which a stair-rod or round length of wood can be inserted to make the fabric hang smoothly and evenly. The rod should extend beyond the fabric at both ends. If the blind should fly up by accident, it will be

stopped by the rod coming up against the two fastening plates. The spring is continually tensioned and should not be over-tensioned by rolling and unrolling the fabric. A loop, wooden ring or ball should be attached to the middle of the lower edge for a handle, which will prevent the fabric getting dirty too quickly.

When you are fixing it to the window, you should either screw the two corner plates firmly to the wall above the ceiling (with or without a pelmet, see diagram) or fasten them to the ceiling. The fabric should always roll from the nearside, not from the window side of the roller.

Sliding curtains

A sliding curtain is a combination of traditional curtains and roller blinds. It combines the sliding rod of traditional curtains with the flat, unruffled surface of the roller blind. Fabrics with large patterns are particularly suited for sliding curtains – unlike ordinary curtains the pattern will not be hidden by the folds, but can be fully effective. The simplest rod is the single-track, plastic, U-shaped rod used for curtains. If you want to use several widths of fabric and push them back one over the other you will need correspondingly more tracks in the rod.

How do you make the widths of fabric so that they are ready to slide? All you have to do is to sew a wide hem at the top into which you can insert a strip of flat

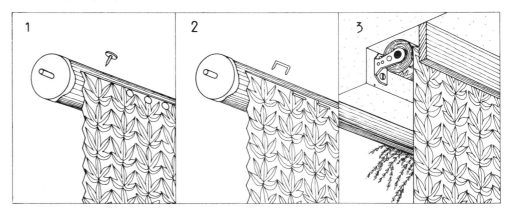

Making a roller blind. The fabric is fastened with either drawing pins (1) or staples (2) to the spring pole, bought to the correct length. The roller is fitted **above the window so that the fabric rolls from the front edge. The blind can also be covered with a wooden pelmet (3).**

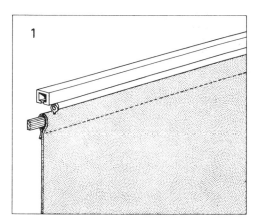

The fabric for a sliding curtain is given a wide hem at the top. A thin piece of beading is pushed through the hem. For hanging, rings are screwed into the beading (but buttonholes are better).

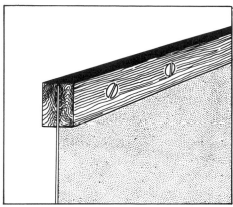

An alternative method of fixing a sliding curtain is to sandwich the material between two lengths of beading screwed together at about 6 inch (150 millimetres) intervals.

Draw-up curtains

Like roller blinds and sliding curtains, draw-up curtains also show off the beauty of modern decorative fabrics better than curtains which hang in folds.

Ring tapes are the main accessory for draw-up curtains. They were used even in our great-grandmothers' days to gather generously cut curtains into romantic billows. They consist of tapes to which small curtain rings are sewn.

The fabric is cut out, allowing for seams, and hemmed all round. The ring tapes are sewn to the back of the two side hems so that the rings on the two tapes are at the same heights. With wide pieces of fabric you will have to sew additional ring tapes to the back at 16-inch (400-millimetre) intervals, otherwise you will find that the curtains will not gather up properly.

The curtain is wrapped round a piece of beading at the top, and this is screwed to the ceiling. A ring is screwed into the beading above each ring tape. Now long cords are drawn through the rings, tied to the lower ring and threaded through the top screw rings and then finally tied together.

wooden beading. On each width of curtain two rings are screwed into the beading which can be hung on ordinary curtain runners. If you want to treat the fabric more carefully, you can sew buttonholes to replace the screw rings. This will prevent the fabric being spoiled and it is also easier to remove for washing or cleaning. In contrast to this method, which is shown in the diagram above left, you can sandwich the fabric between two lengths of beading screwed together. The screws can be quickly removed for washing. The beading can be fastened to the runners with small chains.

If you want to make less work for yourself use a ready-made sliding rod system (diagram above right) if available. Here the fabric is glued to the runners which only fit special plastic rods. The advantage of this system is that the fabric itself goes into the rod, giving a neater finish. With all the methods the bottom edge of the fabric requires a wide seam and is weighted with a pole so that the curtain hangs smoothly and evenly. In general you should only opt for this type of curtain if there is space on one side of the window for the curtains to be drawn aside during the day. Otherwise valuable window space will be used up. Sliding curtains can also be used to make room-dividers.

Vertical venetian blind

Vertical venetian blinds (illustration page 75) are becoming increasingly popular because, in contrast to the normal horizontal blinds, they consist mainly of strips of fabric which are now available in many colours and textures.

To have vertical blinds fitted by a professional is not particularly cheap, but you can do it yourself with a kit. The strips of fabric are clipped into two-piece plastic strips. A second plastic strip, which is clipped onto the bottom also contains a weight. The separate slats are linked by small chains so that they can be pulled to and fro and turned. You must always use special fabrics intended for this system.

The plastic edge strips are made so that they can be used with ordinary one-track, U-shaped curtain rod and ordinary runners.

The separate parts of the kit can be fitted together easily without tools. Even cleaning is easy; the slats can be easily removed from the plastic strips and replaced after cleaning.

When calculating how many slats you will need, start from the window or wall width and remember that the slats overlap by about ⅜ inch (10 millimetres). Bright, plain colours look better than patterned fabrics for vertical blinds.

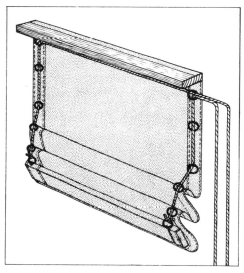

Draw-up curtain seen from the back. The top is wrapped over a piece of beading and screwed to the ceiling. The bottom also has a length of beading to ensure that the folds are even when it's gathered up.

Insulated windows

Windows are usually the weakest part of the house. Wind and cold, sometimes even rain can enter the house here and indeed they are often built in such a way as to afford little protection against the intrusion of street noise too. Can you do anything about this? Aren't heating and sound-proofing measures too complicated and too expensive?

If you intend either making or fitting a window you need to know a few facts about the wall opening in which the window fits and the window itself. Otherwise problems will arise.

Into the wall opening, the window frame (usually an outside frame) is fitted. The casements are hinged onto this, that is, they are fastened with hinges which make it possible to open and close and often to tilt the window. Projecting pieces on the lower outside edge of the casement ensure that rain water runs off.

Single windows can be glazed with plain window glass or double glazed in a sealed unit. Combination windows consist of two linked casements, both of which are glazed, which can be separated for cleaning purposes. Windows are made from wood, metal (particularly light metal) and plastic, and today they are increasingly mass-produced to standard sizes. The main types of casements are shown in the diagram below.

Sound-proofing

Our towns have become increasingly noisy. Most town dwellers are troubled by noise at some time and their sleep can be severely disturbed. Most of this noise comes through the windows. On the one hand glass is a good sound conductor and on the other hand both architects and house owners want windows which are as large as possible. Large windows are undeniably desirable from the viewpoint of looking attractive and letting in more light. But if you are considering noise and heat insulation, modern windows ought to be as small as they were a few generations ago.

Effective sound-proofing is complicated and expensive – it is best to get rid of the old windows and have new ones put in, made with the latest sound-proofing techniques. However, this is rarely possible, so you will have to resign yourself to more makeshift measures, which nevertheless can help to decrease street noise considerably.

Whether you live in an old or a new house – if you want to convert your original windows into sound-proofing windows you must be aware of the following: The thicker the glass, the better it will keep out noise. Glass which is less than ³⁄₁₆ inch (4 millimetres) thick gives no real protection. Window panes should be ³⁄₈ inch (10 millimetres) thick if possible.

It is pointless using traditional window putty for new glass. This hardens; glass is inflexible and so the sound is carried through the putty to the window frames and walls. The glass should be imbedded on both sides with permanently elastic filler.

Loose windows are especially bad at keeping out noise. It is more important to make the windows airtight than to replace them with thicker glass or insulation units.

Many firms sell special windows intended for sound-proofing. Make sure that any window of this type not only allows a gap of at least 4 inches (100 millimetres) between the panes of glass but is also sealed around the edges.

Fitting double-glazed windows to existing windows is often no more effective than using one pane of thicker glass, despite the double layer of glass: the distance between the panes is often too small or the window frames are not airtight. It is best to use two panes of

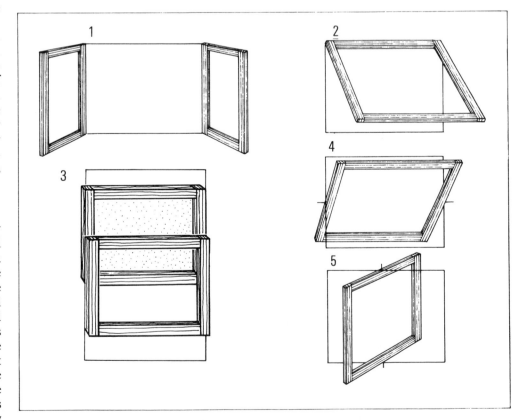

Window designs: (1) Casement window; the casement or casements turn about a perpendicular axis. This is probably the most common type of window. Top-hinged (2) skylight windows are used only for secondary windows (e.g. stair-wells or halls). (3) Sash window; still popular even though it is perhaps a little old-fashioned. (4) Turning window.

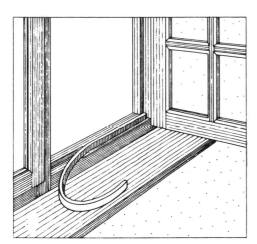

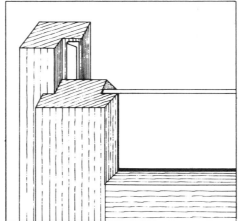

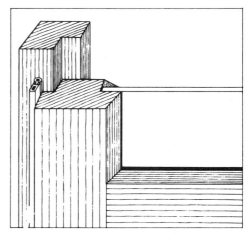

Self-adhesive foam strips can be stuck into the gaps between the frame and the casement. Since it needs replacing frequently and often retains water it should be used only temporarily.

The V-shaped strip opens out when the wind blows on it from outside. This seals the gap between frame and casement. The plastic strip only requires gluing into the gap.

This sealing strip consists of a hollow aluminium or plastic strip into which a synthetic rubber tube is inserted. It can be screwed to the jamb or the outside edge of the casement. It must lie flush.

glass of different thicknesses. The outside pane should be twice as thick as the inner one to prevent it becoming damaged by wind. An ideal sound-proofing window should consist of two window frames placed far enough apart so as to be unable to swing together. One frame at least should be separated from the brickwork by elastic putty, strips of foam or insulation wadding. Both should have a soft rubber edging strip reinforced by an elastic material to keep out the rain.

Heat-proofing

The recess where window frames and casements meet is called a window rebate, and is not airtight, because the casement opens. But the joins between the brickwork and the window frame are usually not airtight either, for these cracks become enlarged quite quickly due to shrinkage in the window frame and weathering of the mortar.

Research has shown that about half of the heat lost through windows disappears through cracks and gaps. The other half is conducted through ordinary panes of glass and the frame.

If the gaps and cracks are sealed up thoroughly you will have gone a long way towards reducing heat loss. Sticking foam draught-proofing strips into the

window cracks does not help since the foam absorbs water easily it soon loses its insulating effect and needs replacing. If you want, and are able, to do more, follow the procedures recommended for sound-proofing, which are for the most part applicable to heat loss as well.

Sash and casement windows can be fitted with a sprung metal or polypropylene strip which is tacked to the frame. Another system consists of a plastic or aluminium section with a synthetic rubber tube set into it. This is fitted to

the jamb and as the window closes it compresses the tube forming a seal. Both these systems can also be used on doors.

The gaps between the wall and the frame must be airtight. They can be sealed with a rubberized mastic putty. The putty is squeezed from the tube onto the cleaned surface and pressed into the gaps with a small trowel. Retaining heat which is lost through the glass can only be done with the methods described above.

It is possible to double-glaze even beautiful lattice windows like this nowadays.

VERSATILE FURNITURE

Nowadays, when you choose your furniture, you can dispense with heavy, large and cumbersome pieces; with ceiling-height wardrobes and large shelf units; with sofas which dominate the room and bulky armchairs; with built in furniture which fits one space only and is useless when you move. You should be able to move it, change it around, combine and convert it in any way you wish. It should not be difficult to change the layout of the furniture in a room if you want to. Even moving from one house to another should present no problems.

Some furniture manufacturers have adapted to the concept of 'take-away' furnishings. Furniture and department stores now sell ready-made cash and carry furniture or kits which are easy to assemble. These can be cheaper than conventional ready-made furniture and there are no extra delivery costs.

Another type is convertible furniture which can be changed with a little manipulation. For example there are sofas which can be dismantled and moved around to form armchairs or landscaped seating areas. Beds which can be pushed or folded back into the wall during the day also come into this category. Multi-purpose furniture of a different kind consists of cupboard units which easily convert into dining or work tables or sideboards, or tables with storage space below them.

For the do-it-yourself enthusiast there are a host of ways of converting your existing furniture into more versatile furniture, or of trying your hand at making mobile beds, tables, work benches, etc.

Low built-up cupboard, shelf or box units are particularly versatile forms of movable furniture. The photograph on the right-hand page shows one example of what can be done with small box units. This central group of storage units in black-stained wood with mahogany edging borders leaves the walls free and makes the room look bigger. The boxes all have the same base area, 24 inches (620 millimetres) square. Some are open, some have drawers or shelves, one contains a cocktail cabinet,

another a writing surface. Ideally, furniture like this should be well finished on every side and you should be able to arrange it in various shapes without any assembly work.

As well as central storage areas, these and similar units can also combine to give rows of drawer units, tall cupboards or movable single items of furniture which are fitted with casters, like a drinks trolley or movable projector stand (films and other attachments could be kept in the drawers). Furniture which is versatile has one additional advantage: there is no difficulty in making an initial arrangement to see how it looks. Because of this you can find the best arrangement at your leisure.

Conventional tall units tend to be limited in their uses. Generally they can only be used against a wall or sometimes as room dividers. Small box units are more versatile. Used as a central storage area (right) the walls are left free and the room looks larger. All units in this system have the same base area of 24 inches (620 millimetres) square.

Using small boxes

Furnishing systems made up from small units are not merely a passing fashion. They are an alternative to tall, build-on units which developed from conventional large storage cupboards – and also to lower level units (about 54 inches [1350 millimetres] high) which have been on the market for several years.

The ground plan of a living room frequently rules out tall units which should ideally be arranged wall to wall. Unfortunately architects and builders do not pay enough attention to furniture sizes when making their plans. One of the most common faults is that windows are too close to corners with walls which are suitable for units. If the window is less than 24 inches (600 millimetres) from the wall, you won't be able to have wall-to-wall units as these are usually 15 inches (400 millimetres) deep. This is also true of doors. Often doors are less than 12 inches (300 millimetres) from a wall which would otherwise be ideal for units. Small units allow for more versatile assemblies, and make you less dependent on the walls. These box units can be arranged in storage areas standing in the centre of the room which can be used from every side. They are easy to use as room dividers which do not obstruct your view across the room. So with box units like these there is no problem in dividing the dining area from the seating area. A further advantage is that most systems require no assembly work, they simply stack, one upon the other, and pins or similar devices prevent them from slip-ping out of place. These systems can be used free-standing in the room provided that they are well finished on every side (including the back).

Almost all these systems can also form ceiling-height wall units. This versatility will be appreciated if you move from smaller to larger rooms. An asymmetrical arrangement of the units can offset badly proportioned rooms. You can build up the units in steps which go up from right or left. Ease of conversion is a prerequis-ite of experimental furnishing. If you require tools or someone to help you, you will lose the urge to experiment. There-fore, when buying you should look for the following points: easy assembly with-out tools; and well finished on every side for free-standing units.

Above left: **The basic units of this build-up system come in almost limitless variations. The drawer units have small fingerholes instead of handles.**

Above right: **In this system the units which have doors can be used upside down, allowing the doors to be opened from the right or left.**

Right: **The tall storage unit and sideboard are from the same system. If you want to change the tall unit at any time you can rearrange the units.**

Cash and carry furniture

Buying furniture usually means a delivery date weeks or even months later, and hours of waiting for delivery men. But it can be different if you choose furniture that you can take away with you, collapsible or foldable furniture which you can easily transport yourself – in or on top of the car, even on the bus, in the lift or up the stairs.

Most take-away furniture comes packed in manageable boxes or bags. Some packing cases – but unfortunately not all – give the volume and also the weight of the furniture.

With boxed furniture, a room can actually be furnished in a matter of hours. The wish to have a particular piece of furniture in your home can be fulfilled immediately.

The choice of tables and chairs is also extremely varied. There are tables with fold-away legs, drop-leaves and draw leaves, and plastic tables with screw-on legs. There is a variety of simple folding chairs in wood, metal and plastic and tubular-steel armchairs with canvas covers that can be dismantled. There are also plastic and metal stacking chairs.

Shelf units or build-up box units are well suited to the cash and carry market. They are based on the premise that the basic units can be combined on the spot to give a large storage area. There are take-away shelf and box units to suit every taste. Ask the retailer to explain exactly how they are put together, ask for an instruction leaflet and find out whether you will need tools (and, if so, which). Some systems are more complicated in their construction than others and can lead to difficulties in assembling them.

Take-away chairs are generally lightweight chairs with loose cushions. They are usually canvas-covered along the lines of a deck-chair design and can be adjusted. There are also many easily transportable types of occasional tables. One advantage of boxed furniture is that you can quickly recognize any faults, for you can examine each piece as you assemble it. This will help you to obtain a replacement at once and will save you a lot of trouble.

The Scandinavian-style beech armchairs and stool (opposite right) with canvas covers, and the matching table are stylish and easily transported.

These tubular-steel chairs (right) are also covered with canvas which makes them very light to carry. The matching trestle table is versatile and can be dismantled when not in use.

In these build-up storage shelves (below) the pine boards are held together with black plastic clips. They can be combined in a surprising number of different ways. They can also be fitted with sliding doors.

Sofa-beds and chairs

The small sofa has a double layer of upholstery. It is 46 inches (1200 millimetres) wide. The foot-stool too is double-upholstered. During the day this sofa shows no sign of its night-time use. If you unfold the sofa and stool and spread the upholstery out on the floor you will make a bed 46 inches (1200 millimetres) wide and 78 inches (2000 millimetres) long – just enough for two people to be comfortable.

Beds are in some ways a waste of space, as they are only used at night. Especially in a small flat or guest room, it takes up more room than you can afford.

Give yourself more living space by hiding the bed or beds during the day! Besides the traditional sofa-bed which converts into a single or double bed with a little manipulation, there is a whole range of armchairs and sofas which show no signs of their dual purpose during the day. When evening comes they convert into comfortable upholstered beds, double beds, guest beds or children's beds. Convertible furniture of this kind need not be makeshift. You don't have to choose between a beautiful armchair which turns into an uncomfortable bed at night, nor a good bed which turns into an ugly sofa in the morning. Convertible furniture should be well designed so that it is equally good for both purposes.

In addition to this it should convert quickly and smoothly. Nobody wants to have to rearrange the whole room morning and evening, to have to undo dozens of fastenings and then have to do them up again, or to have to lift heavy weights.

For the very reason that convertible chairs and sofas are not one of the cheapest forms of furniture, it is worthwhile considering the practical side of everyday use and not merely going by appearances (in both its positions, as a sofa or chair on the one hand, and a bed on the other). So try out the piece of furniture as thoroughly as possible and ask a salesman to explain all the ways in which it can be converted before you decide on a particular one.

The examples on these two pages are shown in both positions to give an idea of the space required, comfort and method of conversion. Both the small sofa and matching stool on the left-hand page have a double layer of upholstery. In the evening the two pieces of furniture are unfolded and pushed together on the floor. This gives a bed 46 inches (1200 millimetres) wide and 78 inches (2000 millimetres) long. This is wide for a single bed, but it could also be used as a double bed. The backrest of the sofa becomes the headboard of the bed. The

Right: **One of these chairs converts easily into a single bed, and two chairs make a double bed. The basic unit is a cushion 30 by 25 inches (750 by 630 millimetres) and 6 inches (160 millimetres) thick; two cushions are linked by a curved piece of metal and a third cushion is added to make a chair.** *Below right:* **double bed made from the three cushions of two chairs.**

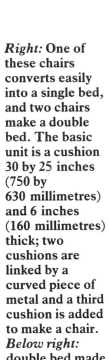

matching bedspread illustrated is our own addition and is not part of the system. Conversion is easy. The sleeping and seating furniture on this page is made up of cushions 30 inches (750 millimetres) wide, 25 inches (630 millimetres) deep and 6 inches (160 millimetres) thick, with removable covers. Each chair consists of three cushions, each of which has a pocket sewn onto the back. Two cushions are joined by means of a curved piece of metal which fits into the pockets. A third cushion is placed loose on top of the floor cushion – and the

chair is ready for use. The backrest can be set at various heights: the metal bracket has a mechanism similar to that on camping chairs. This therefore allows the back of the chair to turn from a position of 90° to one of 180° (or any angle in between).

To turn it into a bed, you take off the top cushion and turn the two other cushions to the 180° position (or to any position which supports the head comfortably, see illustration). The third cushion forms the foot of the bed.

Tables

The illustrations on this page show a cupboard which converts into a table. It can be pushed against the wall when not in use, and is then quite small. Either one or two leaves can be raised to form a table. If you put up the two leaves you get a table surface of 66 inches (1700 millimetres) by 39 inches (1000 millimetres).

This table also serves as a sideboard. Two cupboards under the table top each have two roomy shelves and a drawer providing ample space for crockery, cutlery, table linen, writing and work equipment. Both the table and the swivel supports are on casters.

With the leaves folded down the table measures 21½ by 39 inches (550 by 1000 millimetres). It is in ash stained white or black so that the grain remains visible. If space demands it three people can eat with only one leaf extended. With both flaps, six can eat in comfort (with the middle section used for tableware).

This folding table with the double sideboard makes a particularly good purchase for a small flat. In larger houses it can be a useful piece of extra furniture that can be pushed into a corner until it is needed.

This is a compact, convertible piece of furniture for small rooms. You can see its quality even when it is folded away. The photograph top right shows it folded away to its smallest as a double cupboard used as a sideboard.

The sideboard has doors at each end enclosing a lot of storage space for crockery, cutlery, tablecloths and napkins. Here one flap is up providing space for three people to eat.

When both flaps are in use, a table 66 by 39 inches (1700 by 1000 millimetres) is provided which can seat six. The middle section is for serving dishes, etc.

Making tables from kits

Chipboard or blockboard of at least 1 inch (25 millimetres) thick can be used for a table top. Both types of board are also available veneered or covered with plastic laminate. The edges must be protected with edge strips of wood or plastic.

There are two basic designs in table legs which are generally available in do-it-yourself shops:

Hollow legs consisting of square metal tubing with a fixing plate (for four screws) at one end and a rubber or plastic seal at the other. They are available in various lengths and sections. If the legs are too long they can be shortened by cutting with a hacksaw.

Tapering hardwood legs usually screw at an angle into a wooden wedge. The wedge socket can be screwed or glued into position. This type of leg is rather old-fashioned now, however.

Square steel tubes can be built up to form the frame for tables, tea trolleys (see diagram), chairs, stools and shelf units. Do-it-yourself or hardware shops stock special plastic connectors which, when forced into the tube, produce rigid joints.

Trestles for a trestle table

Simple trestles consist of a piece of squared wood with two legs at each end. A beginner will find most problems when joining the pieces because the trestle must be kept stable.

However, trestles to support a table top can easily be made by the amateur entirely from 3 by 2 inch (75 by 50 millimetre) timber.

Cut eight legs 30 inches (760 millimetres) long and eight cross-members slightly shorter than the width of your table top. Attach a cross-member to the end of one pair of legs by cutting lap joints and gluing then screwing them together. Another cross-member is then lap-jointed to the legs about 8 inches (200 millimetres) from the bottom and glued and screwed in position. Now construct the remaining pieces in the same way.

Join the completed sections together across the top members with butt hinges. Drill a hole through the centre of each

bottom cross-member and insert a rope through both holes, with a knot in each end. The length will be determined by the amount of splay required in the legs. The top of each trestle should now be planed to a flat surface for the table top to rest upon. Also the bottoms of the legs must be sawn to the correct angle. Finally the completed trestles should be smoothed with abrasive paper and varnished or painted.

Construct four frames fixed with lap joints (1) which should be glued and screwed. These should be hinged together in two pairs with string stabilizing the bottom rail. The top and bottom of each trestle must now be trimmed (2) to the correct angle.

There are many ways of making a simple table yourself using easily assembled parts. There are hollow metal legs (1) and screw-on hardwood legs (2). The table top can be cut from chipboard or blockboard and strips should protect the edges.

A tea trolley made from square metal tubing (below). Corner joints and casters make it easy to assemble. Other designs can be made from these components.

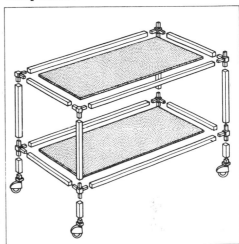

Shelf units

Even if you know very little about do-it-yourself you can feel confident about building a simple shelf unit, especially as there are whole ranges of ready-prepared kits. You should have a look in your do-it-yourself shop for one that suits your purpose.

Making a wall shelf

A wall shelf has many uses, not only for books (over a work table or bed), but also for glasses, vases or condiments (over the dining table, for example), and for the telephone or general storage (in the hall). You can also join several shelves to provide a hanging bookcase.

Stability and appearance depend firstly on the joints used and secondly on the method of hanging. Of course the side brackets and shelf can be merely fitted flush and glued and screwed together, but this method is not very reliable. A tongue and groove joint is better, but here you will have to make sure that they fit correctly to avoid the shelf collapsing under a heavy weight.

Use ¾-inch (20-millimetre) plain pine shelving, or you can use chipboard or blockboard with or without a surface of plastic or veneer. With such boards you will need to cover the edges with plastic strips or veneer.

The hanging device should be invisible. A rectangular metal plate is used for this, which has a keyhole-shaped hole in it. The top of both the uprights are counter-bored large enough to take a screwhead and the plates are fitted over the holes with small screws. To fit the shelf to the wall, accurately measure the centre of the holes and mark the wall,

You can build a simple wall shelf yourself in several different ways. For lengths of up to 39 inches (1000 millimetres), ¾-inch (20-millimetre) wood will be adequate. The width should be about 10 inches (250 millimetres) (1). The concealed hanging device consists of a flat metal socket (2). This method of construction won't take heavy weights (3). The ends can be any shape you like (4), and the shelf can be at the bottom or the top.

checking for horizontal with a spirit level. Fit the screws into wall plugs, but leave them slightly projecting. The shelf is then simply pushed over the screwheads and pulled down.

Plastic storage shelves

If you move frequently, or if you like to move your furniture around, you need furniture which is adaptable and variable. In such cases it is better to choose furniture in kit form which is constructed from individual parts and can be varied in many different ways.

The shelves illustrated above fit this category. They can be built up layer upon layer without requiring tools. There is no difficulty in building up a tall stack of shelves and then halving it to give two low sets of shelves. This shelving system consists of only two basic parts: the 30 by 12 inch (750 by 300 millimetre) shelf sections and the connecting struts available in lengths of 4, 12 and 16 inches (100, 300 and 400 millimetres).

As shown in the diagram, the corners of each shelf unit have sockets: the ends of the struts are shaped to fit the sockets, giving a stable join between shelf and socket, but one which can be undone whenever necessary. If you enjoy designing things, you can make made-to-measure shelves. Both shelves and struts are available in several colours.

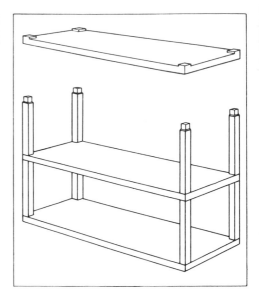

The sections of this serviceable plastic shelving can be fitted together without tools, and taken apart when you move. The shelf units are 30 by 12 inches (750 by 300 millimetres), and the struts range from 4 to 16 inches (100 to 400 millimetres).

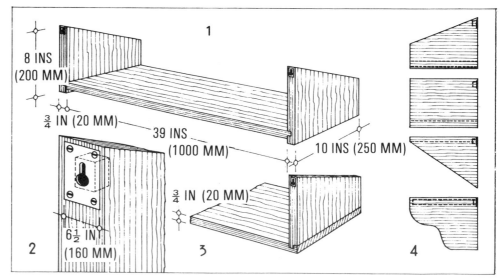

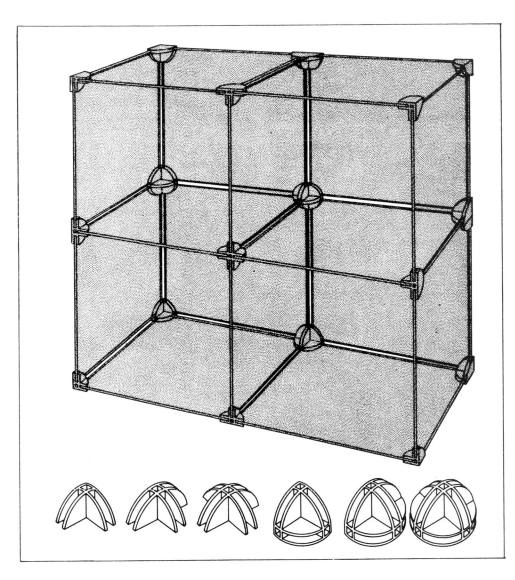

the joining pieces. No other tools are necessary. Nevertheless the corner units give a very strong join so that you can even use the shelves for heavy objects: each sheet of glass can take a weight of up to 50 pounds (25 kilogrammes). The back panel need not necessarily be of glass – you can cut ¼-inch (4-millimetre) hardboard to the same size as the sheets of glass and paint or cover it with plastic before use.

Using space under the wardrobe

Normally drawers are fitted inside a wardrobe, rather than under it as shown in the diagram below. Many old-fashioned wardrobes can be used in this way. They stand on legs 4 to 6 inches (100 to 150 millimetres) long and it is possible to use the space between them for a drawer.

It is simplest to use a plastic drawer with a flat border around all four sides. This is used with U-shaped metal runners which are screwed to the right and left of the drawer. In place of a drawer you could also use a hanging wire basket.

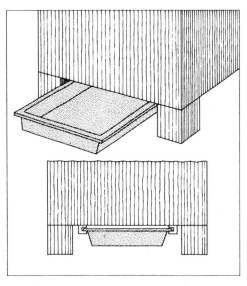

The space under wardrobes on legs is generally not used. You could fit a ready-made plastic drawer here to take tools, dusters or dish-cloths.

You can build glass shelving like this with ¼-inch (4-millimetre) plate glass in sheets 15½ inches (390 millimetres) square. The joining pieces need only to

be pushed onto the glass, so the shelves can be taken apart very easily when you move house, or want to move the shelves into another room.

Glass shelves with plastic joints

The glass shelving illustrated on the right-hand page is one of a host of different designs that you can make with this and other similar systems. This system consists of sheets of ¼-inch (4-millimetre) plate glass, 15½ by 15½ inches (390 by 390 millimetres) in size, and a total of 12 different joining pieces (six are illustrated) which you can use to

make many different shelf units. With a few more joining pieces you could extend the shelves illustrated into a tall stack of shelves or a long, horizontal shelf unit. If you add two more sheets of glass you can separate the unit into two small ones and with four extra pieces of glass you could make four small cubes.

It is simple to assemble. The kit includes a plastic hammer which you can use if the glass is difficult to fit into one of

Using chipboard or particle board

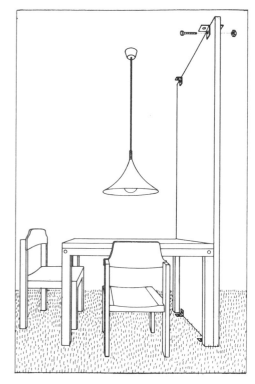

Sometimes a mere piece of wood can help to make your home more comfortable, practical or useful – in the dining area or hall, for example, a work corner or the space above the bed in a bedroom. Nor does it have to be solid wood – a piece of chipboard may be better, for it is easier to work with and you can get it cut in practically any size.

A table by the window
Built-in furniture made from wood and chipboard should be as solid as possible, but you should also be able to take it apart again – in a new house there will probably be somewhere that you can use it.

Somewhere in your house, in the hall, attic or nursery, for example, there may be a window alcove that you can't do much with. An alcove like this is ideal for a built-in work, writing or sewing table. Wooden battens are fixed to the two side walls with wall plugs and wood screws at the required height; 2 by 1 inch (50 by 30 millimetre) battening will be adequate. Use a spirit level to check that they are level. Glue and nail a planed ¾ by 1½ inch (20 by 40 millimetre) batten under the front edge of the table top (¾-inch [19-millimetre] chipboard) to reinforce it and make it look thicker. The table top is pushed onto the supporting battens and held in place with two screws on each side.

Partition
You can divide the dining area from the living area in several different ways, for example, by ceiling-height or low shelf or cupboard units, or by a curtain or screen. The method illustrated below is very simple because you don't need much more than a ceiling-height piece of chipboard.

Here, too, ¾-inch (19-millimetre) chipboard is used by you can also use blockboard (more solid and expensive) up to 1 inch (25 millimetres) thick. The length of the board depends on the height of the room, the width should correspond to the size of the table (see diagram). Remember to fix strips down the side edges to cover the board.

In this case there should be strips of softwood about ¼ inch (6 millimetres) thick and the same width as the board. They should be glued on and held firm with a few small panel pins.

Before fitting into position, sand the board, prime and fill it and sand again, slightly rounding off the corners of the edge strip. To hold the board in position use metal right-angled plates fixed to the top and bottom edges of the board with nuts and bolts. The diagram explains this. If you have cut the board exactly to room height you won't be able to stand it upright once the plates have been screwed on. So fit and fasten the plates first to see where they will go, then take them off.

The other edge of the plates is fastened to ceiling and floor with wood screws and wall plugs. With boards up to 3 feet (or 1 metre) wide you will need four corner plates top and bottom.

It is a good idea to paint the board before it is in position, but then you must mark the position of the corner plates in advance and fit the wall plugs. When the board is in position you can paint the plates the appropriate colour. The plates on the floor should be concealed by the carpet.

Telephone shelf
In small halls it is not always possible to have furniture. The telephone shelf, with an accompanying bulletin board (illustrated below), is a useful and attractive substitute. The back panel consists of ⅝-inch (16-millimetre) insulation board (soft fibre board) painted with emulsion paint before fitting to the wall. It is screwed to the wall with wood screws and wall plugs. The screws should be used with screw caps to prevent them biting into the insulation board.

To support the telephone and writing shelf (made from 1 to 1½ inch [30 to 40 millimetre] spruce wood, 12 inches [300 millimetres] deep, to the same length as the insulation board), screw two brackets to the wall, once again with wall plugs. The shelf can then be fixed to the brackets.

How to divide the dining area from the living room: A ceiling-height sheet of chipboard is screwed to the floor and ceiling with metal right-angled plates. The boards can be painted, covered with fabric or papered to match the rest of the furnishings. The width corresponds to that of the dining table.

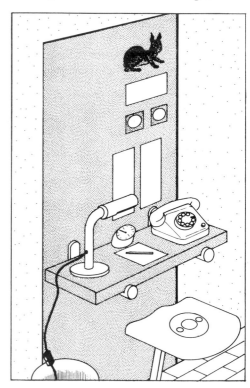

An original idea for a simple telephone shelf in the hall, combining a mini-office and bulletin board. The shelf is 1 inch (25 millimetres) thick and rests on two brackets. The bulletin board panel behind the shelf can be made from ⅝-inch (16-millimetre) insulation board.

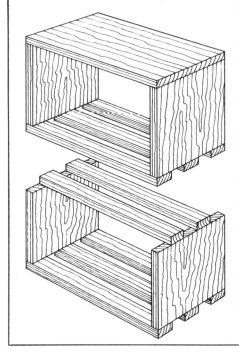

Storage shelf beside the desk

A storage shelf alongside a desk should be 12 inches (300 millimetres) wide to take files. The shelf is fitted to the wall so that the top of it is flush with the desk top. Then you can clear books, files or the telephone from the desk top onto the shelf.

For the shelf, ¾-inch (19-millimetre) chipboard or blockboard is used, 12 inches (300 millimetres) wide. The length depends on the space available, and on how long you want the shelf to be, but it should be at least 6 feet (or 2 metres). Every 18 inches (500 millimetres) you will need a metal bracket with a supporting arm of at least 8 inches (200 millimetres). Steel brackets of this type are available from hardware or do-it-yourself shops. You will also need to buy wall plugs and wood screws to fit the brackets.

Mark the shelf height on the wall to correspond with the height of the desk top, using a pencil and spirit level. It is best to mark the line level with the underside of the shelf. This line also marks the top edge of the brackets which you can then position easily. Cover the

You may need storage space alongside a desk to take books, files, telephone and writing materials. The chipboard or blockboard shelf illustrated here is positioned on the wall so that its top edge is flush with the desk top. The top of the shelf can be painted, covered with plastic laminate or fabric.

front edge of the shelf with a hardwood strip (¼ inch [5 millimetres] thick and the same width as the shelf), place on the bracket and screw down.

Transportable bookshelves

This idea comes from a person who often has to move, and who wanted a bookshelf that could be transported easily – inclusive of books – and which would fit in any room.

After a lot of thought, he came up with a good solution. He constructed his new bookshelves in such a way that they could serve as containers for the books during the move, and therefore did not have to be removed from the shelves. Nor did he have to spend a lot of time rearranging them on the shelves.

The shelves consist of separate units

These bookshelves consist of units with interlocking battens at the top and bottom. Each unit can be lifted off. It is tipped onto its back so that the books stay in it while being transported.

which stack one upon the other – without requiring other fittings or fasteners. The bottom of each unit is made with three battens and the top with two. The battens are arranged so that when the units are stacked they interlock, which provides a flat surface for the side panels. The battens are fixed to the two side panels with a dowel and glue joint. The back of each unit is made from thin hardboard fastened to the rear batten on the base and side panels. Those units which are at the top of a stack should have solid tops instead of battens. The measurements will depend on the size of the books. For books of a normal size a depth of 10 inches (250 millimetres) and a height of 12 inches (300 millimetres) will suffice. The units should be 39 inches (1000 millimetres) long at the most, better still only 24 or 27 inches (600 or 700 millimetres), so they can be transported more easily.

ONE ROOM HOMES

There is a great difference in the sizes of one-room apartments – they range from one tiny room to large, luxury studio flats which are provided with all the comforts. Between the two extremes there is a whole range of apartments to suit different requirements, incomes and age groups.

For young people, a one-room apartment is often their first home. Sometimes it is necessary or desirable to share it with another person. It then becomes the home of two friends, or of a young couple. This can work well, but it will seldom be regarded as a permanent home. This shouldn't mean that a one-room home always has to be makeshift.

However, furnishing an apartment like this can pose a few problems. One of the most important is that of demand. Is it to serve as student lodgings for a few months, as a 'first home' for a few years, or as a home for one or two people for an unlimited period? Should it as a consequence be furnished temporarily and cheaply or permanently and with great care?

When you start looking for a suitable one-room apartment you should also consider what prime purpose it is to serve: Do you prefer to sleep in a living room or live in a bedroom? Do you need room for a dining, work or study area? How can you combine the different demands made on the room? How does it stand with regard to secondary rooms, or areas – is there somewhere for you to cook, do your washing, bath or take a shower? Will you have to store all your belongings in your one room?

You must also think about your life style. Are you a loner or do you like entertaining regularly? Is the apartment merely somewhere where you will spend the night, or do you intend to use it a lot during the day? Do you intend making your own meals at home or do you merely want somewhere to make coffee and a sandwich? Do you have any noisy hobbies (or hobbies which would be disturbed by outside noise)? Once you have answered these questions and decided what you want from your one-room home, it should not be difficult for you to furnish it accordingly.

98

Interlübke

PLATFORM   SHELF UNITS

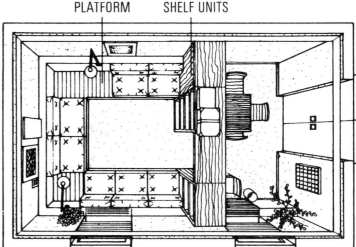

Top: **This large room makes good use of the available space. The bed folds away into a pine unit. A matching unit is placed next to the dining table providing lots of storage space and also acting as a room divider.**

Right: **This room, which is 260 square feet (24 square metres) is divided by shelf units. To the left of it is the living room and the sleeping area with upholstered platforms, and to the right a dining and study area. Storage space is provided by the shelf units. The ground plan for this room is shown above.**

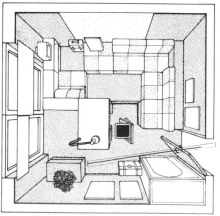

Sparing use of furniture makes the room look bigger. A platform takes up about half of the space, and is extended up behind the cushions from the door to the far end of the backrests, making a shelf 14 inches (350 millimetres) deep. This would provide space for a television or record player. The shelf is covered with felt.

Ideas for a first home

The day always comes when you begin to long for a place of your own – even if it is only rented. But anyone who is lucky enough to find a small apartment at a reasonable price can furnish it quite cheaply. Both of the ideas on these two pages begin with thc same ground area: 170 square feet (16 square metres).

The economically furnished room on the left-hand page was designed for a young engineer. It provides a lot of sitting and lounging room. Strong colour contrasts prevent it from looking too cold. There is a large dining, work and games table, shelves with a lot of room for books and ornaments, and a seating area for ten people, which converts into beds. The cushions are on a platform which takes up half the room.

The second flat, illustrated on this page, was designed for a cosmetics sales-girl. It is a bold and bright mixture of styles. In a first home you can experiment this way with confidence – provided that the items are not too expensive. Here, the furniture is mostly second-hand, and painted and decorated at home. The curtains, covers and patchwork bed-spread are also home-made. Decorating felt was used to cover the cushions.

This is a room for conversation. The old sofa stands opposite the bed and together with the chair this provides seating for seven people. Everyone has the side tables directly in front of him. The special feature of this room is the polished pink floor, but of course carpet could be used instead.

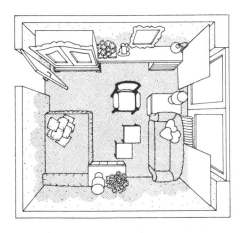

Managing without wall units

The ground-plan of this living room (up to the dining room and kitchen opening) is not at all unusual. The room has been furnished in such a way as to divide it into two areas. As there are no wall units, the storage problem is solved with a row of low shelf units and one higher unit. The row of shelves, which is 27½ inches (700 millimetres) high, also serves as a room divider, separating the seating area from the completely functional work area.

The seating units in the room consist of a pair of two-place sofas, placed at right angles. They are covered in blue denim. A coffee table stands in the corner formed by the two sofas and the same model is used again standing in front of the seating units.

Another comfortable seat is provided by the inexpensive basket chair. The shelving is made up of separate, completely open units which are a little cheaper than models with fall-fronts or doors.

Good lighting is provided by five pendent lamps with metal shades giving direct light – all are red to give a cheerful atmosphere to the room. Together with a few red cushions the lights form a colour contrast with the main blue, grey and brown shades. The dining chairs and screen beside the kitchen are also red.

A lot of money has been saved on window coverings. Simple paper blinds protect against very strong light. Since the balcony window is not open to view there are no curtains there at all. The window which overlooks the street has a transparent voile roller blind behind the paper blind. These window decorations can be replaced quite easily.

There are a few more interesting features of the room: the row of shelf units separating the seating and work areas is covered at the back with an extra panel – unit furniture of this type does not always have a back as it is basically intended to stand against a wall. Hanging shelves above the desk provide space for books and work materials. The hi-fi speakers are built into it to the right and left.

The desk is a trestle table made from two plain trestles and a large work surface. It is fully lit by two pendent lamps, hung so that the lower edge is below eye level.

A screen separates the dining area from the kitchen appliances. In summer the table and folding chairs can be quickly moved from the dining area to the adjacent balcony.

If, to begin with, you only buy the furniture that you really need, you can furnish fairly cheaply and with fewer problems. Bulky wall units don't need to form the basis of your furnishing plan. A row of low shelf units and one taller one allow uninterrupted view across the room illustrated and also divide it into two areas: a roomy seating area and a carefully thought out, functional work area. The living room (without the adjacent dining area) is about 220 square feet (21 square metres) in size.

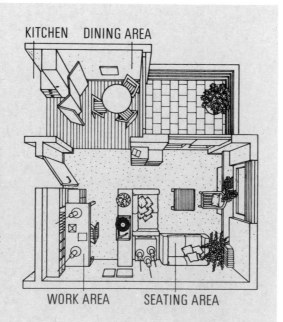

KITCHEN   DINING AREA

WORK AREA   SEATING AREA

Where to put the bed

In theory there are two possibilities: either you emphasize the bed and accept that the room looks like a bedroom or you try to hide it, or at least integrate it into the room so that it does not look like a bed at first glance.

The first option will be chosen by anyone who regards his one-room apartment primarily as somewhere to sleep and who wants a comfortable bed which needs no time-consuming conversion procedure before it can be used. An 'emphasized' bed could be a highly ornamental brass bedstead, or a tall, old-fashioned wooden bed.

A large double bed will also be obvi-

ous. It takes up a lot of room (at least 30 square feet [4 square metres]) and so should only be used if the room is sufficiently large. This is also true of seating landscapes consisting of chair, cushion and lounger units. For if you decide on them the room is bound to lose its versatility.

Both the folding bed and the sofa-bed preceded the current trend towards more flexible and mobile furniture by many years, but both were intended more for the occasional guest than for everyday use. In fact, the sofa-bed has lost much of its popularity, because it was heavy and complicated to operate.

The folding bed, however, has become more sophisticated, so that it is more suitable for use in a one-room apartment. In the simplest form there are single versions which swing against the wall along their length, so that they fit under a shelf and can be hidden by a curtain or blind. There are both single and double beds which swing up along their width into wall units and which when closed look the same as the other storage units. Some versions, once the bed has been swung up, allow for the bed unit to be revolved to reveal shelves and a fall-front writing unit. Some versions fold in half first along their length, so that they can fold into a lower cupboard. There are versions of these where the unit is mobile so that the whole thing can be revolved to show shelves and a writing space in a similar way to that described above. The bedding can be left on the bed, and is usually held in position by two straps. With the growing use of fitted sheets over the mattress and duvets which can be stored easily during the day this is less of a problem than it was with conventional sheets and blankets.

If you don't want this trouble at all, you will have to consider some other way of making your multi-purpose room as pleasant as possible without hiding the bed away, but making it as unobtrusive as possible. One way is to use the bed for seating during the day. This is satisfactory with a foam mattresss or a firm spring interior one, with two or three wedge-shaped foam-filled cushions along the back to act as support. Both these and the bed itself can have matching covers. The pillows also can have zip-on covers so that by day they become cushions. As the bed will be on casters it can easily be moved over to the seating area when needed.

A single bed 77 by 36 inches (1950 by 900 millimetres) which can be folded away full length into the wardrobe (left). The board, which is seen at the foot of the bed, is part of the wardrobe door. There is a shelf in the wardrobe. This technique can also be used for a fold-away double bed.

Built-in unit for a bed which, once it has been unfolded from the cupboard, unfolds further to its full length (right). There is room for the bedding behind the doors of the cupboard above the bed compartment.

A rotating fold-away bed with a particularly sophisticated mechanism (below). When the whole bed has been folded up in one piece the whole inner unit rotates on an axle so that the bed disappears and in its place a unit with shelves is revealed.

How to furnish a long room

Long, narrow rooms can only work if they are cleverly divided up, otherwise they look like long, furnished halls. This one is 42 feet (13 metres) long altogether. The living room alone is just under 30 feet (9 metres) long.

The basis for the division of space was that bookshelves placed across the room divide it into two areas. The seating and sleeping area was placed near the window because of the light. Bedding is stored in a box on casters during the day. The dining and work area forms the second part of the room and is situated nearer the kitchen, giving the owners less distance to walk when they are serving meals. The work area has a table which is used both for eating and working, with shelving units containing files and books near at hand. There is a typewriter on a small table against the wall. The hanging shelf above the table provides easy access to liquid refreshment.

Furnishing, light and colour

The furniture in this apartment is mostly of the kind that you can build or assemble yourself and will therefore probably work out cheaper.

On bright days the wide window area is sufficient to light the whole room. The seating area has been positioned near the window. Artificial light sources have been fitted over the dining/work table in the shape of two reflector lamps. They have the advantage of a direct, non-dazzle, but intense light. The arms are movable. The same type of lamp is also used over the sofa. It can be used indirectly to provide mood lighting or a direct light for reading. This should be complemented by a ceiling light which will provide overall lighting for the rest of the room.

Colours are primarily a question of taste, so we can only discuss the practical aspects of the colours used here. The light blue on the walls makes the whole length of the room look cool but bright. The orange-coloured draw-up curtains give a particularly warm light when it is sunny. A light sandy colour, for example, could be used in this room as an alternative to the blue.

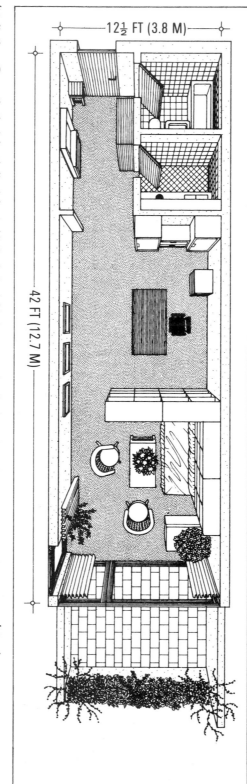

Above: **View from the dining/work table to the wall-to-wall window (above). A practical shelf hangs above the table with lighting fitted under it.**

Left: **The overall length of this one-roomed apartment is 42 feet (12.7 metres). In order to make its proportions more balanced, the interior decorator divided it into two separate living areas.**

Right: **The bookshelves with a few closed compartments are placed across the room to divide this long, narrow space into two well proportioned areas. The dining/work table has been placed behind the shelves, nearer to the kitchen, and the seating area with its coffee table nearer the window.**

Do-it-yourself tables

Together with shelves, tables are one piece of furniture which you can most easily try making yourself. If you are inexperienced, it is better to begin with the side table described on the right-hand page. This will cause you the least problems.

Wooden table

The table illustrated on the right can be used in several different ways: as a work table, dining table, work bench or patio table.

The legs are made from 4 by 1 inch (100 by 30 millimetre) squared wood. For the cross pieces, use planks 1 by 5 inches (24 by 120 millimetres). The table top lies on 1½ by 3 inch (35 by 80 millimetre) battens.

The height of the legs and other measurements depend on the size of the table: the height should be between 30 and 36 inches (750 and 900 millimetres), depending on its intended use, and the size of the table top should be between 24 and 48 inches (650 and 1200 millimetres) by 32 by 72 inches (800 by 2000 millimetres). A desk is usually 30 inches (750 millimetres) high, as should be a dining table. If you are making a work bench at which you will stand to work, it is better to make it between 36 and 38 inches (900 and 950 millimetres) high – depending on your height. A tenon and wedge joint is recommended for the long cross pieces in the frame. The wedge can be taken out and replaced if it happens to become loose at any time. The shorter cross pieces on the other hand could be fixed with a tenon and dowel joint. This is the easiest way of getting a good firm join between the table legs and the rest of the frame.

For the table top you can use tongue and groove planks which should be at least 1 inch (30 millimetres) thick. The two battens which hold the table top in place are set into the planks to a depth of ⅜ inch (10 millimetres) and glued into place. The join can also be strengthened with countersunk screws. Round metal bolts and wing nuts hold the table top and frame together. If you don't want to use planks for the table top you can use

108

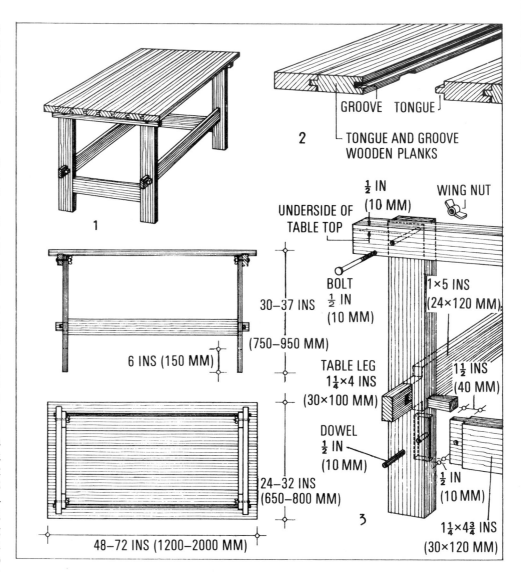

1

2 GROOVE TONGUE ⌐ TONGUE AND GROOVE WOODEN PLANKS

30–37 INS

6 INS (150 MM)

24–32 INS (650–800 MM)

48–72 INS (1200–2000 MM)

½ IN (10 MM)

UNDERSIDE OF TABLE TOP

WING NUT

BOLT ½ IN (10 MM)

(750–950 MM)

TABLE LEG 1¼×4 INS (30×100 MM)

DOWEL ½ IN (10 MM)

1×5 INS (24×120 MM)

1½ INS (40 MM)

½ IN (10 MM)

1¼×4¾ INS (30×120 MM)

3

A solid table which you can have a go at making yourself. You can find tips on the methods used on page 228. Sizes for the frame are shown on the diagram. The table top is made from tongue and groove planks, but you can also use chipboard.

chipboard of a similar thickness but you will have to strengthen the edges with hardwood battens. If the table is to be used as a desk or dining table you can varnish the top, or if it is made with chipboard, prime, fill, sand and paint it. It is better to leave the frame a natural wood colour and merely varnish it.

Folding wall table

Tables which fold against the wall can normally only fold away downwards.

The folding table shown here is a more original idea. Two pegs are fitted into the back narrow edge of the table which run along two grooved uprights, giving the table a variable pivot. The table top can be made from veneered blockboard or chipboard. Two legs, or a square frame, are fixed to the front short edge. Whichever you use must of course be able to fold back. To prevent the legs folding unintentionally, two folding devices are screwed to the legs and table top.

Each pivot peg consists of a bolt about

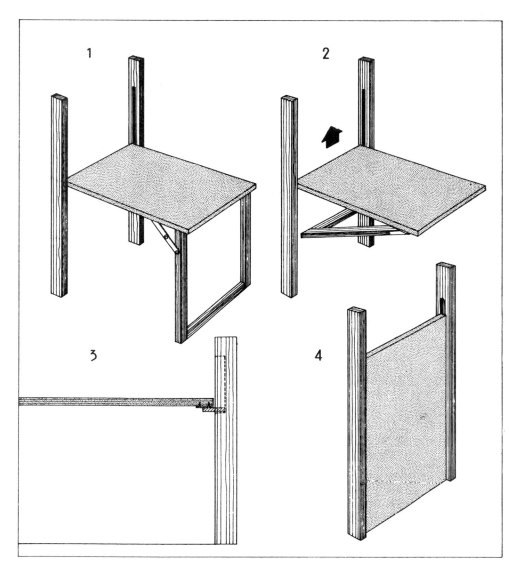

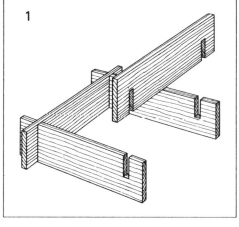

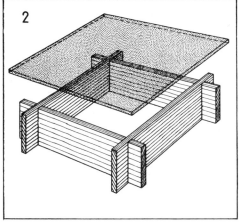

A coffee table that is quick to make. The supports are slotted so that they will fit together (1). The table top is glued on (2). You could also use a sheet of glass for the top.

A side table from four planks

The frame for this side table consists of planks 10 inches (250 millimetres) wide. About 4 inches (100 millimetres) from the end, cut slots with a padsaw. They should be the same width as the width of the planks and 5 inches (125 millimetres) deep (half the depth of the plank).

Use a chisel to clean any rough edges in the slots. When the planks have been fitted together, glue on a top made from ¾-inch (19-millimetre) chipboard. You could also use a ½-inch (12-millimetre) sheet of glass with polished edges (held in position with rubber pads where the planks cross).

Four or five people can sit down to eat at a table this size (1). To fold it away the legs are folded under the table top and the wall end of it is pushed upwards (2). The table top slides by means of a pivot in the grooved upright (3). The table in folded-away position – it takes no more space than the supporting upright (4).

⅜ inch (10 millimetres) thick and 2 inches (50 millimetres) long which is welded or glued to a metal plate about 2¾ by 1½ inches (70 by 40 millimetres) in size. Both plates are screwed under the outside edge of the narrow side of the table so

that the bolts project beyond the edge of table. The pivot pegs now need two uprights which also need a groove made in them. The groove begins at a height of about 30 inches (750 millimetres) and must be as long as the length of the table. The uprights should continue 2 inches (50 millimetres) beyond the top of the groove. They are fixed to the wall (with wall plugs) directly in line with the edge of the table.

Since it is difficult to make the grooves in the uprights cleanly by yourself, you could possibly have this done by a joiner. You could make the uprights from planks and battens with a built-up groove.

Shelving kits

There are two ways of approaching do-it-yourself. One is to try and make every part of a piece of furniture yourself, down to the smallest detail. The other is to remember that many parts can be bought ready-made, which will save you a lot of time and work. In many cases it would not be worthwhile trying to make things yourself, even if it were technically possible – shelf brackets, for instance. Kits can make life much easier for the do-it-yourself person.

Using brass corner plates

For the complete beginner at do-it-yourself, even making bookshelves can have hidden pitfalls. When the sections are cut exactly to size, it is not always easy to get perfectly straight edges or joints which are exactly at right angles. Many home-made bookshelves are not just crooked, but wobbly too, for a lot of work is involved in making solid joints and special tools are often needed, which are not worth buying if you are only making one piece of furniture. You will also find that the larger the bookshelves, the greater the difficulties.

Fortunately there are devices which produce good results even for beginners. The diagram above right shows such a device. These are brass corner plates in L, T and cross shapes, which are used to join the shelves to the side walls of the bookcase. They make all the joints between horizontals and uprights much more stable and precise.

The plates are exactly the right size for ¾-inch (19-millimetre) chipboard, but of course they can also be used with even thicker blockboard. When you have worked out the lengths at home, you could possibly have the boards cut to size by the wood merchant or in the do-it-yourself shop.

The sections of the bookcase are first glued and nailed or screwed together in the usual way. Then the corner plates are screwed in position. Even if the bookcase was rather crooked after the first stage, the brass plates will produce perfect right angles and stable joints. The L-shaped plates are intended for simple corner joints, the T-shaped ones are for use

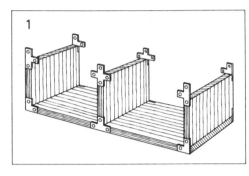

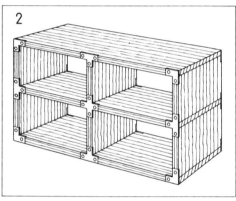

(1) Bookcase made from ¾-inch (19-millimetre) chipboard with brass corner plates used on the joins. The L, T and cross-shaped plates are screwed on.
(2) The finished bookcase – all it needs now is a thin sheet of hardboard for the back. The plates ensure perfect corners.

where one plank is horizontal to another and the cross pieces are used where planks cross.

To form the back of the bookcase a sheet of ¼-inch (4-millimetre) hardboard or plywood is nailed onto the back.

This method can be used to build up a bookcase piece by piece to any size you like. It is of course possible to make several small bookcases which can be placed side by side or one upon the other. As the corner joints are permanent the shelf-unit method gives greater mobility – even when you move to a new house you will still be able to use the small units somewhere.

Wall-track shelving

Wall-track shelving is a further way of using kits for making furniture. There

are a number of different systems from which you will have to choose one which fits your purpose: they range from plain metal shelving brackets to the more sophisticated wall tracks (diagrams right) with their varied attachments. A good system is one which includes both wall tracks and tracks for free-standing shelving, and a variety of brackets for shelves (short or long, horizontal or angled, light or heavy to take different weights) and which can also be used for wardrobe interiors.

Once you have chosen a system you should stick with it, as the parts bought for one bookshelf will fit any other that you might add later. When you move you could combine small sets of shelves into larger ones or divide large ones to give several small ones.

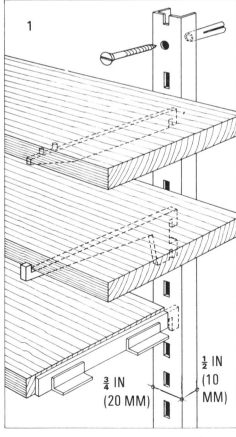

(1) Wall tracks for shelves are fixed with wall plugs. The shelf brackets are then simply pushed into it.

You can choose a type of track which allows for different types of shelving to be used together – for example, shelves of different widths, shelves for newspapers and books, units for built-in cupboards, television and speakers, for a cocktail cabinet or writing surface. In this case all you have to worry about is the correct positioning of the different sections.

Putting up wall-track shelves

The distance between the brackets is fixed by the length of the shelves. When measuring, remember that the shelves should not fit too tightly and that they require a small gap at either end. It is best to lay out two tracks with shelves and brackets on the floor first, to see how they fit together. This will avoid problems later on when the tracks are already

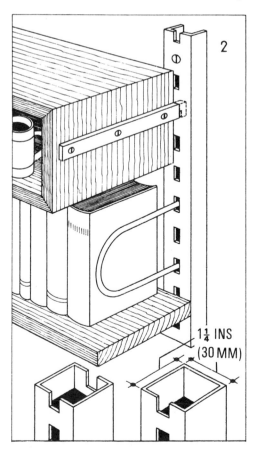

(2) For shelving which is to stand free in the room there are pillar tracks with openings on one side or on both.

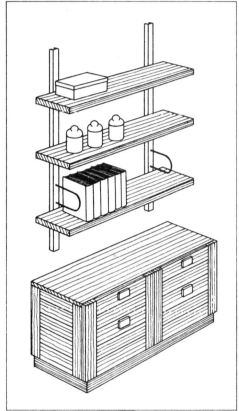

screwed to the wall.

Wall tracks are fixed with wall plugs and wood screws. The tracks already have screw holes. You can buy these tracks in suitable lengths, but it is not difficult to shorten them yourself with a hacksaw.

One track after another is placed against the wall (if you have a skirting board the track will start just above it) and made completely perpendicular with the aid of a spirit level. Then the drill holes for the wall plugs are marked. With wide shelves, fit the two outer tracks first, then the in-between ones. The holes for the brackets must be at exactly the same height, otherwise the shelves will be crooked.

Tracks for free-standing shelves usually come with screw attachments, which ensure that the uprights are firmly tensioned between floor and ceiling.

When the tracks are in position the brackets can then be inserted. The distance between them depends on the

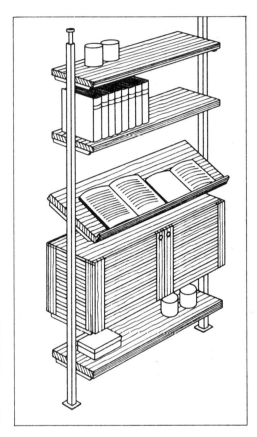

Example of wall-track shelving above a cupboard (above left). The tracks can be bought in the required size, but it is not difficult to shorten them yourself with a hacksaw.

Track shelving used as a room divider (above). A screw attachment in the top of the uprights tensions them firmly between ceiling and floor. Check that they are perpendicular with a spirit level.

height of the books, records, etc. which they are supposed to take. Now it only remains to position and fix the shelves or cupboard units.

If you want to save money you can buy only the tracks and brackets and make the shelves and cupboard units yourself. Shelves which are to carry heavy books must be thick enough to be able to take the weight, and will need extra brackets. You will also need edge strips for the shelf edges.

111

Wardrobes for difficult walls

In many homes, the walls are broken up by chimney breasts, alcoves and awkward corners which make the fitting of storage units more difficult. Although a large number of different wardrobes and other storage units are available it is often impossible to find one that fits exactly into an alcove or fills the space between a chimney breast and a nearby corner.

In this case you will sometimes do better to make something yourself. Here are a few suggestions for made-to-measure wardrobes.

Batten and board wardrobe

If we talk about wardrobes nowadays we usually mean built-in wardrobes. This is the type of furniture that is increasingly bought today. An experienced and keen do-it-yourself person might build a wardrobe like this, but a simple wardrobe made to fit an alcove could be tackled by the less experienced because the sections used are more manageable, and the construction joints are not too difficult to make.

The raw materials for the batten framework consist of planed spruce or pine battens, 2 by 1 inch (50 by 25 millimetres). For a wardrobe 78 inches (2000 millimetres) high, 39 inches (1000 millimetres) long and 18 inches (500 millimetres) wide you will need the following battens: four uprights, 76 inches (1940 millimetres long); four cross pieces 39 inches (1000 millimetres) long; four pieces for each end 18 inches (500 millimetres) long; four pieces for the base and top 18 inches (500 millimetres) long. Two 35-inch (980-millimetre) and two 17-inch (480-millimetre) pieces are also required for the plinth; for fixing the sliding doors in place and concealing the runners you will need one batten 36 inches (900 millimetres) long, the same length of ½ by ½ inch (10 by 10 millimetre) beading and a strip of plywood 39 inches (1000 millimetres) long, ¼ inch (6 millimetres) thick and about 4 inches (100 millimetres) wide. Finally, your list of materials should include hardboard or plywood for the outer casing and blockboard for the sliding door.

The diagram shows how the separate

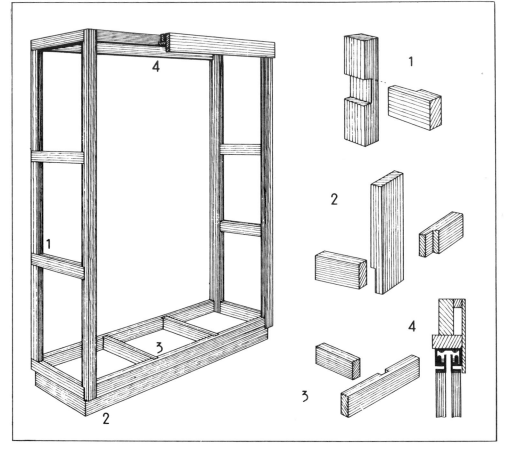

joints are constructed. You will find hints on these wood joints on page 228. All sections which have the same method of joining should be placed side by side, clamped together with a vice and then sawn together. This will ensure that all the similar sections will have similar measurements.

The joints are glued and nailed or screwed. Take care that the wardrobe is absolutely perpendicular.

The base (from inside), the top and sides (from outside) are covered with hardboard or plywood which should also be glued and fastened with small nails. You will not need a back wall if the wardrobe stands against a smooth, clean wall. For the sake of safety it is a good idea to fasten the wardrobe to the wall with metal corner plates. The walls which face into the room can be stained and varnished (for plywood) or painted to fit in with the colour scheme.

For a batten and board wardrobe you first need a framework of 2 by 1 inch (50 by 25 millimetre) planed battening. The diagram shows how it is constructed and the joints used. All joints are glued and also nailed or screwed. In doing this take care to get the joints exactly at right angles. The frame is covered with hardboard or plywood. The wardrobe closes by means of a simple sliding door (example 4). Louvred doors could be used instead.

The sliding door is fitted on runners. If there is no room on either side of the wardrobe for the door to slide, you could use a roller or venetian blind. If you want to be able to open the sliding door completely you will have to lengthen the track, but this is only possible if the wardrobe is flush with the wall.

Interlübke

A wardrobe for the more experienced to make: Adjustable shelves supported on shelving track and brackets make use of a wall with several alcoves. Louvred doors, which can be bought in several sizes, provide a flat frontage.

Plenty of storage space is provided by this built-in wardrobe. It fits inconspicuously into the furnishings because the doors have been papered to match the rest of the walls.

Wardrobe with louvred doors

This method is particularly suitable for a wall with several alcoves of different depths. The louvred doors which open concertina-fashion straighten out the wall and give a unified frontage. Behind the doors, shelves of various widths are fitted depending on the depths of the alcoves. This allows the wall to be used to the full, because the wardrobe does not need to be brought forward from the wall, as would be necessary with built-in wardrobes which have a fitted back panel.

Make the wardrobe deep enough to provide adequate hanging space. This needs to be about 24 inches (600 millimetres) deep. Shelves 12 to 16 inches (300 to 400 millimetres) wide will be sufficient for storing linen, bags, etc. Don't make the shelves deeper than 24 inches (600 millimetres) or you will not be able to see or reach articles at the back of the shelves.

The wardrobe doesn't need partition walls since shelves and clothes rails are fixed directly onto the wall and louvred doors are attached to floor and ceiling, so you don't have to divide up the inside of the wardrobe into separate compartments.

Inside the wardrobe, shelving track with brackets can be used to support the shelves, which can be made from chipboard with the edges lipped with solid wood.

You can buy the louvred doors ready-made in various sizes, and firms that specialize in these will usually also supply hinges, handles and various types of runners for both sliding and folding the doors.

So only the two outer doors are fastened to the floor so that they can swivel. If every other door section is hung on the ceiling runner the doors won't drag on the floor.

LIVING ROOMS

The living room should be the largest, sunniest and most inviting room in the house, as it is intended for family use during the day (as distinct from the bedrooms).

Obviously, everyone has different ideas concerning their ideal surroundings, so it is impossible to offer a single solution to the question of how to furnish a living room. It will naturally be designed to personal tastes and those of the family. Clearly, fashion will play a part, together with the possibilities offered by the room, the quality of life which one expects, one's social and financial position.

The focal point of the medieval house was a kind of all-purpose living area which was used for most aspects of family life and some aspects of work. In the following centuries there was a trend towards specialization and separation. The living room became a salon whose cold luxury was seldom used. Cultivated people used dining and breakfast rooms, smoking rooms and libraries, music rooms and boudoirs, reception rooms and studies, halls and conservatories. Even if people could afford the purchase price, furnishing and maintenance costs of such a house, it would be virtually impossible to engage the necessary domestic staff.

Therefore, society has returned to the multi-purpose living room, to the one room in which people can relax and talk, in which they have the television and hi-fi, in which they read, eat and pass time, in which friends can be entertained. The modern living room should have a comfortable seating area. Here the traditional sofa and armchairs are giving way to more versatile seating units which can be arranged in different ways, and we are beginning to find seating 'landscapes', on which one can sit or lie, talk or simply lounge.

In the modern living room you will also find wall or shelf units with drawers, cupboards, flaps and other built-in features. Here too things are developing, with cabinets which stand free in the room becoming more and more popular.

The dining area can be combined with the living room, and if the table is not too small it can be used not only for eating but as a family table around which parents and children gather to play games, work or make things. A desk may also have to fit into the living room if there is no separate study.

The age of the 'best room', of the 'parlour', is past, but whether it will one day be completely replaced by the universal room, where stiff, formal furnishing has been abandoned, remains to be seen.

The three illustrations here show the same sofa with three different covers. The first gives the sofa a sophisticated and elegant look (above left). The second has a less modern appearance, and is shown here in a setting of antique furniture (above right). The third cover, with its cheerful stripe, echoes the design on the walls, and fits well into this colourful room.

Two schemes for one room

Two interior decorators were set the same problem: to furnish a living room of 24 square yards (or 20 square metres) with an average budget in an individual and practical way. They set about the task separately. Here are their results:

The first of them decided, as one can clearly see, on a scheme arranged along the length of the room (illustrated on this page). The scheme is aimed at balancing practicality and comfort. The room is divided into two sections, without being directly separated, by use of the cupboard made up of small box units placed between the table and the sofa. It is only 54 inches (1350 millimetres) high and both sides can be used.

The furniture was chosen for practicality, so that the seating units are placed together and have removable covers. The box units are interchangeable.

All the furniture is upholstered, constructed and arranged functionally. The dining and work table stands near the door making the distance to the kitchen shorter. For working you can find everything you need stored around you in the box units. Some of these stand on the floor and the rest are screwed to the wall above them with a gap of 16 inches (450 millimetres) between the two.

Colour is used economically, yet the room is not colourless. In the furniture natural colours predominate: brown and sand. The walls have a dark green bulletin board 54 inches (1350 centimetres) high, ending at the upper edge of the box units. A red strip of beading provides a decorative border to the bulletin board, to which you can hang anything you like. The contents of the shelving units add colour and life to the room. Lighting is supplied by four wall lights and one immovable pendent lamp (over the dining table). The wall lights are situated where they will be most used.

The second interior decorator has divided the room across its width (illustrated far right). His main investments were the versatile storage units which can be combined in many ways, so that they will always be useful. The units have a depth of up to 23 inches (570 millimetres). For reasons of practicality they have been

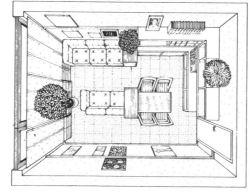

Dining table, cupboard and sofa form a block in the centre of the room.

Example 1 (above): A system of low-level box units with low upholstered furniture makes the room look very open. Since no part of the furniture is taller than 54 inches (1350 millimetres) one can see the whole room at eye level. This is fully exploited by the division of the room into two along its length without detracting from its apparent size. The dining table, cupboard and sofa combine into a free-standing block with room to walk around it. A cupboard made up of box units screens the four-place dining table. This is used to hold crockery, cutlery and glasses.

grouped in a way that allows them to be used from several sides. Four colours determine the mood of the room. Pure white walls would have made the room seem too bare so an eggshell colour was used. The ceiling is painted dark blue. The furniture is white or brown.

Sheets of chipboard 30 inches (750 millimetres) square and ⅜ inch (10 millimetres) thick, covered with upholstering velvet are used. The material is stapled to the underside, but of course another type of flooring could be used.

Three sources of light are used in this scheme, and a lamp with a metal shade has been placed on the dining/work table.

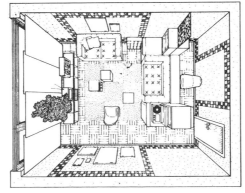

The narrow table is situated near the door between the box units.

Example 2 (above): The same room is this time divided and arranged across its width. Most of the space is taken up by the seating area, the dining/work table being built in between the box units, backing one of the sofas. The sofa can be pulled out to give more room around the table. The tall stacks of storage units can be used from both sides. The decorator has decided against carpets and has instead used ⅜ inch (10 millimetre) thick chipboard covered with material. It is, of course, possible to use other floor coverings. The pattern on the wall echoes the red and white chessboard effect of the floor.

Landscaped seating

It was the pop generation of the 1960s who first introduced a free, flexible, spontaneous style of living. They rejected tables and chairs, armchairs and sofas and transformed their floors into one single furnishing unit by means of cushions, mattresses and upholstered units. This used to be seen as a protest against the consumer society, but along with this was the aim to have more fun out of life. Successful designers, like Olivier Mourgue in France, adapted this easy-going life style to the drawing room, and landscaped seating became accepted.

Landscaped seating can be developed gradually. Begin with a few units, which can be placed together. As more money is available you can buy more units which allow you to re-organize and extend your existing units into landscaped seating. A few footstools to match the seat units will allow you to stretch out in the seats. Landscaped seating can be the focal point of any home. Their widely varied shapes means that you can always achieve an exciting effect. It is best if the other furniture is limited to the bare essentials.

If your room is large enough, you can make your landscaped seating into an island which can be used from all sides. Everyone can find his corner to snuggle into and either sit or lie down as he pleases. One can read, another doze, while a third becomes lost to the world for a while under his headphones.

Landscaped seating is well suited for entertaining. When people sit together quite freely an agreeable atmosphere will follow. It can be arranged so that nobody gets left out of the conversation.

Landscaped seating is more than a new style of furnishing, it is a new way of life. It breaks through the formal barriers of traditional upholstered furniture. You can stretch out, lie or sit on it, change the room by separating individual units or combining them in new ways. One example of this is illustrated, the seating units here being Japanese (left). You can simply lay the units on the floor and sit Japanese style, or you can stack them to form sofas.

In this illustration (above), small double-sided sofas are arranged with matching low upholstered benches to make a large lounging area. In no time at all this landscape can be transformed into conventional seating units. You only need to take out the benches from the centre, leaving the two sofas to right and left of the fireplace.

Antique furniture

Antiques have an aura of venerability and it is the awe with which we regard the past which determines their price.

A single piece of antique or reproduction furniture can stand in a modern setting and, while its isolation emphasizes its exclusiveness, it will also enhance the surrounding modern furniture and accessories.

Old furniture tends to dominate a room so it needs space but it should be closely integrated with the modern furniture and accessories (as shown in the examples on these two pages). The modern furniture should be carefully chosen to complement the antique or reproduction pieces.

Do no sacrifice comfort; to this end the Biedermeier sofa (opposite), on which one must sit too upright for modern tastes, is complemented by modern seating units. For this reason too, choose modern lighting which gives a better light than old-fashioned lamps.

Do not be afraid to touch antique pieces. They can be renovated if necessary with modern fabrics, so long as their intrinsic value is preserved. The sofa and chair (opposite) have been covered with a modern fabric in which only the stripe is reminiscent of Biedermeier, but which nevertheless goes with the style of the furniture and at the same time forms a link with the modern furniture.

You do not necessarily need an oriental rug to add the final touch to your antique furniture. Toning wall-to-wall carpeting is often more effective. A roller blind of decorative printed curtain material is preferable to pleated curtains. Do not use boldly patterned wallpaper with your antique furniture. Its true value stands out more clearly against plain walls. If you find plain walls too boring, choose a wallpaper with a small pattern.

Above right: **An Empire-style secretaire bookcase with a drop front.**

Right: **An elegant and stately Biedermeier dining room. The glazed cherry-wood display cabinet can house fine glass and porcelain. The simple ash chairs are later Biedermeier.**

Below: New covers were made for this antique sofa and armchair, to harmonize with the modern seating units. The cherry-wood sofa dates from 1830, and the armchair is slightly earlier. The cream colour of the modern seating units ensures that the natural colours in this scheme are consistent, and they combine to draw attention to the antique furniture.

Dining tables and dining areas

Mealtimes can be either a boring routine or a pleasure to which one looks forward and this does not only depend on the meals which are served, or the company at the table.

It is important to be comfortably seated with plenty of space at mealtimes – or when playing games around the dining table. If exasperation and an uncomfortable position can be eliminated, mealtimes will be more enjoyable.

It is also important where and how you eat. In a house with a separate dining room you can buy a dining table of suitable size that is big enough to take the family and also to cope with visiting friends and relations.

In smaller, newly built homes, there is usually no separate dining room, but space in the kitchen or living room (particularly if it is L-shaped or 'open plan') for the table can usually be found. In these cases, a drop-leaf table and some folding chairs offer the best solution. Do not forget that you must leave an area free of furniture to allow the table to be extended.

Also you must have room to pass

Above: **Round dining tables are bigger than they look. This plastic table could seat six comfortably.**

Below: **This table forms a meeting place for the whole family. The delicate colours make the room inviting. The uncomplicated furnishings emphasize the basic materials used.**

behind the chairs to your place without making those at the table get up again to make way for you. It may be better to save space by doing without a sideboard than to battle continuously against furniture which is too big.

Before buying a table think carefully what shape and size will best suit your home. This will depend on what you intend to use it for, whether you will need it for entertaining or working as well as for mealtimes. Bear in mind that chairs have to be pushed back.

Table shape

Is a round table more practical than a square one? This is not only a question of taste. Round tables may be more sociable because they bring all those sitting round them into close contact. But they need more space and create corners which are sometimes difficult to use. They also restrict the area of each place setting and provide less space for serving dishes.

Square tables are recommended only for a small number of people, otherwise the table would need to be so big as to become impractical. Rectangular tables make the most of the space available and are therefore the most practical. They are available in a large number of lengths and widths, but the height is fairly constant. There is by no means a standard height, though ergonomists recommend a table of 28 inches (720 millimetres) with a seat 17 inches (440 millimetres) high. However, tables can be 30 inches (760 millimetres) high, and chairs 18 inches (460 millimetres). If you buy period furniture you will find even higher tables and chairs. You must test to find which height is best for you and your family – preferably by sitting in them. Do not trust a manufacturer's claim that a table will seat six or eight. You can calculate as follows: To eat in comfort each person needs a width of 22 to 24 inches (550 to 600 millimetres) and a depth of 12 to 16

inches (300 to 400 millimetres), but it would be advisable to allow more, where possible.

If one allows 8 to 12 inches (200 to 300 millimetres) for tureens and serving dishes, then a rectangular table to seat four should be a minimum 42 by 32 inches (1100 by 800 millimetres) and up to 48 by 36 inches (1200 by 900 millimetres). If two extra people are to sit along the sides of the table it will need to be 63 inches (1600 millimetres) long and 39 inches (1000 millimetres) wide, (36 inches [900 millimetres] might do).

A drop-leaf table with the extra leaf of the normal 20 inches (500 millimetres) could provide two extra places.

Four people can sit at a round table 36 to 39 inches (900 to 1000 millimetres) in diameter, five or six with a diameter of 48 inches (1200 millimetres), six or seven with a diameter of 52 inches (1300 millimetres), and eight with a diameter of 54 to 60 inches (1400 to 1500 millimetres).

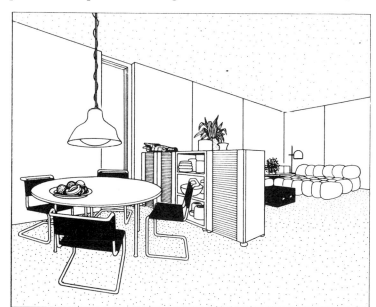

This illustration shows a dining area contained in a living room, which is separated from the seating area by a tall sideboard. This sideboard can be used from both sides, but of course this is not essential. The dining table stands between the wall and the sideboard where the light is good during the day- and night-time. There was sufficient space to allow for a round table. Extending models can be turned into a large oval table seating six to eight.

A screened dining area in a living room of about 270 square feet (25 square metres). This solution is easily achieved by putting up a shelf unit across the room. It does not necessarily have to reach the ceiling. Open units will look best in this position. A drop-leaf table can be used, so that more space can be provided, and all the necessary tableware can be stored in the shelf unit and sideboard. The height of the lamp is adjustable to avoid glare.

Upholstered furniture

The sofa, matching armchairs and attendant coffee table have to some extent become outdated and replaced by newer seating systems.

The range of upholstered seating units has become wider and more varied. Much can be achieved quite inexpensively with some of the simple but attractive units now available. By the use of simple compact chairs you can obtain more seating space for the same amount of money as a smaller number of overlarge chairs. Well shaped, light armchairs are now available at a moderate price, made of metal or wooden frames with canvas as a popular covering. Chairs like these are particularly suitable when furnishing a small room, and they are light to carry.

It is generally a good idea to have one or two extra chairs, possibly folding ones, in the house, which can be brought into the living room when you are entertaining. Seating that is arranged in a circle is particularly inviting and sociable, but will need more space than a rectangular arrangement. These extra chairs can also be used on a patio or balcony.

Living rooms do not necessarily need to have matching chairs. You can feel free to make a collection of different types of chairs in your seating area. Even widely differing models will go together if you bear in mind a few basic points:

Plain-coloured chairs set few problems so long as colours go together. More flair is necessary with patterned covers. If you are not sure, stick to plain covers.

Above right: **Seating units arranged in an L-shape are both practical and attractive. Shelf units which are half the height of the room divide the seating and dining areas. The television is well positioned so that all the chairs in the seating area give a good view.**

Right: **Another good solution is offered by a horseshoe arrangement of chairs, for it appears most inviting. Two shelf units divide the dining area from the seating area. Good lighting is provided by variable-angle lamps fastened to the corner tables.**

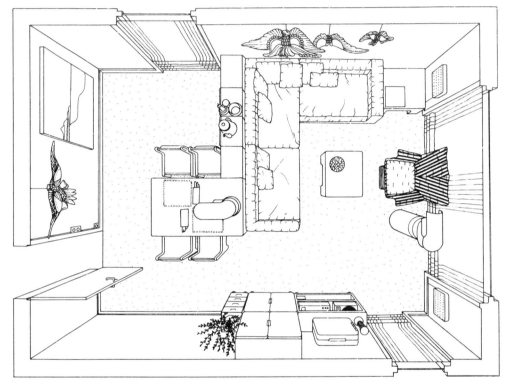

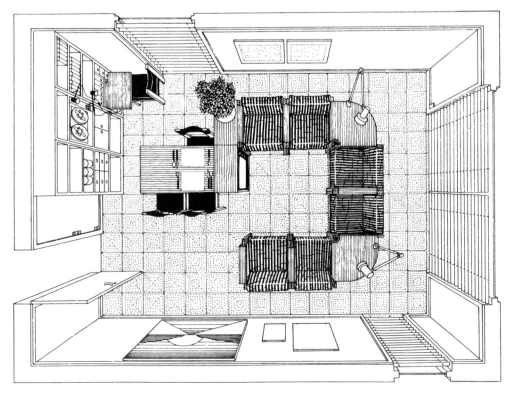

You can successfully combine wood-framed chairs with fully upholstered models if you obey this rule: rustic wood with simple textiles and finer woods with more luxurious covers.

If your favourite chair does not go with the new ones – choose the favourite every time.

The combination of antique and new furniture is always attractive, its charm being due not least to the interplay of different shapes. Antiques bear the marks of use and in a way tell a story. This is true whether it is a piece from the rococo period or a modern classic chair from the 1930s.

A seating area need not be made up exclusively of chairs. You can use sofas which in fact have two advantages: they can seat more people, and also you can stretch out occasionally if you feel like it.

Build-up units

Even in the upper ranges of more expensive upholstery, you will find mostly sofas and chairs which can be combined to form larger units. This arises as much from the demands of manufacturing costs as from the increased mobility and flexibility demanded by changing lifestyles. The basic type is the seating unit (a chair without arms) which can be combined with other identical units to form various sizes of sofa. Corner units or attachable arms are used to form the ends of the sofa.

The most important thing to watch with build-up units is the method by which they are joined. For only a firm join will allow a sofa made up in this way to act as efficiently as a traditional solidly built sofa. This point is even more important if the furniture is on casters. Every manufacturer of quality upholstery offers a wide choice of fabric or leather covers for each model. The quality of the covering will determine the price of any model you see, but more expensive covers do not add comfort, though they will probably give longer wear.

Fully upholstered models in the upper price range should have an all-over covering. Loose cushions should have zip fasteners.

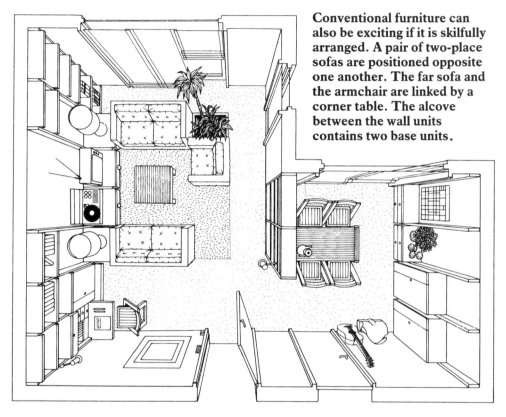

Conventional furniture can also be exciting if it is skilfully arranged. A pair of two-place sofas are positioned opposite one another. The far sofa and the armchair are linked by a corner table. The alcove between the wall units contains two base units.

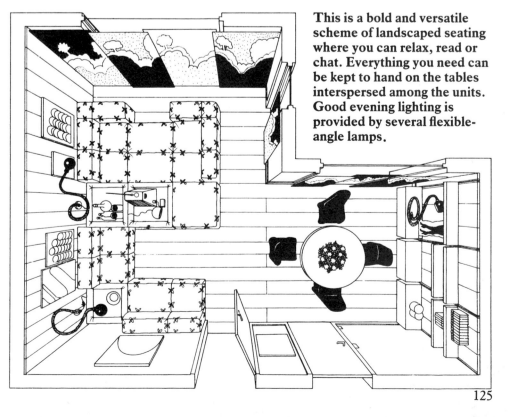

This is a bold and versatile scheme of landscaped seating where you can relax, read or chat. Everything you need can be kept to hand on the tables interspersed among the units. Good evening lighting is provided by several flexible-angle lamps.

How to frame and hang pictures

It is hard to imagine a home without pictures. Even when furnishings are limited to the bare necessities you will usually find a picture, photograph or poster somewhere. Pictures are chosen for the home because they are pleasant to look at, because they awaken memories, because they are decorative. So it is important how they are framed and hung.

Framing a picture

Here are a few basic points to consider when choosing a frame:

Narrow frames are generally best for small pictures, wider frames for larger ones. This rule does not always apply, for a striking print, though small, will succeed in a wide frame while a more delicate picture would be dwarfed by it.

The bigger the picture, the more striking should be the frame. But strangely it is also possible for a small landscape to be put in a wide frame, for the 'peep-show' effect will add to the appearance of depth in the picture.

Very ornate frames risk standing out so strongly that they appear more important than the picture. If in doubt always opt for the one with the least decoration.

Coloured frames will show off a picture best if they echo its main colour. You must also consider how the frame goes with the furnishings of the room; the colour of the frame must also fit into the colour scheme of the room. In general coloured frames are recommended for less expensive pictures: reproductions of old engravings, coloured topographical views or similar motifs. In these instances a white border should always separate the picture from the frame so that the bright colour of the frame does not overshadow the more delicate colour of the picture.

Oil paintings should not be put behind glass for this will lessen the effect of the colours and texture.

Changeable frames are used mainly for graphics, prints, reproductions, etc. There are numerous framing kits among which are those where only glass is visible from the front, allowing the picture itself to produce an effect. With some kits you buy the complete frame, with others you buy only the clips.

The hanging loops should be fixed so that once the picture is hung they are invisible or only partly visible.

Hanging a picture

It is very important where a picture hangs. It should not be hidden away but in a prominent position. One often sees pictures placed too low, too high or in a dark corner.

The whole wall forms a frame for the picture, so the proportions of the wall must complement those of the picture. There are two possibilities: either balanced symmetry or an exciting asymmetry. There must be a harmonious balance between the furniture which stands against the wall and the picture.

A picture must also harmonize with the general furnishings of the room. The effect of a picture can actually be increased when it fits into the room both through its style and positioning, when one can see the interior as a complete 'work of art'.

It is not easy to hang one picture on its own correctly. Grouping several pictures

Pictures should be hung at eye level. These have been arranged so that they are at eye level when one is seated. An exception is when large groups of pictures fill the whole wall.

together may appear easier, but even here you encounter difficulties. The group must work as a whole – and yet every picture must be fully set off. If it is done badly you will only get a disconnected, uninteresting relationship which cannot catch the eye and which does justice to none of the pictures.

Pictures can help to correct a room or to emphasize the particularly fine proportions of a wall. This in no way lessens the value of the picture; on the contrary – if the wall, the room and the picture harmonize perfectly, each of these separate elements can only profit by it.

Since there are no standard wall sizes and a multitude of different pictures there can be no standard solution for all the problems of picture hanging. However, the following tips will answer questions which crop up repeatedly:

Pictures should not be hung too high. You do not want to crane your neck to look at them. Pictures are generally hung at eye level, measured either while standing or seated. The background should be as plain as possible. A white wall is ideal, but pictures can also be hung effectively on a coloured wall, provided that they are not overshadowed by the colour of the wall.

Mounts help pictures to stand out against a patterned wall. Align the edges of the frame with guidelines in the room, such as door or window frames or prominent lines in units or furniture. Pictures and furniture should complement one another. For example, hang the picture over a chest of drawers, the dining table or the sofa.

Do not hang large pictures over delicate pieces of furniture, for too large a picture can 'kill' the furniture. Similarly, too small a picture will look lost over a wide, heavy piece of furniture.

The symmetry of a room demands a symmetrical arrangement of pictures. When seating units are arranged symmetrically against a wall with small cupboards, intervening tables, table lamps, etc., the picture should be placed at the centre of the wall.

Asymmetry must be balanced. If you put up a picture to one side of the wall you must consider optical balance. For example, if a picture is hung to the right of the bed, it must be balanced by something like a lamp placed on the left.

Imaginary guide lines help to arrange larger groups. The group begins with one picture (usually the most important or largest). Then one makes up a row (with the same upper or lower edge). Then the group can spread upwards. Do not leave too large a gap between the pictures, or the group falls apart visually and no longer has the effect of a complete unit. Vertical rows make the room seem higher. This kind of arrangement will be good, for example, on very wide walls. On the other hand, horizontal groups make the room look wider.

Small pictures can be combined within one frame, with or without borders, depending on the type of pictures.

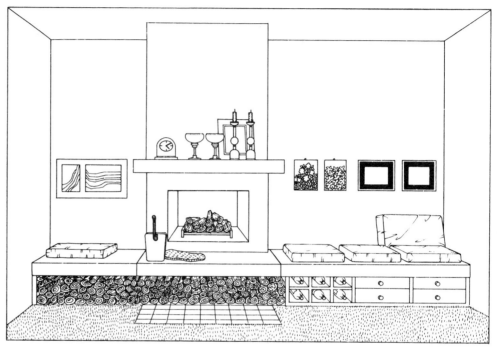

The perpendicular and horizontal edges of the frame can be aligned with other lines in the room. Here the mantelpiece acts as a guideline.

If the furniture standing against the wall is arranged symmetrically, the picture (or group of pictures) should be hung in the centre.

STUDIES AND RECREATION ROOMS

The need for office space, of some kind, in the home is obvious, but this need is generally overlooked in an initial furnishing plan, so that writing paraphernalia comes to be scattered throughout the house. Whenever you need something you have to think hard and search carefully. Did I put the letter from the insurance company with the unanswered letters in the kitchen drawer or with the insurance policies in the wardrobe? Is the guarantee for the projector kept with the films or with the bills in the kitchen drawer?

The aggravation caused by such time-wasting searching can be easily avoided. Almost every home has some corner that can serve as a miniature office. It need not be a complete study, nor need it look like an office. The main idea is to have such things as insurance policies, tax returns, unanswered letters, cheque books and passports, birth certificates, instructions for the washing machine, recipes and newspaper cuttings in a fixed place where you can find them immediately. Various types of files can help you to keep household documents in order; box files or storage boxes, loose-leaf folders and filing cabinets, briefcases and document files – and, of course, a waste-paper basket.

A home office is an obvious necessity for both the man and woman of the house, but there are many other ways in which you can add to your standard furnishings to allow better use to be made of your home and to adapt it to your individual habits and hobbies. Everybody needs somewhere to sew, mend and iron. You could use the kitchen or bedroom, but it would be much more practical to have a kind of utility room next to the kitchen. But very few architects include this in their plans – space is always limited.

The household 'music equipment' – the hi-fi or record player, cassette recorder or tape deck are generally found in the living room. You can buy special hi-fi units to house them if required.

Do you collect anything? You will need room for your collection of stamps, minerals, engravings or beer mats; enough room to allow them to be arranged and housed visibly and also to allow you space to work on your collection. Only you know how much space you will need for your books. Don't forget that any collection seems to grow involuntarily, so remember to allow room for growth.

Every home should have somewhere for a writing or work corner, whether in a bedroom, kitchen, hall or living room. This one is in a bedroom, and the fitted wardrobes were planned with this in mind. There are models that, together with the usual clothes and linen cupboards, also have writing desk units.

Finding room for a desk

Where can your office go? You will need a comparatively large space for a full-scale writing desk with built-in or adjacent storage. But you do not necessarily need an 'office-sized' writing desk, you can choose one of a convenient size which can also be used for other things. What can you do if, however you try, you have no space large enough to take a special table? There are many different ways of solving this common problem – one way, a writing desk forming part of the bedroom units, has already been illustrated on page 129. There are many others.

What about a built-in writing desk in the kitchen? If, when planning your kitchen units, you find that the whole wall area is not necessary for wall units

and kitchen equipment, you could build a writing section into your row of wall units using a drawer-unit without a base, a work surface placed at the correct height for writing and possibly storage space provided by a shallow wall cupboard.

Even the space above a normal size refrigerator could be used, not of course for a writing desk at which you can sit and work, but for a kind of desk at which you stand. For this you will need to build a chipboard framework over the refrigerator. There would also be room for a sloping writing surface directly over the refrigerator where you can jot down recipes or make out a shopping list. Above it, you can fit shelves for cookery

books, files for letters from the insurance company and bills. The shelves need only be half the depth of the refrigerator.

In bedrooms the corner between the wardrobe and the window is often unused. You might fit a writing surface between the wardrobe and the wall with a few shelves above it to house files. You should make a fold-away writing surface so that if space is limited you can hang a folding chair on the side of the wardrobe.

Another way is to buy a small cabinet on casters which can be pushed under the writing surface when 'the office is closed'. You can keep all your documents to hand in the cupboard.

Often the dining table also has to serve as a writing table. As a rule it stands quite

Left: **This spacious desk is in mahogany with brass-bound corner pieces and drawer handles, and has a fine leather top. The chair is also mahogany and leather. Based on the style of the European military campaign chests, this desk would only be suitable for a large study.**

near the kitchen so that while you are dealing with your correspondence you can keep an eye on the cooking. In this case, storage space should be available near to the table.

Some systems of built-in furniture include desk units. Find out whether the manufacturer of your living room units makes one with a writing flap. A small household with little writing paraphernalia to store can often manage with a mini-desk in the hall perhaps by the telephone. You can get plastic shelves which only require screwing to the wall, and there are also many systems for fitting adjustable brackets to the wall for chipboard or glass shelves.

Above: **Large and small boxes not only support the writing table but make up the complete shelf unit.**

Top right: **The writing surface in cream-painted wood is supported by two tubular-steel trestles. You can lift off the top, stand it flat against the wall and clear away the trestles.**

Above right: **Above the drawers, on either side of this desk, there are open storage compartments.**

Right: **Pine is used for this chair and writing table. The drawers can be placed to right or left as you wish.**

Good working light

Experts have shown that around 80% of the nervous system and 25% of domestic energy consumption are used merely to see by. So the choice of a good light to work by will ease the nervous system, cut down fatigue and make your work easier.

We have already explained (on pages 28–9) what you need to know about light and lighting as a means of giving shape to a room. Here we are exclusively concerned with lighting the household work area. Its importance increases with the regularity with which you use your writing desk – and is most important for those who work at home at a desk or drawing board. The photographs of these pages show four ways of lighting which will soothe the nerves. We will summarize their advantages and disadvantages:

Lamp over the table: pendent lights can be hung so as to illuminate the whole table top quite evenly, but cannot be directed to light one particular section of work, as is the case with adjustable models. Also pendent lights are stationary, so that the work surface cannot be moved either. However, some flexibility can be achieved if the light is adjustable for height.

Lamp screwed to the table: variable-angle lights give the best form of lighting for a work table. The plastic or metal

Above right: The lamp is hung over the table. To light a normal work table, you need only use a pendent lamp with an opaque shade. The light is cast directly onto the work surface. Hanging lamps like the functional lamp illustrated, with its fluorescent tube, will seldom suit a living room.

Right: In this case, the lamp is fastened to the table. Variable-angle lamps are screwed to the table by means of a swivel clamp. Anyone who regularly works at home – even on a typewriter – could choose one of these practical and inexpensive lamps. This lamp with its plastic shade is probably too functional to be used in a living room.

shade eliminates any dazzle from the tungsten light. Depending on the design, these lights can be adjusted in many different ways. The whole table top can be illuminated or the light can be directed onto a smaller area. The functional appearance of the light may make its use in living rooms rather limited. The screw clamp is not recommended for a very thick table top.

Lamp placed behind the table: a floor lamp takes up none of the work surface. It is completely movable and allows for directed light. It can also be used in other parts of the living room when it is not needed in the work area. But not all floor lamps can be used over a work table for they can only fully illuminate a small area.

Lamp placed on the table: table lamps are mobile, which enables you to move the work table without having to move any fittings. They look right in a living room and can be used elsewhere. But the base of the lamp can get in the way on a small table – it needs comparatively more space. A light placed to one side can never uniformly light the whole table. Often they have no variable swivelling shade.

There is no ideal solution, and it is a matter of taste which kind of light suits you best.

Above right: **Here the lamp stands in front of the table. A floor lamp (like a hanging lamp) takes up none of the table space. It should be swivel-mounted and adjustable for height so that the light can be directed onto the work surface. The lamp illustrated has been turned through 90°.**

Right: **Here the lamp has been placed on the table. Table lamps are the usual lighting for a domestic writing or work table. You can use one with a more attractive style if you want to avoid an office atmosphere. The lamp should be able to swivel and be adjustable, if possible.**

A corner of your own

Have you never wished for a quiet corner to keep your personal things? Most people need a corner for keeping their own bits and pieces, or for indulging in a hobby, where nobody else will interfere, 'tidy up' or borrow things.

The photograph below illustrates a possible solution to the problems of restricted space – a make-up table combining with a mini-desk in a corner of the bedroom. Many systems of built-in furniture offer box units like those which are here mounted on the wall. Both have flap lids, and a mirror is mounted inside the right-hand one. A bright, fully adjustable light comes with it. Cosmetics can be stored in the left-hand side and anything which will not fit (such as tall jars and bottles) can stand on the shelves above the units.

You could also have an additional cupboard under the right-hand unit. In this unit itself, you can keep writing materials and files containing important family and domestic documents. The corner is made to stand out from the rest of the bedroom by using a different wallpaper.

The best place for sewing, mending and ironing is a small room directly linked to the kitchen. It should have a large table to allow sewing to be spread out and which can also be used for handicrafts. Shelves or cupboards, either from a system of built-in furniture or made in your own workshop will provide a lot of space for tools and sewing-machine attachments, for the iron, for dress fabrics or knitting patterns.

The photo on the right shows an ideal collector's cabinet. Here it is used for a collection of minerals, so that most of the drawers are only 3 inches (70 millimetres) deep – rocks are heavy and must be placed separately in small drawers. These specimen cases are made up from a system of built-in box units, which also includes different units (e.g. cabinets with doors). The table stands directly in front of the units which are only 9 inches (230 millimetres) in depth. When you want to reach the lower drawers it can be easily moved to one side. The open shelves at the top are used to display particularly fine pieces.

Perhaps the best place to have your own 'domain' is in a divided bedroom. With careful planning, both partners can have enough space for their own hobby or work.

If the bedroom wardrobes don't fill the whole wall, you will have space for a make-up corner. It can also be combined with a writing surface (left). A shallow box unit with a flap lid is mounted on the wall, a mirror is fastened to the inside of the lid and finally a shelf is built.

This impressive cupboard, used for a collection of minerals, looks as if it has been specially made to fit the room, but in fact it is made up from box units. The individual units are 20 by 20 inches (500 by 500 millimetres) and 9 inches (230 millimetres) deep, and so take up a comparatively small floor space. They are fitted with drawers 10 inches (250 millimetres) wide and either 10 or 3 inches (250 or 70 millimetres) deep. The front of the drawers are used as display shelves for any particularly good pieces.

Listening to music and reading

A comfortable armchair can be placed anywhere, it need not necessarily stand near the bookcase. As it will generally be used during the evening it will need particularly good lighting for reading. A floor lamp with an adjustable shade is the conventional source of light for a reading chair, because it allows the light to be concentrated onto the reading area. If the chair is near to the bookcase or the wall, a spotlight could be fixed there instead.

The illustration on the right shows a leisure centre for listening to music, reading and watching television. It is separated from the rest of the room by units half the height of the room. All the technical equipment has been installed close to the reclining chair.

Hi-fi platform

Often enough when units are built for a hi-fi or tape deck you forget that every time a record needs turning or a tape needs changing, you will have to go over to the deck. Often you also forget that not only the hi-fi but also an increasing number of records and tapes will have to be housed, preferably in a clear, ordered, yet space-saving way.

So hi-fi fans will prefer to sit in a place which will allow them to operate the equipment without having to move, and where they can easily reach their record and tape collection. The scheme illustrated below right has several good points. The raised platform along the length of the wall provides visible storage space for records and also allows the hi-fi equipment to be set up within reach.

How to make the record rack

The record rack is let into the platform, which is about 14 inches (350 millimetres) high, but it can also be made as a separate unit. The method of construction is shown in the detailed diagrams on the right.

The main material used is ¼-inch (5-millimetre) plywood sheets. This is used for both the outside and dividing walls of the rack. The records stand in narrow compartments. The end panels and partitions are held together by four pieces of wood. The dimensions are determined by

the size of the record covers. That is: the inside measurement of each compartment will be 13 inches (330 millimetres) wide and 11 to 12 inches (280 to 300 millimetres) deep (the records stand slightly above the level of the rack so that they are easy to get hold of). The space between partitions should be about 4 inches (100 millimetres) wide. The number of compartments you make will depend on the size of your collection.

Four lengths of 2 by 1 inch (50 by 20 millimetre) battening are used as the framework. Into these small notches (½ inch [10 millimetres] deep and ¼ inch [5 millimetre] wide) are cut at 4-inch (100-millimetre) intervals. Sheets of plywood measuring 12 by 4 inches (300 by 100 millimetres) are glued to the battening in between these notches, and then the dividing walls, measuring 14 by 12 inches (350 by 300 millimetres) are pushed into the notches and glued.

You can cut wide slits into the dividing

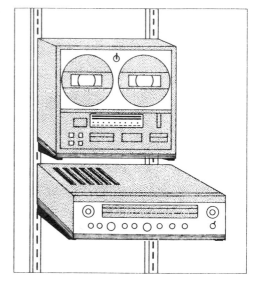

Above: **Wall shelves for record and tape decks. This position ideally suits the record deck because the very sensitive stylus is less affected by floor vibration.**

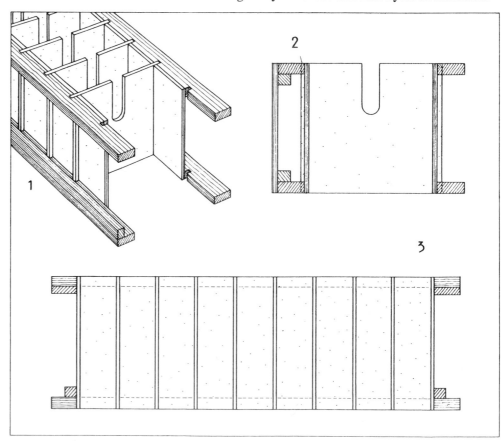

Left: **A corner for listening to music and reading, separated from the rest of the living room by units half the height of the room.**

Below: **A platform about 14 inches in height is constructed against the wall to fulfil three functions: a rack holds the record collection (the diagram below left on page 136 indicates how it is made); the decks are housed alongside the record rack; and the rest of the platform, which runs along the whole wall, can be used for plants or books.**

walls before gluing them into place (see diagrams 1 and 2) so that it is easier to get hold of the records. The slits are made in the following way: drill a hole about 1¼ inches (30 millimetres) in diameter, 4 inches (100 millimetres) from the top edge. Then saw twice into the wood, meeting at the drill hole. It is important to smooth the top edge of each dividing wall thoroughly.

Wall unit for hi-fi equipment

Modern record players are very sensitive, and any vibrations can make the stylus jump out of the groove. Therefore, the record player must stand as firmly as possible.

The best solution is for the record player (together with other hi-fi decks) to be housed in a wall unit and not in a piece of furniture that stands on the floor.

The shelf illustrated can be constructed with two vertical metal channels (diagram far left) and brackets of the required length (these are both standard components from a number of manufacturers). The shelf should be slightly larger than the hi-fi equipment all round and could be made from chipboard or blockboard. Several pieces of equipment may be housed one above the other.

Where to position hi-fi speakers

In many living rooms it is impossible to arrange speakers in the way recommended for ideal stereo reproduction. How can one, in spite of this, listen to perfect stereo (or quadro)?

The problems

Advertising literature and instruction manuals almost always deal with the ideal position for speakers and listener: the two speakers and the listening position should form a triangle with equal angles and sides. This ideal set-up is reproduced in many hi-fi shops and is generally found very impressive. But in your own home there will often be difficulties. Here are the three problems which crop up most often.

There is not always only one listener to the music. Often several people will want to listen, so that the stereo reproduction should, as far as possible, sound balanced and harmonious from any seat (or at least from more than one). Because of this, you should aim not only at an ideal listening point, but an ideal listening area.

Very few rooms reproduce sound like a demonstration studio. The ideal is for the wall behind the speakers to be hard so that the sound is reflected well – and for the two side walls to be of similar quality. Then you not only hear sound directly from the speakers, but also from indirect sound sources. There will be variations in the sound quality where there are differences in wall finish – such as wood, plaster, or curtains. The wall behind the listener should, on the other hand, be 'soft' to cut down the volume of interfering reflections.

But in practice a person often has to cope with quite different walls. Often the hard wall is behind the listener and the soft wall is the one where you want the speakers to stand.

It is rare to find rooms which are the ideal shape for hi-fi installations – they are very regular in shape. Many rooms are quite irregular, with alcoves, built-in bookcases, etc.

Very few people would go so far as to consult an acoustics expert when planning a living room. Because of this you

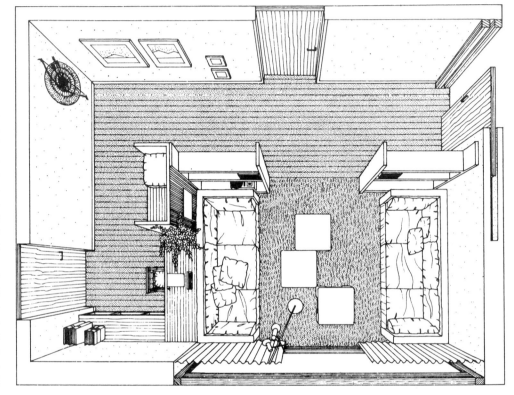

will have to try and make the best of your room. The only way to do this is really by trial and error.

Positioning your speakers

Three different rooms have been chosen for the illustrations on these two pages. These are ground plans for a large-scale building scheme and so are of a fairly common shape. First of all an interior decorator planned the furnishings, then a hi-fi specialist suggested the best possible speaker positions to suit each furnishing scheme.

Speakers are not of course of a uniform size or shape. They also have varying performance and sound characteristics. There are flat speakers which hang on the wall like a picture. There are spherical speakers from which the sound emanates in all directions. There are large box speakers which stand on the floor, and there are the smaller bookshelf speakers which can also be screwed onto the wall, leaving more floor space.

Perhaps you will find similarities with your own home in the diagrams, which

Two ceiling-height shelf units separate two sofas from the rest of the room, giving an enclosed seating area. Naturally, the speakers must be positioned within this area. The best idea here is to use small bookshelf speakers. Since they only have to fill a small space, speakers with a low output are sufficient (but of high quality nevertheless). You would have to test to find the best position.

will help you to choose the best position for your own speakers, and the best way of arranging your seating area. You need not necessarily feel that your existing hi-fi reproduction is imperfect, nevertheless you should try alternative positions in case you discover a better one for them.

There is one thing that you should avoid: do not assume that new (and possibly more expensive) speakers will give better results in the same position. Every speaker has different sound characteristics and those of the new speakers may not be as suited to the original positions.

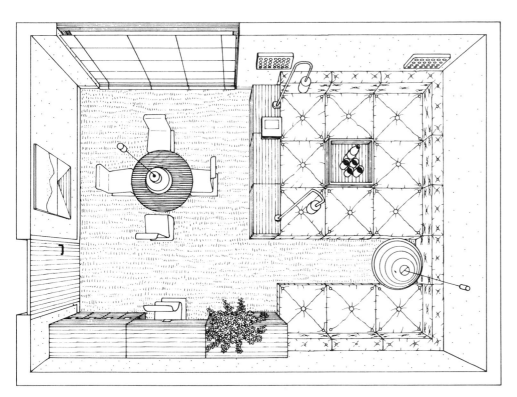

Stereo and quadrophonic sound

Our ears pick up sounds separately, and generally a sound will reach one ear first and then the other. From this slight time difference the brain establishes the direction of the sound. In a concert hall, for example, you find that you can work out from where the sound is coming even if you have your eyes closed. Therefore, we have three-dimensional hearing.

Stereophonic sound works like the ears. It records music through two channels, and gives out sounds through two speakers, thus keeping a three-dimensional sound providing that you place the speakers far enough apart. If they are too close together the sounds will merge and the music will not appear to have been recorded in stereo at all.

Quadrophonic sound also takes account of the fact that when you sit in a concert hall you not only hear direct sound but also indirect sound reflected from the walls. So four channels are used, and you need two sets of speakers – two in front of the seating area, and two behind it.

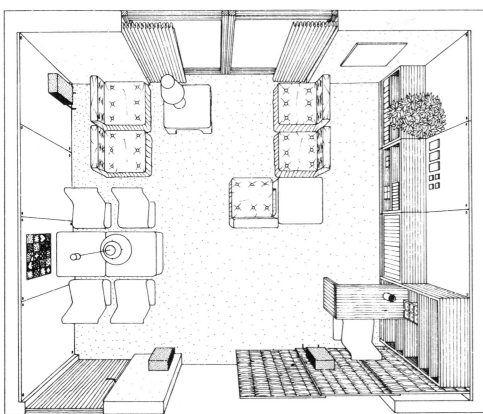

With landscaped seating there may be nowhere, or nowhere particularly suitable, for standing speakers. In this case you can get good stereo reproduction from flat box speakers which hang on the wall (covered with perforated board in the diagram above right). In this sort of room you could consider using four speakers (provided your deck can take four) to give greater intensity of sound.

Here the seating area is much more open so the expert advises using three speakers. They must be arranged to eliminate any 'sound vacuums' between the separate speakers. Otherwise you would get a 'ping-pong effect': the outputs would not flow together to give a three-dimensional sound but would separate into a kind of echo effect. If in doubt you will have to try it out.

139

Space for work and hobbies

In these two pages we start by showing you how to set about making a table for the space below a window, to be used for sewing or writing.

The kitchen whose ground plan is shown in the diagram on the right measures 7 ft 9 in (2.35 metres) wide and 12 ft 2 in (3.7 metres) long, and thus has a floor space of almost 95 square feet (9 square metres). It was originally furnished with only a cooker, sink and a base unit. The new occupant added only the essentials: white built-in units, a tall cupboard for cleaning equipment or for general storage (near the door) and a round drop-leaf table.

The space in front of the window was left free for a handicraft table the same height as the windowsill. The work top, made from ¾-inch (19-millimetre) chipboard, stretches from the left-side wall to the units on the right and is 24 inches (600 millimetres) wide. It can be fixed firmly by use of metal right angles or battening supports. But it is also possible to make the whole or part of it fold down, so that it is easy to reach the window or the built-in units on the right.

If there is a radiator under the window you will need to allow both air and warmth to pass freely: you will have to saw slits or drill rows of holes in the windowsill or work surface.

Any materials needed for work can be stored on a shelf which you can build on the left under the work surface. Since it is difficult to keep an open shelf tidy, and an untidy one would not look good in a kitchen, you could use coloured plastic drawers like those used by craftsmen to sort and store their tools and small pieces of equipment. You can enquire about these in hardware or do-it-yourself shops.

The shelves are also made from ⅝ to ¾ inch (16 to 19 millimetre) chipboard. The front edges should be covered with wood or a plastic iron-on strip.

A sewing table

If you sometimes want to use your bedroom as a sewing room during the day, you will need only a minor conversion job. You will probably need to get rid of the bedside table – instead you can fix a narrow shelf above the head of the bed – and to push the bed as near as possible to the wardrobes leaving just enough room for the doors to open. This should give space by the window for a work surface stretching the whole width of the room.

The sewing table is built onto the windowsill (diagram right). It consists of a sheet of 1-inch (30-millimetre) chipboard, cut to fit the projecting windowsill. The table top rests on brackets with supporting arms of at least 12 inches (300 millimetres) which should be screwed to the wall with wall plugs. A table depth of 20 inches (500 millimetres) will be sufficient, allowing the window to be reached without difficulty.

You can put a storage shelf about 8 inches (200 millimetres) wide over the window, again using brackets, but this time above, rather than below, the shelf so that they are not visible from below. You can gain further storage space from a container on casters which will fit between the bed and the sewing table. Its top can be used as a bedside table.

You can build in plastic drawers or plastic-covered wire baskets beneath the work surface – and screw on removable hangers which you can use to hang up material which has been cut out ready for sewing or half-finished work. There is room for a bulletin board above the table which can be covered by a roller blind at night like the one over the window. In this way it will be easy to keep this bedroom sewing area tidy.

A reading corner

One suggestion which is more suitable for a single bedroom or one-room flat than a double bedroom is to build in a reading corner.

The window wall can be used for this. On this wall you might attach a shelf unit up to the windowsill and stretching the whole width of the room – or if you need a lot of space for books you can cover the whole window wall with shelves.

Various methods are possible. You can screw metal channels to the wall and place the bookshelves on matching brackets. You can build a large bookcase from veneered chipboard (at least ¾ inch

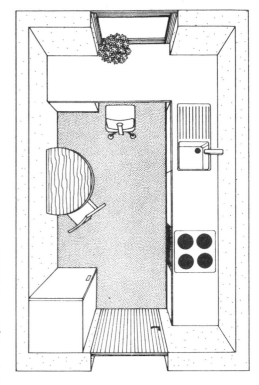

Above: **The ground plan shows the top view of a kitchen which has, in front of the window (at the top of the diagram), a handicraft table with many shelf compartments. It can also be used as a sewing or ironing table.**

Below: **This standard bedroom had room for a small writing table to the right of the window. A small cupboard to the left of the window holds work materials – in this case a bedside table has been dispensed with.**

Right: **This sewing table is extended to provide an additional work surface. The lamp can be swivelled.**

Below right: **The same bedroom as in the diagram below, this time with a sewing table which takes up the whole window wall. There is a lot of storage space under the work surface.**

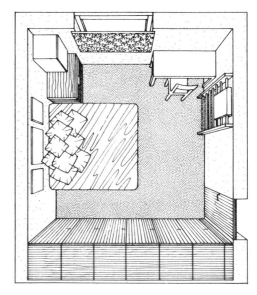

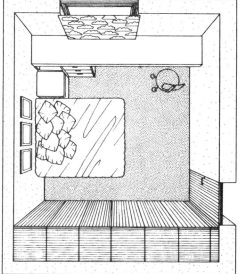

[19 millimetre] thick) but you will need to cover the front edges of both shelves and uprights with suitable plastic strip.

You could also mount small or large box shelf units on the wall, whether from a ready-made system of units or made yourself (from chipboard or blockboard). A shelf depth of 10 inches (250 millimetres) will be enough.

The best position is kept for the reading chair – perhaps a rocking chair. You will also need an adjustable floor lamp or a light which can be clamped onto the shelf.

Chairs on casters
Several times in this chapter we have recommended chairs on casters, with adjustable seats and backrests, to be used with a writing desk or other kinds of work places.

These office-type chairs, usually adjustable in height also, have a base with a centre column with four or, in more sophisticated models, five splayed feet each with a caster. Tests have shown that chairs with only four legs are more accident-prone than those with five: four-legged chairs tip over more easily than those with five legs. All chairs of this type share a further tendency to roll away when they are not meant to and should therefore be used with care.

Useful items to make yourself

Cocktail cabinet

This is a useful piece for the advanced handyman to make: a cocktail cabinet which opens from the top and which can also be used as a table. One special feature of the design is that to reach the contents you need not lift the whole lid, but only part of it. In order to be able to reach all the contents, a revolving shelf which is divided into four parts is built into it.

First of all you construct a square box from chipboard or blockboard, the length of the sides being determined by the depth of the sofa beside which it is to stand. It must be deep enough to take bottles of the normal height. You can stand the box straight on the floor or you can make a base from 2 by 2 inch (50 by 50 millimetre) squared wood, depending on the style of your sofa. It is best to avoid casters as bottles, especially bottles of wine, should not be moved to and fro.

This unusual cocktail cabinet consists of a simple box with a revolving shelf inside (1, 2). The top has only a quarter opening (3).

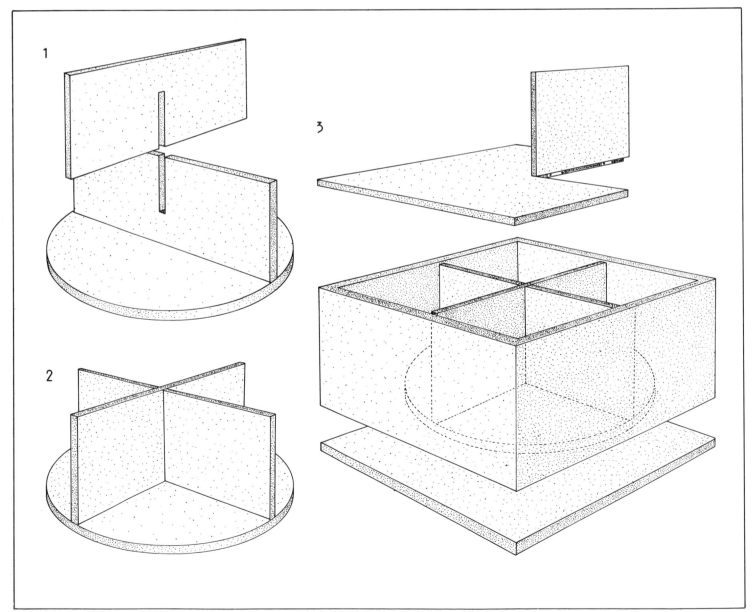

The revolving shelf is a circular piece of chipboard or blockboard. Its diameter should be about ½ inch (10 millimetres) less than the diameter of the inside of the box. Two pieces of chipboard or blockboard must have slots cut in the centre to half the width, so that they can be fitted together into a cross. This cross is then glued and screwed onto the circular base. The rotating mechanism consists of two spindles, one fitted under the circular base at the centre, the other into the intersection of the two cross walls. You also need two for the housings for the spindles, one fastened to the bottom of the box and the other under the lid. Ideally, the spindles and housings should be made of metal, but you could use dowel for the spindles and blocks of wood drilled to the appropriate size for the housings. A little wax would help to lubricate a wooden mechanism.

You will also need to fix three or four small casters under the revolving shelf so that it will turn smoothly. The lower rotating mechanism (spindle and housing) must match the height of the casters. You can, for example, mount the lower housing on a piece of wood to make them the same height.

The last thing is the lid. Saw one quarter out of a square of chipboard or blockboard and then join one side of it to the remaining piece with a long hinge. The cocktail cabinet can then be filled, primed, sanded and painted in a colour that matches the upholstery.

Lighted display shelves

If you collect glasses you won't want to put them in a cabinet: glass looks best in the light, if possible with the light behind it. Only then can the effect of the transparency of the material, the colours, the interplay of light and shade between the thin and solid parts of the glasses, goblets and decanters be fully appreciated.

A unit with glass shelves, built in front of a window, would be the ideal place for a collection of glass, but it is not very practical, because the window needs to be opened and cleaned. So you need shelves with artificial light which gives a similar effect to daylight.

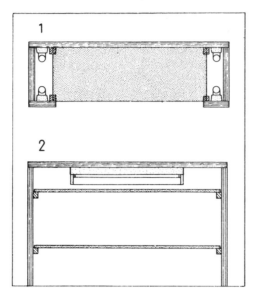

Two examples of display shelves with built-in lighting. The fluorescent tubes can be placed at the side (1) or above (2). Translucent glass reduces the glare.

A shelf with a lighted rear wall is a good solution. It should be deep enough to take a fluorescent tube with an opaque shade in front of it along the back wall.

But light from above or from the side can also give an interesting effect. The diagram above gives hints for building a shelf unit like this.

Shelves with side lighting: Place 4 inch (100 millimetre) wide shutters in front of the side wall, behind each of which you can install a row of fluorescent tubes. A further row is placed in front of the back wall. Translucent glass or plexiglass shades close off the two side light compartments. These are fastened by means of thin beading. The shelves are of ¼ or ⅜ inch (6 or 8 millimetre) plate glass and are supported by horizontal brackets.

Shelves with top lighting: Fix a fluorescent tube or several lights to the top of the shelf unit, a translucent glass or plexiglass shade beneath them and an impermeable wooden shade in front of them, so that the light will not dazzle anyone looking into the cabinet. If you use lights you will need to drill venti-

lation holes into the top of the cabinet, to avoid overheating. This cabinet, too, is fitted with glass shelves. If possible cover the back wall of the cabinet with dark felt, for the glasses will show up under the light to best advantage against this background.

Fabric utensil holder

Writing materials, handicraft equipment and sewing things are best kept next to the place of work. If there is no space available you may find that a utensil holder on the narrow side of the table will prove very useful.

You need canvas or strong muslin. You will need a piece that is slightly larger than the side of the table for the edges will have to be hemmed. A few smaller pieces are sewn on to make pockets, which can vary in size depending on what you want to keep in them. Use a particularly strong thread for the hem and pockets or sew both by hand using a large needle. When the utensil holder is finished sew six to eight large press studs to the underside and nail, screw or stick the other halves to the side and legs of the table. Then button the utensil holder onto the table so that it will hang straight even when it is heavily loaded.

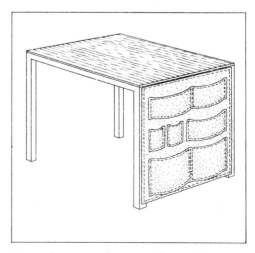

A good means of storage for writing or sewing equipment or even handicraft materials is provided by this fabric utensil holder fastened to the table.

BEDROOMS

With the increasing costs of land and building, rooms, and particularly bedrooms, have become smaller in an attempt to get three in where there is really only room for two. The result is that the old bedroom suite of large wardrobe (possibly another smaller one also), dressing table, chest and bedside tables plus a bulky double bed, became increasingly less suitable and more difficult to contain. Now the bedroom suite is more or less defunct and it has been replaced by ranges of units offering a wide variety of arrangements. For those who still have large rooms, there are some more pretentious ranges, especially in the more expensive price bracket. But if you only have a small room, it can still be furnished pleasantly and comfortably without overcrowding. However, it is obviously better to delay buying the furniture until you know the size of the room, and then to go to the store with the plan and select those units most suited. But you should also select furniture that is flexible enough, and could perhaps be extended to suit another room, should you decide to move.

Fitted wardrobe units that can be taken apart and reassembled differently are more versatile, for example, than an ordinary wardrobe. Twin beds which you can place either together or separately are more flexible than a large double bed which generally has to be placed in the centre of the room. A dressing table, 'that altar to vanity crowned with its triple mirror', is unnecessary because it is firstly impractical and secondly too bulky. Nor are traditional bedside tables really necessary, for there are more elegant and practical ways of storing necessary items beside the bed.

Since the sun does not always shine into a bedroom, white walls often look grey and pale colours lifeless. Many people do not mind this, and those who put out the light immediately and go to sleep do not even notice. Brightly coloured bedrooms, however, like the one seen on the right, are pleasant and cheerful. Here are three tips for those who want to try a bright colour scheme:

Use strong, calm colours which will be less glaring in rooms with little sun than in a sunny room. Stick to perhaps two basic colours, and small touches of other bright colours can be used in curtain and cushion fabrics, for example.

Try using patterned materials. Look for fabrics with different but harmonizing patterns in your favourite colour. Remember that large checks or wide stripes will appear merely as contrasting surfaces if combined with heavily flowered curtains.

Turn your cool, nocturnal bedroom into a dusky cave. Fill the room with dark colours on the walls, floor and wardrobes. To find your way around this dark sleeping cave you will need to include a few points of light to act as landmarks, such as light patches on the bedspread, lamps, mirrors or brass fittings.

The indigo carpet could look too solemn if it were not enlivened by the predominant colour, yellow. The fitted wardrobes (not in picture) which have sliding doors, the bedside tables and the bed are all in yellow-stained wood. The natural-coloured wicker trunk, in which extra pillows and blankets can be stored, looks light yellow. The sparkling flower pattern of the duvet covers makes a bedspread unnecessary, and tones well with the colours and pattern cf the curtains.

Beds

Above right: A smart hand-made patchwork bedspread covers a metal bed with brass fittings. The poster fits in well with the nostalgic atmosphere.

Right: A wooden four-poster bed. This one has been constructed and painted in the original style. This collector's item can be bought with or without the canopy.

Left: The chromium-plated double bed gives a very modern feeling to this bedroom. Beds of this kind need not necessarily be combined with materials of the same kind (here enamel and plate glass have been used). However, the accessories in this room would all have to be very modern, and even wood would look out of place in it.

Above: Even the most solid furniture made in light pinewood will not appear over-heavy and cumbersome. Here it makes a charming contrast with the dark beams of the sloping roof. Window blinds and bed covers are in the same material. Matching pine bedroom furniture completes the rustic appearance of this room.

Storage space

The original bedside cupboard was primarily intended for slippers and the long-forgotten chamberpot. The drawer usually contained a dusty collection of medicines. The top provided space for the bedside lamp, alarm clock and glass of water. The need for surface and storage areas around the bed has not decreased. Space is still needed for books and magazines, framed photographs and an alarm clock, for night clothes which may not be used during the day, perhaps for a second television set and also for a breakfast tray.

Here are a few ideas on how to get rid of your bedside table and still have plenty of storage space:

Chests on casters to both left and right of the bed could provide an open space at the top with drawers or a cupboard below, or many other arrangements. The tops of the chests offer surface storage space for alarm clocks, etc.

Even more space is offered by a tallboy like the one illustrated opposite above. This one includes a pull-out flap below a deep, open shelf where you can store all the things you might need in the night. Below the shelf are drawers and above a cupboard or shelf unit. The one illustrated has another open shelf above the cupboard unit. The height of this tallboy is 54 inches (1400 millimetres).

If no space at all is available alongside the bed, you can put up a shelf above the head of the bed, placed high enough to avoid accidentally knocking something down during the night. A plank 10 inches (250 millimetres) wide should be large enough. The lamp can be screwed or clamped to the shelf. You could possibly put up several shelves one above the other, but you must be absolutely confident that they are going to stay there! If you have the room, the next suggestion is better from the safety point of view.

A large shelf unit at the head of the bed (illustrated right) is mainly recommended for a multi-purpose bedroom. It provides a lot of space for books, ornaments and also the things that one might need during the night. A space for bedclothes could also be included.

The space under the bed is often used to store bedding. A bedding drawer with a lid can be pulled out to act as a bedside table at night. This system has one disadvantage – when you want to put the bedding back in the drawer in the morning you will have to clear the top before you can open the lid.

Many systems of built-in furniture include low units with drawers to stand beside the bed or hang on the wall. The unit directly next to the bed should have its top surface within reach. Next to it you can put a unit double the height (two small units stacked) and in this way you will gain extra storage space.

There are a variety of possibilities for storing bedding apart from those already mentioned (see illustrations on this page). Built-in chests which are the same height as a bedside table have the advantage that you can store the bedding away in a deep drawer or behind a flap and still use the top of the chest for surface storage. In the chest illustrated above left, half the top is a flat surface on which items can be placed, and the other half a lid which can be raised. Linen chests also come in cupboard form, as benches or corner units, but whatever shape or form they are, they must have ventilation slits or holes so that the bedding can be well ventilated while in storage.

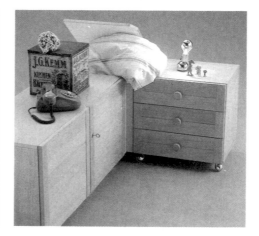

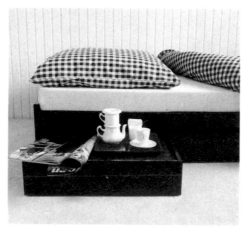

A linen chest (above) in which the front half of the top opens upwards, so that items on the bedside table can be left in place.

The linen chest pictured above right allows every inch of corner space to be used. This model is veneered in oak.

A linen drawer (right) which slides under the bed also has a lid which can be used as a table when the drawer is pulled out.

The shelf and cupboard units behind the bed (right) in this large multi-purpose bedroom offer ample surface and storage space. The bed with its boldly patterned cover is slightly recessed into the shelf unit. Everything is to hand, book, alarm clock and bedside lamp. The lamps are clamped onto the shelf and can be turned to any angle. The high window has a blind which matches the bed cover.

If the bedroom is not large enough for several units to stand side by side, you will have to use the height of the room. The arrangement of units (right) is 54 inches (1400 millimetres) high and comprises drawers, an open compartment and a cupboard above this providing a lot of storage space. In addition it has a stable pull-out leaf. Some systems of built-in furniture include units like this, even those which are intended mainly for the living room or the children's room.

Wardrobes

Unless you are fortunate enough to buy a place where the wardrobes are built-in as part of the structure, you will have to provide these yourself, and in many cases you will find that the space allocated does not match your requirements.

Most wardrobes seem big enough at first, but over the years they will begin to burst at the seams. So it is worthwhile allowing for as large a wardrobe as possible from the start. In theory, you should be able to buy additional units, but unfortunately ranges go out of production – so in practice it is not always possible. Even when the range is still available, you will probably find that the colour will be different to that of your own, because the latter has been exposed to the light.

Wardrobe space

If you are building or converting a house, you can save money and create space by arranging the partition walls so that they form the wardrobes as part of the structure.

A wardrobe need not always stand along one single wall, but can be arranged around a corner, or in the recesses on either side of the chimney piece. If space is limited, choose wardrobes with sliding doors instead of the usual hinged doors. These can stand nearer other furniture such as the bed, and you need not worry about the doors getting in the way of the door of the room.

If you are buying your first bedroom furniture, choose a wardrobe which allows you to vary the interior, placing the rails and shelves wherever you wish. Rails for dresses, suits or trousers can be placed at different heights. If longer clothes become fashionable you can raise the rail, and vice versa.

The room above and below the hanging space is occupied by drawers, shoe baskets and open shelves, which are today used mainly for sweaters, for it is better to hang up shirts and blouses. You could keep spare towels in the wire baskets.

Wardrobes with variable compartments have many advantages. In this wardrobe (below) you can decide for yourself where and at what height to place the shelves, wire baskets and rails.

Buying a wardrobe

The standard depth of a wardrobe is 24 inches (600 millimetres). You must allow this much to avoid squashing the shoulders of suits, coats and dresses. For this reason wardrobes which are less deep have hanging rails placed front to back, which can usually be pulled out for easier access. Heights vary considerably between around 68 inches (1720 millimetres) for an ordinary wardrobe, to 94 inches (2400 millimetres) for units which reach from floor to ceiling. Sizes of units and doors will also vary considerably according to the kind of system employed, but on average doors will be between 20 inches (500 millimetres) and 24 inches (600 millimetres) where units are intended to reach the ceiling. If there is a small gap between the units and the ceiling, this can usually be filled with a piece of chipboard or similar material. The more flexible is the range, the more effectively you will be able to fill the wall area. Large spaces can be filled with matching units, but if a space of approximately 8 inches (200 millimetres) or less is left over it can usually be filled in the same way as the space at the top.

Older, standard type wardrobes with a fixed interior tended to have too much unused space. In a well designed wardrobe the position of the hanging rails, partitions and runners for the drawers can be varied. The more comprehensive the divisions in the wardrobe, the easier it is to find things, so you will save time, trouble and temper. To make the most use of the wardrobe's depth it is best to have drawers, or wire and plastic baskets, as well as shelves for storing folded clothes, shoes, etc.

Walk-in wardrobes

A walk-in wardrobe is a very large built-in cupboard which will provide room for all your clothes, linen, bags and cases, and if there is still more space you can use it as a dressing room.

The interior fittings can be assembled from simple do-it-yourself materials which you may already have, such as cheap whitewood shelving or cupboards, rods (for hanging clothes) or a clothes rail on casters like those used to display clothes in shops, or seen sometimes in cloakrooms. You can also use plastic clothes containers.

Do not try to economize too much on the external construction, to the extent of spoiling the appearance of the room. You should in any case be able to build your fitted walk-in cupboard for less money than you would have to pay for the same area with a conventional range.

The walk-in wardrobe illustrated on the left is made as follows: a dividing wall (known as a stud partition) separates the wardrobe from the rest of the room. The framework is made of squared timber 2 by 2 inches (60 by 60 millimetres) which must be fixed to the wall, ceiling and floor. An upright is then positioned about every 24 inches (600 millimetres) with a horizontal piece halfway up between each upright. Then it can be covered with ⅜-inch (10-millimetres) plasterboard or chipboard. A cross-beam must be fixed to the ceiling between the end of the dividing wall and the wall of the room where the doors are to hang. Attach the track for the doors to the underside of the cross-beam. The wardrobe and the area in front of it can be fitted with hanging lights. Finally the dividing wall must be papered or painted on both sides. Fit out the wardrobe space with cheap shelving. Plastic boxes or wire baskets can be used for socks, sweaters, etc.

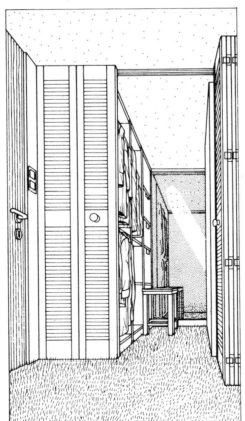

Front view of the walk-in wardrobe illustrated above. Folding louvre doors close it off entirely. The diagram below right shows the framework of the wardrobe before it is covered.

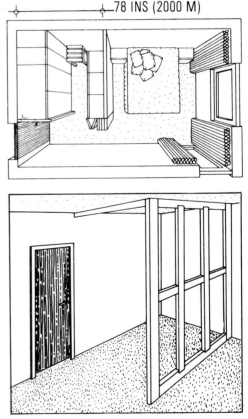

78 INS (2000 M)

The ground plan shows how a walk-in wardrobe can be used even in a room which is fairly small. It takes up less than 45 square feet (4 square metres) of the room out of a total of 165 (15).

151

Advanced bed-building

The quickest and simplest way of making a bed is to buy a foam-rubber mattress and place it on the floor. With some kind of support for the head it can be used as a lounger during the day, and it can be combined with other mattresses, if you have enough room, to give a landscaped seating area. If you prefer a more conventional type of bed, the next two pages will be of interest. They contain various suggestions for the home handyman.

Double bed from two doors

You do not need to be an expert carpenter nor even an experienced handyman to make this double bed. You will need no tools other than a drill (with various bits) and a medium-sized screwdriver.

Buy two veneered doors 33 inches (800 millimetres) wide and 78 inches (2000 millimetres) long. They must, of course, be thick and strong enough to bear the weight of two people. They are linked top and bottom with hooks and rings. Steel hooks about 3 inches (80 millimetres) long will do the job. Screw the hooks and rings to the doors as shown in the diagram. The long sides have two dowel joints, for which the holes are drilled with a ⅜-inch (8-millimetre) bit. They should be positioned 18 inches (500 millimetres) from the end and ¾ inch (15 millimetres) from the top edge.

Base for a double bed made from two doors. The bed supports are on casters (1). Two dowel joints hold the long sides in place (2). The doors are also held together by hooks.

Push two wooden dowels, ⅜ inch (8 millimetres) in diameter into these holes (these are available from do-it-yourself shops). If you want to take the beds apart you need only undo the hooks and push the doors apart. In normal use they will remain firmly joined.

Screw four furniture casters to the underside of each door. Only use casters fixed with a flat mounting plate otherwise they may be difficult to fix into position. The mounting plates should be screwed into place with four wood screws 1¼ inches (30 millimetres) long. Each plate should be ½ inch (10 millimetres) from the outer edges so that the screws cannot break off when a heavy weight is placed upon the bed. If you want to paint the doors they must first be sanded and the edges slightly rounded. To do this it is best to wrap the sandpaper round a cork sanding block or a block of wood. Then the doors must be primed. The underside can be left unpainted. Any unevenness should be treated with filler. When dry (after a few hours) lightly sand again. Then paint, preferably with two even coats. Instead of paint you could use white or coloured sticky-backed plastic, with which you need only cover the edges, allowing it to overlap about 2 inches (50 millimetres) onto the main surfaces. In this way you can save time, materials and money.

On top of the bed base place a foam-rubber mattress of the same size. This should be covered with a plain or patterned cover to match other furnishings or the bed linen. It will not be necessary to fasten down the mattress.

Four-poster bed

A four-poster bed is not only romantic, but it can be very practical as well if your bedroom ceiling is too high. It need not be all frills and lace, nor even painted with rustic designs and with checked sheets, but can be made quite differently as the example illustrated right shows: elegantly striped with a slight rustic air, but definitely suitable for a modern home. The stripes of the mattress cover, canopy and rear wall can be echoed in some of the other furnishings of the room, like the cushions and even in a roller blind at the window.

The basic frame for the four-poster is made from squared timber (planed pine) with a cross-section 2 by 2 inches (60 by 60 millimetres). From this you cut the posts about 75 inches (1900 millimetres) long. The long sides of the top frame are 75 inches (1900 millimetres) to 78 inches (2000 millimetres) long, and the cross pieces should be 66 inches (1600 millimetres) long.

You can find the various ways of making a neat job of the corner joints on page 228. Simple nail or screw joints will be insufficient here and you will need hole and plug joints or dowels – this also applies to the joints in the lower part of the bed.

You will also need squared timber for the base. As these timbers will subsequently be covered by sheets of plywood, as shown in the diagram, you can use thinner 2 by 1¾ inch (50 by 45 millimetre) wood (for ¼-inch [10-millimetre] plywood). This timber is used to build three sides of the base with one piece for

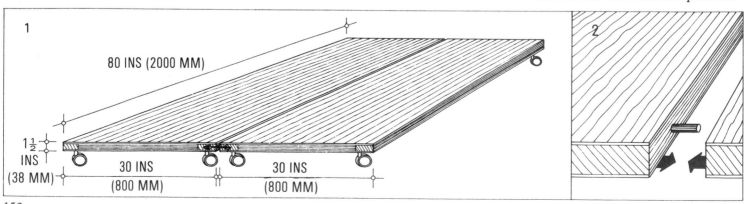

1

80 INS (2000 MM)

1½ INS (38 MM)

30 INS (800 MM)

30 INS (800 MM)

2

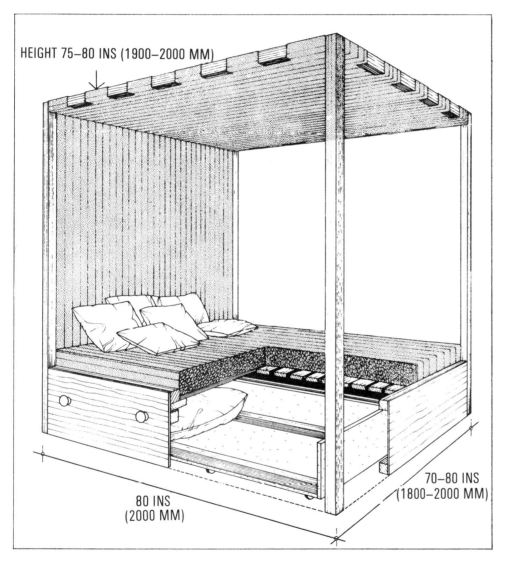

HEIGHT 75–80 INS (1900–2000 MM)

80 INS
(2000 MM)

70–80 INS
(1800–2000 MM)

both the upper and lower joins. On the fourth side leave out the lower piece of wood and include only the upper, otherwise you would not be able to pull out the drawers which run on casters.

Making the base and roof
You must now make the supports on the two long sides for the planks on which the mattress will lie. For these use timber which is 3 inches (80 millimetres) wide and 1 to 1½ inches (30 to 40 millimetres) thick. Glue and screw them to the underside of the upper frame timber. When you have fixed the planks that support the mattress and covered the bed with

A make-it-yourself four-poster bed. The base is made out of plywood or blockboard, into which you can build a large drawer or two smaller ones, which run on casters and will store the bedding during the day. The mattress lies on boards.

plywood you have completed the basic bed base.

You must then decide whether the storage space under the bed is to be one drawer which is the full width of the bed or whether you would prefer it to be divided differently. For example, you could have two drawers of the same size

side by side, or a large drawer for bedding (occupying two-thirds of the width) and a smaller drawer for other things (one-third). Remember that smaller drawers are easier to move than large ones. The drawers are made as follows: a base of ⅝-inch (16-millimetre) chipboard should be reinforced along the front and back edges with 2 by 2 inch (50 by 50 millimetre) battening. The side pieces, excluding the front covering, should be 10½ inches (270 millimetres) deep to fit a bed 12¾ inches (330 millimetres) high, to allow for the depth needed for the casters and ¼ inch (5 millimetre) margin to ensure the free movement of the drawer. Therefore, it is best to get the casters (you will need six for a large drawer) before cutting out the drawers.

The side pieces are glued and carefully nailed together. You can use metal right-angle brackets to reinforce the corners. The front consists of a sheet of plywood, the same height as the sheets used to cover the edges of the base. If the floor is uneven or carpeted it is best to take ¼ inch (5 millimetres) off the lower edge.

Do not fit the front until you have screwed on the casters: one under each corner of the drawer and one in the centre of the back and front edges. You must also fix handles to the front, preferably wooden ones. All surfaces must now be sanded, primed, filled, sanded again and painted. Red paint was chosen for our model.

The covering fabric has narrow red stripes. While the paint is drying, make the covers for the foam-rubber mattress bought to the size of the bed, for the roof and for the wall covering (this consists of a thin sheet of chipboard covered with foam).

The roof will look smarter if instead of covering the entire top frame, you leave pieces of the painted frame, showing through at regular intervals. Here the material is nailed to the inside of the frame. Where the fabric completely covers the frame, the fabric is wrapped round the frame and nailed into place along the top. If this is too difficult you could probably have it done by an upholsterer.

153

A good bed will help your sleep

One needs great freedom of movement in bed. In the course of eight hours of sleep you will change position about 30 times; a healthy child will turn over or curl up every ten minutes. You need room for this natural movement in sleep.

This means a large enough bed with no hollow in the mattress. It means a light cover which will not place too heavy a load on the sleeper. It also means that the bed should stand free in the room. If possible the bed should not stand lengthways against a wall, but with the headboard to the wall. The proximity of the wall makes you turn instinctively towards it, for you feel more protected, so you will spend eight hours lying on your side, which can lead to restricted circulation.

Bed mattresses

Just as you can put up with back ache, you can put up with a sagging mattress and uncomfortable springs, but it is neither pleasant nor healthy to sleep in such conditions, for you can neither rest nor sleep properly. We spend one-third of our lives in bed, so why do so many people make this third of their life so uncomfortable?

If the bed is too short you cannot move freely. In a bed which is too short and too small you will be cramped. If the mattress sags you can lie only on your back and will possibly snore. Also it can lead to blockage of the blood vessels and back strain.

Old mattresses not only lose their elasticity but also become slightly musty. During our sleep, we lose liquid through the skin which is absorbed by the bed covers, linen and mattress. Even with regular cleaning (every two years) a mattress will not last longer than ten to 15 years.

Bed bases

A better bed begins with the base, and if you place an expensive mattress on a worn-out base, you are simply wasting money. On the other hand, even a cheaper type of mattress will be improved if combined with a sound base of the right type.

You may see references to 'posture-springing', which in fact refers to both the base and the mattress. The springing of the base and the mattress it supports should give under pressure from the body weight only at the point of pressure, and not over a larger area, so that the body is kept in a level posture and is not allowed to sag.

There is a wide variety of bed bases. The simplest is a diamond-mesh spring suspended on a metal frame, which may have legs, or may be supported by attachment to the head and foot ends of the bed; a similar type has a mesh top and spiral springs; there are box springs which are wooden-framed, fitted with spiral springs, upholstered and covered to match the mattress, and supported on metal 'side-irons' fixed to the head and foot ends of the bed; this last type has to a great extent been superseded by bases which are of similar construction but have their own legs usually fitted with casters for ease of movement. There are two main types: sprung-edge – these are generally more expensive, as they have springs right to the border; and firm-edge – these are, on the whole, more practical as the edges cannot be so easily broken down as the sprung-edge type when people sit on the edges of the bed. Finally there is a newer type of base, referred to sometimes as the 'duck-board' type, which consists usually of a wooden frame in which springy wooden slats, connected by strips of rubber webbing, are mounted across the width of the bed on toughened rubber supports.

Spring or foam?

Up to a few years ago a battle was raging in the bed industry between the manufacturers of sprung and foam-rubber mattresses. Now it has turned to healthy competition, for the good of the public. The manufacturers of foam-rubber mattresses have moved away from the use of a uniform soft foam to work with layers of foam of different densities. Sprung mattresses have become lighter, as manufacturers have tended to turn away from the very deep mattress which had also technical disadvantages.

Spring mattresses adjust to weight differences through the elasticity of their springs. There are two main types: open and pocketed springs. In the former, which is the most common and less expensive type, the springs are usually of the waisted type and are linked together with insulated clips to cut down noise, and the whole unit has a border wire all the way round at both top and bottom. These border wires are also linked in different ways, according to the manufacturer, with the purpose of reinforcing the border against the strains of people sitting on the edge of the bed. In the pocketed type the system is similar, but there are a greater number of straight-sided springs, each in a calico pocket more closely linked together than in the open type.

Foam mattresses consist of foam rubber (latex = natural rubber) or some other foam material (polyurethane = synthetic product). The natural advantages of a foam-rubber mattress, its elastic cells and air pockets, can be incorporated into a synthetic foam mattress with little technical difficulty.

Test before you buy

Here are some points to watch when buying a mattress. Always buy the mattress with the base. Do not be afraid to test a mattress as thoroughly as possible in the shop. Foam mattresses (latex or synthetic) should not be too thin or have too large cells. Bed bases and spring interiors should not squeak or grate.

While it is true that the traditional striped cotton union ticking is still the best covering for a mattress from the point of view of wear, bedding is sold to a great extent on the patterned and glossy coverings offered by manufacturers at all price levels. These covers may well be less hard wearing, and in fact some people cover them with a plain white cotton mattress cover in addition to a sheet.

Traditionally the upholstery of a mattress is held in place by tabbing or buttoning, and this method is still widely used on spring-filled mattresses. It does not apply to foam mattresses because of their quite different construction.

This comfortable-looking bed is screened from the rest of the room by curtains which are made from the same material as the bedspread. The curtain over the window, which has a roller blind instead of net curtains behind it, is also of the same pattern.

CHILDREN'S ROOMS

Most reasonably priced apartments, and some houses, are too small for families. The average family – father, mother and two children – generally finds it has to manage with three rooms, kitchen and bathroom. The third room is usually smaller than the other two and is therefore allocated to the children, even though it is probably unsuitable for more than one child.

Usually all you can do is to restrict yourself to the bare essentials when furnishing the children's room and to try and save as much space as possible – with bunk beds, for example, and versatile furniture with built-in tables and space-saving shelving. In addition you can often provide extra playing space by making a playroom in the attic, cellar or hall.

There is another way of giving the two children more freedom of movement, and that is to reallocate the rooms. The parents move their bedroom into the nursery.

This is not always practical, of course, but if the large bedroom is seldom used during the day, and is really only used for eight hours each night, then for 16 hours every day the largest room is being wasted. If your home is small and lacks a nursery, then it is worthwhile considering giving the children the larger room.

If the parents do give up their large bedroom for the sake of the children, and move into a room which is a lot smaller, they will have to put up with a lot of inconvenience. There will be too little wardrobe space, the bed will probably be too big for the limited space, and some of the bedroom furniture will even have to be left out. However, this is at least a possible way of improving the family life as a whole.

Whether you decide to give the children the larger or smaller room, here are some points that you should consider when choosing nursery furniture.

1/ The furniture should be easily transported, even by children.

2/ It must be extremely solid and serviceable.

3/ It must stand firmly and not tip over easily.

There should be no sharp corners or edges.

4/ Surfaces should not be treated with paint or other substances containing lead, for this is poisonous. Use non-toxic paints.

5/ Seats on children's chairs should be horizontal, hollowed out to a depth of about ½ inch (10 millimetres) towards the back of the seat. This makes for a body angle of 3–4° when seated.

6/ The backrest must be curved sufficiently to fit the natural curve of the child's spine as well as possible.

7/ Worktops on children's tables must be sufficiently large and should be set at an angle (about 16° for reading and writing).

8/ Foam mattresses are best for children's beds and should lie on a firm base. Only in this way can damage to the spine during sleep be avoided.

Children tend to think of furniture not only as a way of furnishing a room but also as playthings. These coloured plastic boxes suit both these purposes. You could furnish a whole nursery with them, but they can also be combined to provide varying play elements – a boat, a shop, a castle or a train, for instance. Each box has drill holes so that they can be joined together with nuts and bolts – even by children.

An adventure bedroom

Children need a room which offers them many opportunites for play and movement, especially if they live in town and have little opportunity for playing outside the home. They need a room which will stimulate their imagination and where nothing can inhibit their wealth of ideas.

Rooms of this kind are called adventure rooms. They can be inside the main part of the home – essential of course if the child is to sleep there – or could be in an attic or a cellar.

The adventure room illustrated on this page has a double floor and other additional play facilities. You can fit the second floor yourself, 27½ inches (700 millimetres) above the original floor, if the room is high enough (it should be at least 9 feet [or 3 metres] high). This children's paradise also has wall bars for climbing, a trapdoor in the floor for the child to climb in and out of, and in this instance a climbing rope hanging down in the middle of the room above the trapdoor (you may wish to omit this if you think it might cause problems).

The bed (to the left of the photograph) is at a raised level and with its 'peephole' looking out towards the door it becomes part of the play area. A roomy cupboard and a number of small drawers built in under the bed provide storage space for linen, clothes and toys. Additional storage space is provided by shelves and low built-in cupboards around the writing and play table by the window and along the back wall. You could use your attic, cellar or even a large hall to make a playroom along similar lines, which could be used as a hobbies room and playroom. It should be near the parents, but not too near, otherwise they would be disturbed by the noise. The furniture must be the right size to suit the age of the child. Good light is also important. Of course the room must have heating as it will be most used in winter.

This adventure room is ideal for young children. Although very few homes will allow you to put the entire scheme into practice, the room offers suggestions for furnishing a 'children's paradise'.

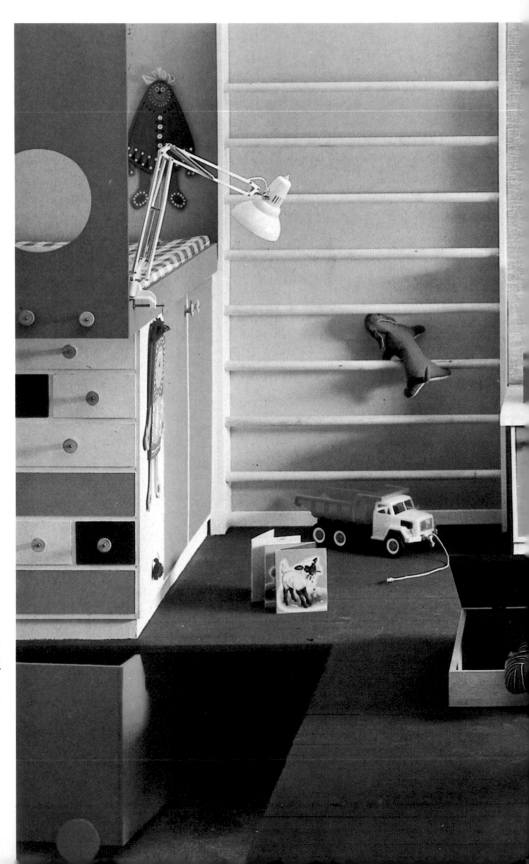

Small bedrooms for children

Children need a lot of space if they are to be happy at home: room to play, read, sleep and to do their homework. But their rooms are usually too small and in addition two children often have to share the same limited space. This makes nurseries difficult to furnish in general, for the furniture has to grow as the child grows. Also the furniture has to withstand more wear and tear than that in other rooms. So most parents take the easy way out: they spend as little as possible and try to bridge the gap between baby furniture and a teenage room by using furniture that is no longer needed in their own bedroom or in the living room, together with a certain amount of home-made furniture.

Children's furniture should not be too expensive – but neither should it be cheap and improvised. Children, as much as adults, need a stimulating yet functional environment; in their rooms, too, you should use colour to create the right atmosphere and exciting accessories to create pleasant surroundings.

Many parents believe that they should use soft, pastel colours in a child's bedroom. In fact, most children love bright colours – not only in the pictures they paint, but also in their rooms. There is no point in worrying whether such strong colours will make the room look smaller. This may be a problem for adults, but children will only consider the work and play area available.

As children's bedrooms are usually so small, they can only take a limited amount of furniture. There is probably no room for anything else. Therefore you should not have to spend a lot of money on furnishings. On the other hand, for this very reason, you can ensure that these few items of furniture are practical and of good quality.

Another of the main failings in most modern children's rooms is that there is not enough lighting (and sometimes it is also badly positioned) and not enough suitable space for homework. Children should be able to sit on a chair that they feel comfortable on, and be able to reach the table without stretching, and not be bent over it because it is too low.

This wide-angle photograph is deceptive, because this room for two 12-year-old boys has an area of only 100 square feet (10 square metres). The fact that it looks larger is due to the cleverly planned furnishing scheme. The unusual positioning of the bunk beds has four main advantages: it provides sleeping accommodation for two; provides additional shelf storage in the framework supporting the higher of the beds; provides room for a work table under the top bunk; and a playing area on the bottom bunk. The top bunk, a simple box bed, lies across two shelf units (with a lot of storage space) and is also screwed to the wall at the head end. If you are good at do-it-yourself you could copy this idea.

'Cave' beds

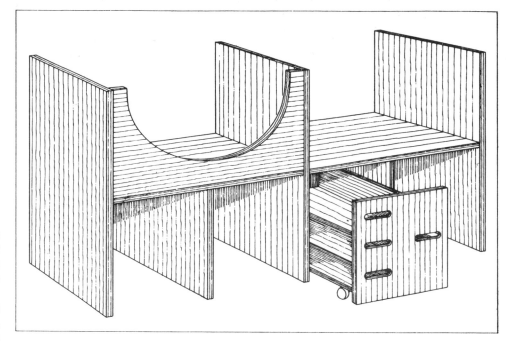

From just looking at the picture, you can see that these beds are not only for sleeping in. They are a sort of cave where a child can hide and play and let his imagination run wild.

But it is not only the beds that make this bedroom so pleasant for children. The clever and imaginative father, who designed and built it all himself, has also made room for toys and clothes and for folding tables which can be hung on the wall when the children want to play. Another feature of the room is a long multi-purpose pole below the ceiling to which lamps and climbing ropes can be fastened. You could also hang a Punch and Judy tent from it, or the backdrop for a shadow theatre. It can also take a curtain room-divider and in wet weather a badminton net. This pole of 2-inch (50-millimetre) tubular steel is screwed to the built-in beds on one side of the room and to a very firmly anchored wooden shelf on the other side.

How to build the berths
The framework for the 'cave' beds, illustrated on the left-hand page, provides space for two sleeping berths. It takes up a whole wall and is built to fit the size of the wall (about 12½ feet [3.8 metres]). You can build half the unit for only one child. This will generally leave room for shelving which can be built onto the narrow end of the bed.

For the basic construction, ¾-inch (19-millimetre) blockboard was used. You will need three boards the height of the room for the ends and middle wall, also the two boards on which the mattresses will lie, as well as two partition walls under the mattress base, which help to support it as well as dividing off the storage space for the clothes containers.

The precise measurements depend on the wall size against which you are building your berths. The beds should preferably be about 72 inches (1800 millimetres) long and about 36 inches (900 millimetres) wide. The mattress bases should be at a height of about 39 inches (1000 millimetres) – if they are higher than this you will not have enough space above the beds, and in addition if the

containers are too tall they will be difficult to move.

The simplest way of fastening the sheets of blockboard together is with screws. To fasten the mattress bases onto the side walls, screw 1½-inch (30-millimetre) square battens to the side walls and nail the bases onto them.

The frame around the berths is made from ⅜-inch (10-millimetre) plywood. The semi-circular cut-out is drawn with a string compass and cut out with a padsaw. It is fixed into position as follows: 2 by 1 inch (50 by 20 millimetre) battens are glued and screwed to the front of the upper side walls and mattress bases. The frames are screwed into position behind the battens.

Making and fitting the boxes
The boxes, which are on casters, are made from ¾-inch (19-millimetre) blockboard or chipboard. The base is slightly raised so that the casters (four to each box) are not visible. Slots are sawn into the front with a padsaw or a coping saw. Each container under the right-hand of the berths needs two slots side by side where one can grip to pull it out. Each container under the left-hand side has two additional slots (see diagram) which the children use for climbing into bed. The containers are constructed by screwing 1 by 1 inch (25 by 25 millimetre) battens to the rear of the front section, and the partitions are screwed to the battens.

You can vary the inside compartments of the containers. You can build them like boxes, but remember that it will be difficult to reach right into them. It is more practical to fit shelf compartments as shown in the diagram. The dividing wall can be exactly in the centre, or you can arrange it so that there is space for a clothes rail. The number and arrange-

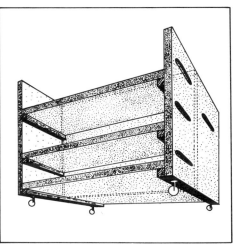

Top: **The assembled double berths. The mattress bases are about 39 inches (1000 millimetres) from the floor, leaving about 60 inches (1500 millimetres) space to the ceiling. For the main structure, ¾-inch (19-millimetre) blockboard was used and the frames around the berths were made from ⅜-inch (10-millimetre) plywood. The box containers (above) are on casters and each one can be divided up as you wish.**

ment of the compartments will depend on what you want to keep in the box in question: toys or craft materials, clothes or linen. All visible edges of the chipboard must have an edge strip for the rough edges might chip.

When assembled, the box should be sanded, primed, filled, sanded again and given at least two coats of paint. For mattresses, use foam cut to size, and cover it with ticking.

You can build additional shelves into each berth (see photograph) – for all the little things that children like to have by them.

This is a bed which is more than just a place to sleep. It is a cave full of treasure, a refuge for small dreamers, a castle of their own. An imaginative father designed these 'cave beds' and also built them himself. Underneath them he used large roll-out drawers – you can almost do without wardrobes in this room. The tables can be moved around or they can also be folded up and hung on the wall so that the floor can be used for playing.

Compact furniture

If your child's bedroom is small, you will need to use a lot of imagination if you are to give the child enough play space, or to prevent the growing teenager suffering from claustrophobia. The two examples on these pages show how you can make more play space by building compact furniture for a child's bedroom.

Bedroom unit for a teenager

This idea, which combines bed and table, shelves and bulletin boards, provides a teenager with almost all the furniture that he needs.

The shelves can also support a swivel-mounted spotlight, which can be positioned so that it can light both the writing surface and the head of the bed. In the example illustrated the height of the table and work surface is 27½ inches (700 millimetres). For smaller children you would have to make it 23½ inches (600 millimetres) high. A revolving chair would be a sensible addition in both cases. One particularly good point for do-it-yourself people is that the whole unit consists of only two types of wood: ⅝-inch (16-millimetre) chipboard and 1 by 1½ inch (28 by 35 millimetre) pine wood (which should be planed even though it is mostly used for the sub-frame).

How to build the unit

The diagram below will help you to compile a list of the lengths of wood required. You can see from the diagram where you have to deduct ⅝ inch (16 millimetres), which is the thickness of the board, from the total measurement given.

Gluing and additional nailing provides for sufficient stability. Since chipboard tears easily if you nail into the back of it, use this trick: Drill through the sheets which are to be joined, both together, with a very fine bit. Apply adhesive to the surfaces which are to be joined, allow it to set slightly, in accordance with the instructions for use, bring the two parts together and nail into the pre-drilled holes using countersink nails.

Begin with the table section for the rest of the unit will be built upon it. For the pull-out drawer use four furniture casters

164

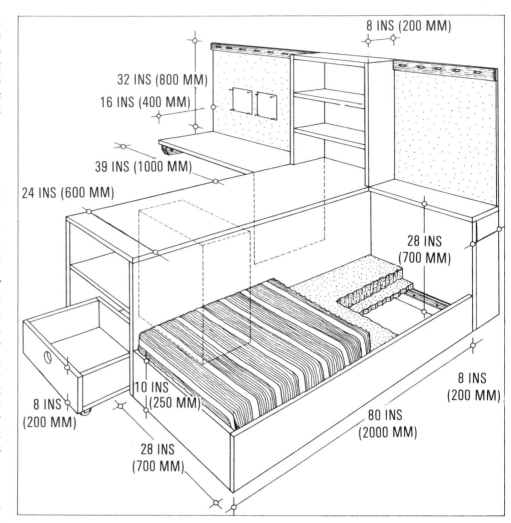

Bed with built-on table and shelf units designed for a teenager's bedroom.
This versatile unit consists exclusively of ⅝-inch (16-millimetre) chipboard and 1 by 1½ inch (25 by 35 millimetre) pine

screwed to the base. The wood battens are used to support the bed base, for fastening the writing surface to the wall and for the row of hooks above the bulletin board.

The bulletin board is made from cork tiles; but you could also use insulation board. The row of hooks has ⅜-inch (10-millimetre) dowels set into it. Drill holes with a ⅜-inch (10-millimetre) bit, glue the dowels and knock into the holes.

The finished unit is primed, filled, sanded and given two coats of gloss paint.

battening. It will present no special problems to the experienced do-it-yourself person. Cork tiles are fitted to the wall to serve as bulletin boards. The unit is finished with a gloss paint.

It is best to cover the edges of the chipboard with PVC edge strips, but you could also use hardwood strips of ¼ by ⅝ inch (5 by 16 millimetres).

Bed with storage below

The best way to make more space in a small child's bedroom is to make more use of the height of the room. The diagram on the right shows a combined bed and cupboard which fulfils this requirement.

Small children's clothes are not long

enough to require a full-length wardrobe. A wardrobe about 39 inches (1000 millimetres) high will probably be enough. There will be about 60 inches (1500 millimetres) space above this wardrobe to the ceiling, so that you can put the bed above it. The child will neither have to sleep at a dizzy height, nor feel too restricted when he sits up in bed. There is enough space for him to stand up as well.

The advantage of this is that bed and wardrobe are combined into a space of about 20 square feet (2 square metres). For separate items of furniture you would need at least 30 square feet (3 square metres). This leaves more floor space free for playing. The bed cupboard illustrated is one that you can make yourself. The cupboard and drawer units could be standard units modified to suit this special arrangement.

Making the cupboards

This combination unit which you can use to save space in a child's room consists of two low cupboards which are the right height for hanging a small child's clothes. You can place the cupboards directly together or you can push them apart sufficiently to make room for a simple ladder between them.

On top of the cupboards, you lay a sheet of ¾-inch (16-millimetre) blockboard which is screwed firmly to the cupboards and surrounded by four strips of blockboard about 8 inches (200 millimetres) high. This forms the bed which needs only a mattress to complete it.

If the cupboards that you have bought are unfinished, you can either stain or polish the whole unit, or paint it according to your own choice.

A sleeping platform made from two cupboards with a bed above them. You can make the cupboards yourself from chipboard or blockboard, but it is easier to use matching ready-made units. In the latter case you need only make the bed box to correspond with the size of the cupboard units. You can fit a simple ladder between the two units.

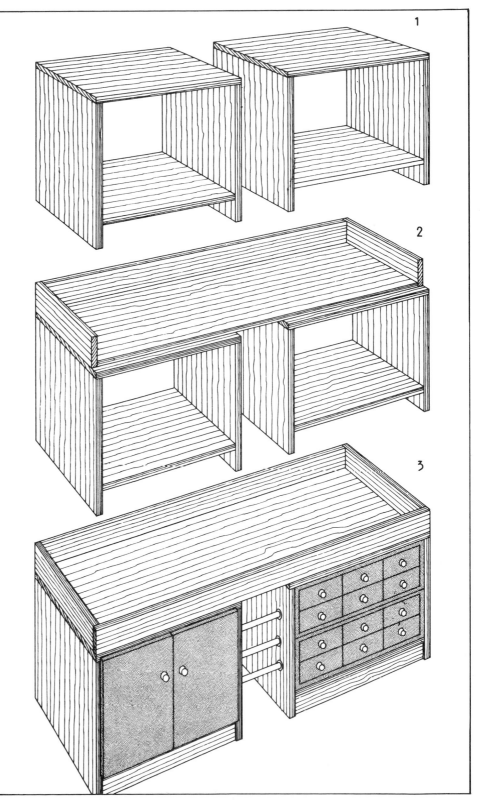

Good ideas for furnishings

Often only little things need to be changed or added to make a home more suitable for children. Here you will find suggestions that will help.

What are the main features of a home that is ideal for children? It must be comfortable for the child, so it must be warm, light, airy, adequately fenced outside but with no restrictions inside for the occupants. It must also be safe to avoid accidents to the child or damage to the house. It should be made easy for the child to keep his toys and clothes tidy for this will encourage him to put things away when he's finished with them.

Children under six

Homes which are pleasant for children are usually pleasant for the parents too. They are practical and functional as well, because they save the adults the need to run around after the child and to worry about his safety. Since our homes are generally built for adults you can help by insisting on childproof furniture and furnishings.

Children need a lot of play space. Tables in the home are too high for them. If you have an old kitchen table you could shorten the legs and fit casters to make it a useful, mobile item of play furniture.

Chairs which you can raise, and lower and which have adjustable backrests make it easy to accommodate any child's shape. If they have casters they can be pushed to the place where they are needed without any difficulty. Also every nursery should have a shelf that the child can reach easily, and under it you could keep movable toy boxes.

A mirror not only serves our vanity. For children it is also important as a means of achieving self-confidence. It should be low enough to be used without the child needing to climb onto a wobbly chair.

Children will be particularly reluctant to wash themselves when their noses hardly reach the edge of the basin, when they can't reach the taps, and when the water ends up running up their arms into their sleeves. A small stool would help here. If it is covered with towelling it will

be more inviting and warmer on bare feet. If you have a slippery floor you should make the stool slip-proof by attaching felt or rubber pads to the bottom.

Not only stairs inside the house, but also entrance stairs in blocks of flats, stores and hotels, should have an extra low hand rail for children. Unfortunately, this is rarely so, but at least in the home it may be possible to fit an additional rail or rope to make it easier for a child to negotiate the stairs.

A gate across the top of the stairs will prevent accidents but will still allow contact between mother and child. You can buy gates which are adjustable to the size that you require, have them made or make one yourself (about 30 inches [800 millimetres] high). They can be fastened to the banisters with ordinary hinges and be removed when no longer necessary.

Table for under the bed

Children's rooms are often so small that there is just enough room for one work table. What can you do when two or three children want to make something at the same time? Two folding trestles, a door (about 36 by 76 inches [900 by 1900 millimetres]) and four casters will solve the problem. The casters are screwed under the door so that it can easily be pushed under the bed when it is not in use. You can make the wooden trestles yourself – the instructions are given on page 93.

Seat made from a crib

The day will come when the baby's crib is no longer needed and is taking up unnecessary storage room. You can turn it into a seat fairly easily. Remove the front set of bars and position the top cross bar as low as possible (otherwise the bed, which is now open at the front will not hold together). Cover the mattress and foam for the backrests with bright fabric. The back cushions are fastened to the crib frame with tape tied in a bow. The converted crib can be repainted to match the colour of the fabric. You must make sure that it is sturdily constructed in the first place, otherwise it will collapse.

Children from six to twelve

Children of this age need more than just space to play. They also need room to keep their toys, books and records. A good solution to the problem of storing these things is the use of 'bed shelves'. Shelves fastened to the foot of bunk beds (see diagram below) will take all the articles that need storing away, yet are required to be handy for use. The shelf for the record player and records is slightly deeper and if there are two battens to support it, this will provide extra insurance against it tipping over. A spotlight provides full lighting for this section of the shelves if required. It can easily be fastened to any shelf although you must be careful that the flex is hidden, otherwise it might trip the child up. You could buy shelf units suitable for this, though you would probably have to extend the shelf for the record player, so it would possibly be a better idea to make the whole thing yourself. The bedding is stored in two boxes beneath the bunks.

An ordinary bookcase fastened to the foot of bunk beds will take all the things that children continually need to hand. The bedding is stored in two boxes on casters under the bunks.

A multi-purpose play bench

A bench on which several children can sit, either in their room or outside, is a useful addition to the household's furniture. You can combine several units of this kind to make tables or tunnels, bookcases or a shop counter, a complete doll's house or a stage for a puppet theatre. If you make the benches slightly higher you can keep toy boxes under them.

The bench is 32 inches (800 millimetres) long and about 16 inches (400 millimetres) wide. The height can be about 10 inches (250 millimetres) – or more, depending on the main purpose for which it will be used, and on the age and size of the child.

If you make it from ¾-inch (20-millimetre) blockboard it will be able to withstand rough treatment. Cut one 32 by 16 inch (800 by 400 millimetre) piece and two 10 by 16 inch (250 by 400 millimetre) pieces for each bench. You will also need a strip (or plank) 4 inches (100 millimetres) wide and 30½ inches (760 millimetres) long for the cross pieces

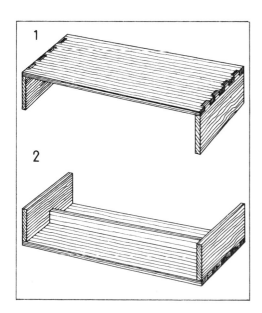

A play bench is a useful piece of furniture for the nursery. It can be used as a seat, but it will also make a good shop counter or a stage for a puppet theatre.

under the seat. You will find instructions on page 231 for the dovetail joints used to join the seat to the sides. The cross piece should be glued and dowelled. Round off all the edges, stain and seal, or paint the bench. Older children will be able to finish the wood themselves.

Bed with storage drawers

You can make a bed like this yourself quite cheaply from either chipboard or blockboard and wood planks. You need three 4 by 1-inch (100 by 25-millimetre) boards, each of which is 11 by 33½ inches (280 by 850 millimetres) in size. To these cross pieces you glue and screw ¾ inch (20 millimetre) thick planed planks (63 inches [1600 millimetres] long) after slightly rounding off the edges. Leave a gap of about ¾ inch (20 millimetres) between each plank, to give a kind of duck-board effect. The planks and cross pieces should be pre-drilled. For No. 8 2-inch (50-millimetre) countersunk wood screws use an ⅛-inch (3-millimetre) bit for the cross pieces and a ⅙-inch (4-millimetre) bit for the planks. The screw heads should be countersunk.

The drawers, which can be used for toys or perhaps bedding consist of ⅝-inch (16-millimetre) blockboard or chipboard for the side walls and base. The front and back will be visible when the drawer is pushed under the bed and so should be made with the same wood planks as the bed base.

The drawer bases are 30 by 35 inches (750 by 900 millimetres), the two side walls 8 by 30 inches (200 by 750 millimetres). The back is a plank 37 inches (940 millimetres) long and the front of two planks of the same length. Casters are screwed to the base of each drawer. If the drawers are to be used for toys, you can divide up the interior using ⅝-inch (16-millimetre) chipboard.

The whole unit should now be thoroughly sanded, rounding off all the edges (this should have been done already for the mattress base). The bed can be varnished or, after priming, filling and resanding, painted. Finally a mattress that has been made to size is placed on the frame.

Adjustable shelving unit

The shelf units of the type illustrated below can be bought ready-made. They have adjustable shelves, and can be used for toys, school books, records etc. The lowest shelf can be extended to form a work surface, and can be adjusted to suit a child. The whole unit must be fixed securely to the wall, otherwise it will tilt forward. The desk lamp, which is also fully adjustable, can be screwed to the writing surface or to one of the shelves above. Both the seat and backrest of the chair are adjustable.

If you are good with your hands you could make a bookcase like this yourself. The four corner posts can be made from 2 by 2 inch (50 by 50 millimetre) squared wood. They are held together at the base by a frame covered in ⅝-inch (16-millimetre) chipboard and at the top by a covering sheet of the same material, which is also used to make the actual shelves.

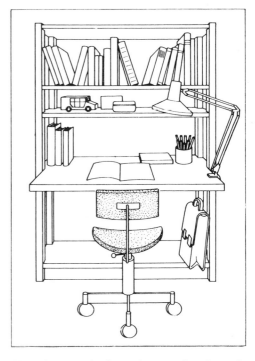

Here is a work place that can be altered as the child grows up. The shelves are adjustable and the work surface can also be raised or lowered depending on the size of the child.

Practical tips for the nursery

Scarcely any other room in the home offers as many opportunities for do-it-yourself as a child's room. Even mothers and fathers who are thoroughly tired of do-it-yourself will reach for their saw and hammer when it is a question of making a toy box or a bench, a bookcase or writing desk for their children; for often you can't buy exactly what you want. In addition you save money – but this does not mean that any wobbly box that you make yourself is good enough for the nursery.

A space-saving toy box

Children seem to amass toys very quickly, and they should all be kept somewhere that enables the collection to be moved from one room to another as easily as possible, and preferably in something in which a small child can rummage about, without having to deal with sides of the box that are too high. It would also be advantageous to have a box that can be put under the bed or shelves and which is not too heavy.

The building materials are as follows:

A simple toy box is constructed using ¾-inch (19-millimetre) chipboard or blockboard. All the joints are butted together and fixed with wood glue and nails or screws. The interior could be sub-divided using the same material.

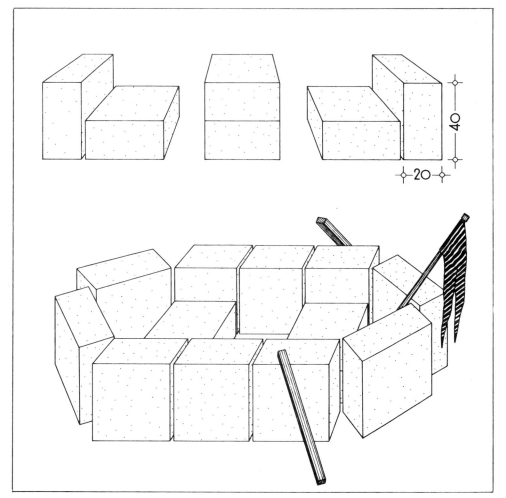

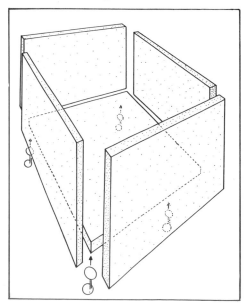

¾-inch (19-millimetre) chipboard or blockboard for the base and sides of the box. Don't make the box larger than 18 inches (500 millimetres) square or it will be too unwieldy. The height should be between 10 and 12 inches (250 and 300 millimetres). If the box is to be kept under the bed, you will have to make it fit the height of the bed accordingly, remembering to allow for the height of the casters. All the sections are assembled with glue and nails (or screws). When you place this in position you must ensure that the sides are at right angles. The casters should be screwed to the base at each corner, slightly in from the edges. Round off all the edges, then the box is ready for priming, filling and painting. Attach a handle to one side.

Foam blocks are light and not too expensive. You can cover them with fabric or waterproof material. Each block is 16 inches long and wide, and 8 inches high. You can use one block as a stool, two to make a children's table. With four blocks you can make a doll's bed. Six blocks will make a complete seating area (top). The ship (below) is made from 12 blocks.

Foam blocks for playing

Four of the brightly coloured foam blocks illustrated above make a doll's bed, six of them will make a table and two chairs. But to get endless use out of them you would need at least a dozen. Each block measures 16 by 16 by 8 inches (400 by 400 by 200 millimetres).

To cover each block you will need 48 inches (1250 millimetres) of 36 inch (900 millimetre) wide material. You can easily work out how to cut the material from the size of the blocks. Use a 32-inch (800-millimetre) zip fastener around three sides of the block (8-16-8 [200-400-200]) so that you can take the cover off for washing or cleaning.

Hard-wearing cotton and synthetic materials are best for covers. For blocks that will be used on the patio or in the garden use a waterproof cover and a strong tent zip. Canvas or sailcloth make particularly hard-wearing covers. Don't hesitate to vary the colour of each block.

Twelve blocks in two piles of six, stacked one on top of the other, give a block the size of a wardrobe (48 inches [1200 millimetres] high, 32 inches [800 millimetres] wide, and 16 inches [400 millimetres] deep). You could also store the blocks under the bed, so they don't take up much space.

Twin desks

Before you begin work, see if you can get hold of two old cupboard units from a typing desk. If you can't find any you could use any other small cupboard which is about 24 inches (600 millimetres) high, or you could make suitable shelves yourself.

If the cupboards are too high, you could maybe make them lower by reducing the height of the base. Cupboards which are too low can be raised by increasing the height of the base. In either case they should give a desk height of 24 to 26 inches (600 to 650 millimetres) for smaller children and 26 to 28 inches (650 to 700 millimetres) for larger children. Your wood merchant might cut three sheets of chipboard for you: one ¾-inch (19-millimetre) piece 51 by 39 inches (1300 by 1000 millimetres) for the dividing wall, two ⅜-inch (10-millimetre) pieces for the work surfaces which should measure 37½ inches (1260 millimetres) in length and 1½ inches (35 millimetres) narrower than the depth of the cupboards.

Glue and nail 1½ by ¾ inch (40 by 20

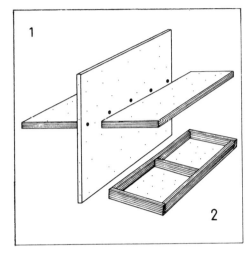
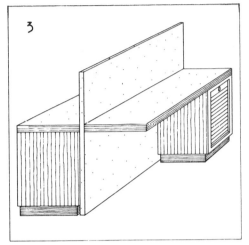

millimetre) battens on edge around the two thin sheets of chipboard. This will strengthen the thin sheets and also protect the edges. The battens are also used to fasten the boards into position. They can simply meet flush at the corners or be mitred (a more stylish solution).

To establish the height of the writing surface, lay one board across one of the cupboards and mark the top edge on the dividing partition which you place alongside it. Drill through the partition and the battens on either side to take the bolts. Before screwing on the nuts from the opposite side, place washers on the bolts.

Now push the cupboards under the table tops and screw to both the work surface and the back wall. Sand all surfaces (rounding off the edges), prime and fill, resand and paint.

One suggestion for a practical twin desk: It consists of a dividing partition (chipboard or even blockboard) with writing surfaces screwed to it. Example 2 shows the underside of one of the writing surfaces, with its frame structure. The writing surfaces are supported by two cupboards.

A toy-car roadway

If the toy-car roadway is mounted on a board on casters which fits under the bed, you will not need to assemble and take it apart continuously. Screw a 1 by 1 inch (25 by 25 millimetre) batten under the front edge of a sheet of ⅝-inch (16-millimetre) chipboard and attach a piece of wood to it to take two handles. Then screw four casters to the base of the board. Now it only needs priming and painting.

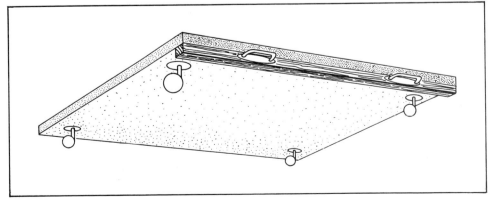

To save the time involved in setting up and dismantling a toy car roadway, mount the track on a sheet of chipboard mounted on casters.

KITCHENS

The kitchen is first and foremost a place to work. If it is to function efficiently it must be functionally planned and equipped. This has become an increasingly complex operation and for this reason there are likely to be more mistakes made in planning the kitchen than in any other room. Unfortunately, they usually don't occur to you until it is too late. Therefore, this section deals mainly with points to watch when planning your kitchen.

Keep in mind the activities which have to be carried out in the kitchen. Primarily, these are food preparation and washing the dishes, both of which require water, so they are centred around the sink area. Next in sequence, and really an extension of food preparation, comes the mixing zone; this is followed by the cooking zone centred around the cooker; finally, there is the serving zone.

In planning these zones, your aim should be to have a continuous work surface so that the progress from one to another is made easier. In the preparation area there should be work surfaces on either side of the sink, although in effect this will probably be the drainboard on one side. On the other side there should be at least 24 inches (600 millimetres) of work surface which will lead into the mixing zone; this area requires some 35 inches (900 millimetres) and leads to the cooking zone. In this case there should be, if possible, 12 inches (300 millimetres) either side of the cooker or hob, and ideally these surfaces should be heat-proof. Where there is a separate oven there should also be a work surface adjacent. If there is sufficient space the work surface beyond the cooker can be extended for a serving zone.

It is unlikely, and in fact undesirable, that this layout will be in one straight line (a 'galley' kitchen). The more usual layouts are L-shaped or U-shaped, or in cases where the room is long and narrow there may be units and work surfaces on only two parallel walls. In the first two layouts the progression from one zone to another is the same as in a straight-line layout, but in the last one it is best if you can arrange the sink and cooker on the same wall, with a preparation area on the opposite wall.

One way of assessing the likely success of a layout is to measure the distances which have to be covered between sink, cooker and refrigerator/storage unit (these should be adjacent). Taking into account both the size and shape of the kitchen, and the provision of sufficient work surface, the overall length of the three sides of the triangle should be between 12 and 20 feet (3.6 and 6 metres) and the distance between sink and cooker, the route most used, should be between 4 and 6 feet (1.2 and 1.8 metres).

There is now a very wide range of interior fittings for the base units, with shelves and drawer units and carousels or swivel units which fill the corner spaces, so that every storage requirement can be satisfied.

You may find that shelves that you make and fix yourself will not only prove to be very useful but will also save you money. Correct lighting plays an important part in the efficient working of any kitchen. A central light on its own is insufficient since wherever you are working you will be standing in your own light. This central light is necessary for an overall light for the room, but you will also need to provide extra lights for the work surfaces.

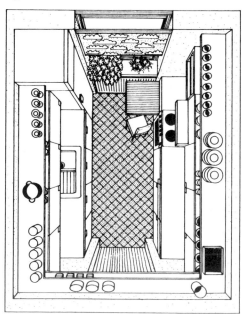

A small kitchen which has nevertheless a sophisticated atmosphere. It has a floor area of about 70 square feet (7 square metres). The ground plan explains the layout: the space between the units is only 4 feet by 9 feet 9 ins (1.20 by 3 metres). This is not really a disadvantage as all the work surfaces are within reach.

Three kitchens

You can of course become used to a poorly equipped kitchen – just as you can get used to a sagging mattress. In time, you will scarcely recognize what it is that makes your work so difficult.

It may be that the cooker is in the wrong place, the refrigerator not directly within reach, or a badly positioned sink makes washing the day's dishes one of the most irritating jobs.

The three kitchens illustrated on these two pages presented some difficult planning problems. The first appeared impossibly small at first sight. The second, though quite large, was in an old property and had a depressing appearance. The third really was small and probably presented the most problems. All three kitchens were improved by logical planning and the use of the best and most suitable units and appliances. Planning and well designed equipment can succeed in even the most hopeless situations.

Kitchen 1 (above left): This reorganized room originally had a small larder next to the window, making the installation of base units with a continuous work surface impossible, so that the basis of the replanning was to remove the larder. The removal of non-structural walls is not too great an undertaking, and can often be the answer to a planning problem. New units and appliances were bought, keeping only the existing dishwasher. This

A kitchen of 65 square feet (6 square metres) (above right). Light pine units make this small room pleasantly cheerful and they tone pleasantly with the original floor tiles. This photograph shows how the removal of the larder has made possible a continuous work surface round a compact U-shape.

This galley kitchen 6 feet (1.90 metres) wide and 11 feet 10 ins (3.60 metres) long has fittings along two adjacent walls in an L shape (right). Along the narrow wall there is the sink with the dishwasher below the drawer. On the long wall there is a hob with a built-under oven and a pull-out table.

172

was covered by a pine panel to match the new units (front right in the photograph).

The floor tiles were also kept and since they toned with the colour of the wood they no longer looked unattractive. The cooker was built in on the window wall. The windowsill was below worktop height. The window was not altered, so now it can no longer be opened, only swivelled. The venetian blind is set into the window recess (obviously curtains would be very dangerous above a cooker). Heat from the radiator in front of the window rises between the window-sill and the base units.

The units were arranged around three walls to make full use of the available space. The wall units extend to the window wall. One tall unit (front left, not in photograph) holds cleaning materials. The continuous work surface in the new kitchen has proved most effective. Originally there was only one work surface, in front of the window.

Kitchen 2 (above): 'Now that we have had our kitchen for a few weeks, I can tell you briefly how we like it', wrote the owner of this kitchen after it had been refitted. 'My work has become consider-ably easier, and many jobs can now be done much more quickly and efficiently. I am very pleased with the high-level refrigerator and oven, the continuous work surfaces (very easy to clean) and the rearrangement of the units.' This kitchen of 150 square feet (14 square metres) is larger than average, but the main work area takes up only one row of units (left in the photograph). Opposite the work surface there are tall units in which other appliances are stored (not in the photo-graph). The family gathers for meals around the large dining table in front of the window.

Kitchen 3 (below left): Even if you have little kitchen space, you can avoid many mistakes by spending some time at the

A roomy kitchen of 150 square feet (14 square metres) (above). The row of units on the left contains the hob and the dishwasher. The oven is in a high-level unit. For meals the family gathers around the large dining table by the window. The right-hand wall (not in the photograph) contains another wall unit.

planning stage. Here underfloor hot-air heating is used (you can see the heating grate on the left of the photograph). Beyond it are the sliding doors onto the patio, which help to conserve space in the kitchen. Good use has been made of wall cupboards, which have ordinary hinged doors, while the base units include a rotating metal saucepan rack in the corner.

All the units are oak-fronted and are finished so as to be acid- and alkali-proof, making them almost as resilient as plas-tic. There is sufficient circulation space in front of the units.

A new look for a dull kitchen

There are kitchens which are perfectly furnished and equipped, but still look as cold and clinical as an operating theatre.

These two pages show three ways of brightening up a dull kitchen without changing all the fittings. Each of the three schemes began with the same kitchen (photograph below).

No fault could be found with the modern white built-in units and labour-saving appliances. The cooker is well positioned with storage units and work surfaces on either side. Above it is an extractor hood discharging directly outside. The main work surface is in front of the window with sink and dishwasher to the left of it. The vinyl-tiled floor does not show the dirt since its flecked design and its neutral colour goes well with anything. In short, this kitchen is furnished very practically. Small spots of colour are added by a geranium, bread-bin and oven glove – and that is all. How is it possible to give this, as it were, perfect but boring kitchen a new look?

This is what the original kitchen looked like (above). There is nothing wrong with its practical furnishings. The cooker is well placed with storage units and work surfaces on both sides. Above it is an extractor hood, discharging directly outside. The main work area is in front of the window. To the left of it stand the sink and the dishwasher. There is no lack of labour-saving appliances. However, it is rather dull looking.

Scheme 1 (below): Stripes and bold colours have made this dull kitchen more cheerful. White walls are essential for this method of giving the room more character. If the old wallpaper is still in good condition you can simply paint over it. Here, blue is emphasized and stripes provide the main theme. The striped pattern is produced by sticking adhesive tape onto the white walls and tiles. Casters smarten up an old kitchen chair which has been painted blue. You can make the three sets of shelves yourself from chipboard.

Scheme 2 (below left): Sometimes it is enough merely to change the wallpaper. Here a blue paper with a white flower pattern was chosen. Since you can get fabric with the same design, the roller blind was made and the revolving chair covered to match the wallpaper. Other points of colour are provided by the spice shelves painted grass green and the blue door (not in the photograph). A metal tube was fitted above the cooker on which implements hang on 'S' hooks (be careful none of them drop). To the right, on the wall, is a small bulletin board.

Scheme 3 (below): Wood and straw determine the character of this particularly cosy kitchen. The walls have been timber-clad. The timber must be completely coated with a protective agent to withstand cooking fumes and condensation. The wood (Scandinavian spruce) has been stained a reddish brown.

The rush matting is well suited to the high humidity level usually found in kitchens. It is laid loose on the floor. The checked curtain hangs from wooden rings. The dark green pendent lamp lights the window area in the evening.

Moving with a fitted kitchen

A fitted kitchen can only function properly in the space for which it was designed and into which it is fitted, so moving kitchen units is not usually possible or desirable. However, it can be done if you decide that you may want to move it with you when you buy it.

The photographs and diagrams on these two pages show that if you plan ahead you may be able to fit your new units into a new kitchen. The units were bought for kitchen A. The numbers showing separate units on both diagrams show that almost all fit into kitchen B.

The points to remember are: Only buy units of 20 inches (500 millimetres) or less, as these will be easier to change around. Choose doors which open out frontwards. You won't be able to take your work surfaces with you as you probably won't want to cut them up – you will have to buy new ones.

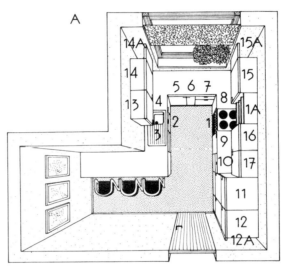

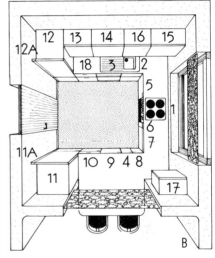

Kitchen A (right): It is about 120 square feet (11 square metres) in size. There is room for a wide breakfast bar which rests on one of the base units. The chairs should be about the same height as bar stools.

Kitchen B (left): After the move. The room is slightly smaller. The base units are covered with laminated plastic.

Planning a well laid-out kitchen

Whether you can save time with your daily housework depends to a great extent on the way your kitchen is arranged. The motto 'Good planning saves time' is applicable here. On these and the following two pages you can find out what changes to make in your kitchen to save time and energy and to increase your free time.

First, you should be clear on how to work in your kitchen, where most of your work takes place: in all probability you will find that most of your time is spent around the sink and the adjacent work surfaces in preparing meals and, of course, washing up; next in the area around the cooker and finally in fetching food from the refrigerator and the larder.

Make a note too of the number of times you walk across the kitchen every day between the different work areas. Then note for a whole day how often and how far you have to stretch, bend and straighten up again in the course of your work, and how many things you have to lift and carry. An analysis of these figures will help you to determine whether your kitchen could be better planned.

Try to adapt the kitchen units and appliances as closely as possible to your own method of working. Sometimes it may be enough to change or swap round the interior fittings of the units. It is best to keep pots and pans near the cooker, and crockery should be near the sink. Small items of crockery should be kept in the wall units and large, heavy casserole dishes in cupboards or large drawers which are easier to reach.

A trolley can be very useful in your daily housework. Anything heavy that you don't want to carry yourself can be moved around the kitchen or through the whole home on it. Or you can use it to carry crockery from the kitchen to the dining table and back again or from the sink to the cupboard. A small trolley will save both time and energy.

Dining area in the kitchen

The larger the kitchen, the further you have to walk between the separate work surfaces. So if you have a large kitchen, don't furnish all the space as a kitchen,

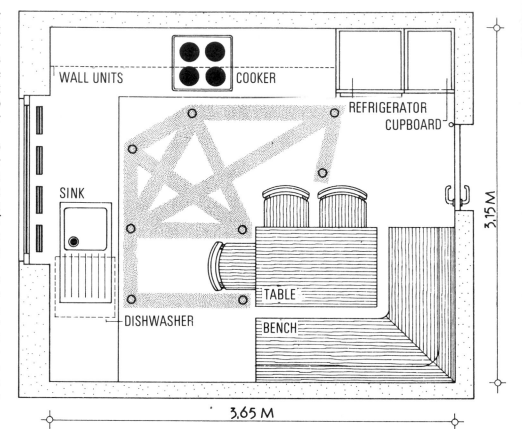

Network of movements during daily work in the kitchen. The distances you have to cover every day are marked onto the ground plan of the kitchen. It is most dense of course by the main worktop under the window.

but make it a kitchen with a dining area. Nowadays, if it is well planned, neither the family nor your guests will mind if they are asked to eat in the kitchen. This can be very pleasant and has several practical advantages. The main one is that you don't have to make a detour through the hall to get from the cooker to the dining table.

One of the many possibilities is shown in the photograph below left. Here the kitchen is separated from the dining area by a row of base units. The worktop over the units continues round into a dining table. At meal times, plates and dishes only have to be pushed along into the right place.

Clearing away after the meal is just as easy, and in this instance after-dinner coffee can be served in the lounge, which is sited directly off the kitchen/dining

area (situated front right in photograph).

You will be aware of the advantages of a large room throughout the day, for you no longer have to work shut away in a poky kitchen, and you can get other members of the family to help as there is plenty of room.

Another method is to place the dining table in the centre of the kitchen, if the room is large enough – but not in such a way that a large table gets in your way every time you go to and fro between cooker, refrigerator and sink. Here, dining furniture which is easy to push aside and/or fold away is particularly suitable. Then they can be moved out of the way easily for cleaning.

In many cases you can fit low units between the cooking and dining areas to separate them clearly, but they could also be decorated in different colours.

A superimposed photograph showing daily housework (left). You have to take two or thrce steps to and fro and make a few arm movements when transferring crockery from the dishwasher to the storage cupboards. The composite photography shows the advantages of a well planned kitchen, saving work and energy.

In any kind of housework, walls and doors are obstacles that you have to bypass over again during the day. If the kitchen and dining room are combined as in this open-plan flat (below), you can work in both rooms simultaneously and save a lot of time. The kitchen is separated from the dining area by a row of base units. The dining area leads into the living room at the right of the picture.

Important points when furnishing

When you are choosing your home, or planning the building of a new one, there are a few points that you should watch:

There should be enough room for fitted units by the door.

There should also be enough room for units below the window.

You must not totally enclose radiators under the window, but must allow the heat to circulate freely.

Each separate work surface in the kitchen should have a light.

You can never have too many power points in the kitchen.

A kitchen arranged around three walls is the most labour-saving.

Furnishing hints

If everything in the kitchen is to harmonize and to function as practically as possible, you will have to give a lot of thought to every detail of furnishing. Here are a few tips:

Floor covering: If the kitchen has a wooden floor it should be scrubbed. Wooden planks will add charm to your kitchen, but you will have to be prepared to clean them properly. For a long time tiles in various shapes and colours have been popular. Vinyl flooring is easy to care for, and the foam- or felt-backed versions are more restful for your feet.

Wall coverings: Wall tiles are traditional for kitchens. They are hard-wearing, easy to clean and available in many designs and shapes. You could also cover the walls with plastic tiles, or a waterproof vinyl paper. You will find out how to hang tiles on the next two pages.

Window coverings: It is best to choose a covering which neither collects dust nor hangs in generous folds over the worktop. Fabric or plastic roller blinds have proved their worth in the kitchen. You can get papers suitable for the kitchen and material for roller blinds with the same pattern. Venetian blinds are practical for you can position the slats to regulate the amount of light allowed in. Sliding curtains are also popular for they never get in the way and are easy to clean.

Units: They should not only look homely and attractive, but above all should be easy to keep clean. As well as units finished in plastic laminate or painted wood, you can get wood units which are veneered rather than solid wood. Wood for kitchen units should be carefully treated so that they are as practical to use and to keep clean as plastic ones. Decorative mouldings make the wood surface more interesting, but can collect dust and dirt and will need regular and thorough cleaning. Don't forget to test the handles or handle grooves on the doors and drawers. Not all of them are practical, and there are some designs on which you will continually break your fingernails.

Worktops: Work surfaces in a kitchen must be able to withstand cutting with a knife and should be heat- and acid-resistant. Plastic laminate worktops are most common, but you could also choose ceramic tiles (e.g. marble), stainless steel or solid wood or a mixture of these surfaces.

Dining furniture: If you are going to have your dining area in the kitchen it is best to choose furniture which can be cleared away easily, such as collapsable tables and chairs which you can fold up or at least stack. Here too you should choose materials which are easy to care for.

Door wall: The door should be at least 25 inches (650 millimetres) from adjacent walls so that base and wall units will not overlap. If you are to have tall cupboards by the door you will need even more space to allow for a light switch.

Window wall: On this wall you will probably have your sink or, in any case, a main working surface, on account of the good light. The length of the wall on either side of the window should be at least 16 inches (400 millimetres) so that wall units which are 12 inches (300 millimetres) deep can be fitted on the return walls. Use roller or venetian blinds for the windows as they will not get in the way when you are working.

A good oven saves time

To save cooking time you need the right cooker and the right pans, but this doesn't necessarily mean that you will have to buy new ones. Make sure that your electric hot plates and pans are the same size so that your pans are neither too big nor too small and choose pans with a flat 'sandwich' base (steel-copper-steel). If you have a gas cooker, the flames shouldn't lick up the sides of the pans. Heat will then be absorbed quickly and evenly. You can save time with an automatic oven. It cooks and bakes without you having to watch over it. To get used to an automatic oven it is a good idea to start by baking a cake: place the

cake in the pre-heated oven, check the clock is at the correct time and set the time switch. You can now get on with something else without worrying. The oven will automatically switch off at the end of the cooking time. Automatic hot plates can also be connected to your timer: place potatoes on one plate, vegetables on the other, set the cooking time and the time at which cooking is to finish. The plates will switch on automatically at the beginning of the cooking time, and off at the end. There are ovens available which also switch on automatically. This means that you can go to the theatre, cinema or away for the whole day and have a hot meal ready when you return.

Self-cleaning ovens have been available for some time. With an oven like this you set a switch to 'Clean' and all the baking and roasting stains burn away to a small pile of dust in the course of two or three hours and are then wiped up with a damp cloth. For this the oven heats to a temperature of about 500°, and therefore glass door panels are of specially treated heat-resistant glass. Later types of oven, with some form of fan circulating the hot air rather than having concealed elements, are virtually self-cleaning during the cooking operation saving a lot of time and temper. If the oven is used a lot you are recommended to clean it two or three times a month.

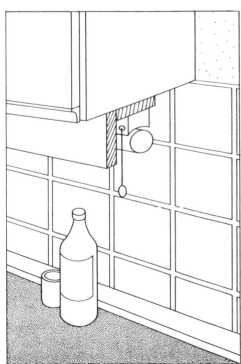

Lighting: A light in the middle of the ceiling can serve only as general lighting. With this lighting you will be working in shadow, because you stand in your own light. Tube lighting under the wall units to light each work surface is a practical way of lighting. They can be switched on and off at the light or at the switch by the door as you wish and depending on the available connections.

SieMatic UK

This kitchen is well designed and has plenty of storage space and worktops. The double oven is built into the units. The most interesting feature in this kitchen is the central area. As well as the hob, there is also a grill for steaks and hamburgers, and an extractor hood to allow smoke and steam to escape. There are extra taps in this area as well, so you would not even have to walk to the sink to add water to anything.

How to hang wall tiles

If you want to hang wall tiles yourself the instructions on these two pages will help you. You should remember that wall tiles will last for years and if you choose a very striking pattern you may get tired of it, and they cost too much to change often.

Careful preparation

A professional will usually hang wall tiles in cement mortar. It takes time and much practice to learn how to apply the thick layer of mortar smoothly to prevent the tiled wall looking crooked and uneven. At your first attempts some tiles will fall off, and the gaps between the tiles will not be perfectly perpendicular and horizontal. If you want to use this method of hanging tiles you will have to get an experienced tiler to teach you.

The so-called 'thin-bed' technique is much more practical for beginners. Here any type of tile (ceramic, plastic, light metal) is stuck to a (smooth) wall with a thin layer of special adhesive. Even a beginner can make the tiles adhere firmly and look good, so in this section we will deal only with the 'thin-bed' technique. It has long proved successful. The preparation of the wall for using tile adhesive is the same for all types of tiles. The surface must be firm, even, dry and free from dust and grease. Any wallpaper, distemper, emulsion or gloss paint must be removed (with wallpaper stripper, washing down with water or solvent, rubbing down with sandpaper). Any unevenness in the plaster must be smoothed out with filler. Absorbent surfaces should be primed with thinned tile adhesive (one part adhesive to five parts water).

As well as plaster walls, plasterboard is also suitable for tiling, together with any wood surface such as plywood, chipboard, hardboard, blockboard. Here too the surface will have to be treated correctly. Hardboard should be fixed with its back, textured surface outwards, as this will give better adhesion for the tiles.

Where to begin hanging

Tile adhesive will not adhere well to any smooth surface – it should be scratched with a piece of hardened steel to provide a 'key' for the adhesive.

The second step, once the surface has been prepared, is to mark the boundaries of the area to be tiled. This will depend to some extent on the size of the tiles. The most common tile size is 6 by 6 inches (150 by 150 millimetres), but there are other sizes available. These will depend on the country of origin and other factors. While tiles are more usually square and rectangular, there are hexagonal and diamond-shaped tiles and curved shapes, such as the traditional 'Provençal' shape. Before deciding on a particular type of tile you should see a large area of them. The basic rule when marking the area to be tiled is that as few tiles as possible should have to be cut.

First you must find out if the floor, skirting board or work surface is properly horizontal. If this is not the case, position a tile at the lowest point and draw a horizontal line (using a spirit level) extending from its top edge, along which you will lay your first row of tiles. The row below the line will have to be cut to take account of the uneven floor.

Proceed similarly with the vertical edges. Don't start in the corner with a complete tile unless a plumb line has shown that it is perpendicular. This will not usually be the case, so you will have to divide up the wall so that the first tile begins at least 4 inches (100 millimetres) from either the right-hand or left-hand corner. This will avoid having to cut narrow strips of tiles to fit into the corner. The corner row will be stuck on last.

You will also have to take any gaps for light switches, powerpoints or pipes into consideration. If possible they should not come in the middle of the tile, but at the edge – or better still – at a corner. This will make cutting the tiles easier. When you have determined how the wall is to be divided up, the starting lines are marked with a pencil (one horizontal and one perpendicular). Take care not to lay the tiles too close together but leave a gap of between $1/16$ and $1/8$ inch (2 and 3 millimetres) all round. Some tiles have small projections, which are covered by the grouting, to keep the tiles automatically the right distance apart.

Sticking on the tiles

Sticking on the tiles begins with applying the adhesive. It is spread onto the wall with a comb spreader provided by the adhesive manufacturer.

Plastic combs which are used to spread adhesive on a plastered wall will quickly wear out and no longer work efficiently, so have spare combs as it is important to spread the adhesive thoroughly.

The adhesive must be worked wet and should not dry out before the tiles are fitted. Don't apply more adhesive than you can tile in ten to 15 minutes.

The tiles are placed in position on the adhesive and pushed down. To get even gaps between tiles insert small pieces of wood prepared in advance between them. They must be removed before the adhesive begins to harden, so don't leave them for longer than 15 to 20 minutes, or they will stick firm. When pulling out the spacers hold the neighbouring tiles lightly in position with your hand to prevent them coming away.

Instead of the small pieces of wood you can use wooden matches, though they will be less easy to remove. There are cross-shaped pieces of plastic which act as spacers where the tiles intersect. They are pushed right in and do not need to be removed as the grouting will cover them.

About 24 hours after you have stuck on the tiles you can fill the gaps with grouting. Any extra can be sponged away.

Cutting tiles

Ceramic tiles are cut on the glazed side with a glass-cutter, then broken smoothly in two on two nails (see diagram) or a knitting needle. The outline of small cuts into the edges of a tile must be scored with a cutter and then broken away carefully with pincers. To make a hole in a tile use a masonry bit in a drill. To make a large hole, you should initially drill a smaller hole then score the outline of a large hole with the cutter and break away the rest of the tile with pincers.

Plastic tiles are generally cut with a sharp carpet knife along a steel rule.

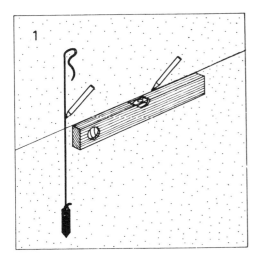

(1) Mark the upper edge of the area to be tiled with a pencil using a spirit level, and the vertical edge with a plumb line. Precise measurements will save frustration and bad tiling.

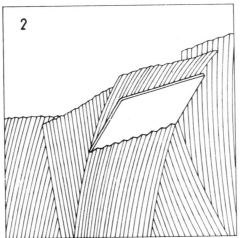

(2) Tile adhesive is applied with a comb spreader to the clean, well prepared wall. The spreader ensures that the adhesive is spread evenly.

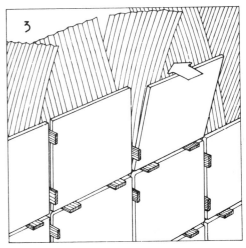

(3) When pressing the tiles into position small pieces of wood ensure that the tiles are evenly spaced. You can use cross-shaped pieces of plastic instead which, unlike the wood, can be left in the spaces.

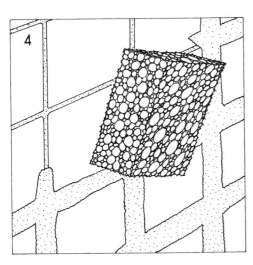

(4) When the adhesive is dry the spaces are grouted (preferably with a rubber spreader). Any excess grout is washed off the tiles immediately with a sponge.

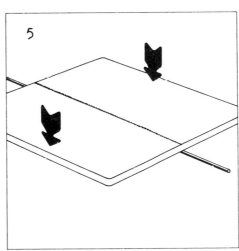

(5) Ceramic tiles are scored with a glass cutter and broken in two over two nails or a knitting needle. Plastic tiles, on the other hand, are cut with scissors or a knife.

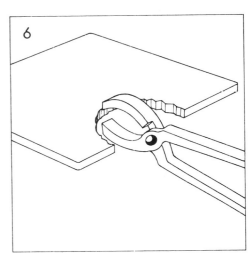

(6) Round holes are broken out of ceramic tiles with pincers. This must be done very carefully a little at a time, or you can break off more than you intended.

A more practical kitchen

Often you will not notice how your kitchen can be improved until a long time after you have moved into a new home. Usually it is only little things, but these can be annoying if you are bothered by them day after day. There are many ways of solving these problems yourself. A few have been collected together on these two pages.

Seldom will it happen that the worktop in front of the kitchen window is the same height as the windowsill. It is often a few inches lower so that the windowsill juts out over the worktop. In such cases, dirt can collect between the windowsill and the worktop.

If both worktop and windowsill are the same height, you can easily have the top cut to give a clean join. As an additional protection you can push or stick a T-shaped strip of plastic between the sill and worktop.

Raising a worktop

If the worktop is lower than the windowsill you can raise it, providing of course, that it will still be comfortable to work on. To do this, you simply unscrew the work surface, place a batten framework under it and screw it back into position. Any edges of the battens which are visible can be covered with plastic laminate. If the windowsill juts out, you can cut away part of the worktop to accommodate it and fill the join with a T-shaped strip.

If the surface of the worktop is no longer very good, you can place the batten framework on top of it and screw on a new worktop. This should be made from ¾-inch (10-millimetre) blockboard which is then covered with plastic laminate to cover the windowsill and hide any joins.

Herb and spice shelves

Herbs and spices are usually bought today in glass bottles or jars with a good seal. In many homes they seem to collect very quickly and there is soon no more space to store them, and moreover, you get tired of having to rummage in the cupboard to find the right one. To solve this problem, you could have herb and

184

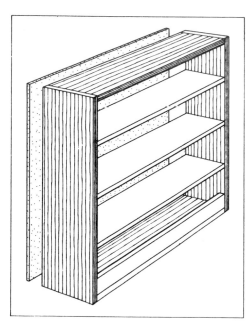

Kitchen herb and spice shelves, home-made from pine planks with a hardboard back. The size depends on the height of the jars.

spice shelves where all the bottles are visible and easily found.

The measurements of the shelves will depend on the space available but this home-made version should fit somewhere in your kitchen. Perhaps you have a suitable space between the base and wall units, or maybe it can stand on a base unit without taking up too much work space, or be screwed to the side of a tall cupboard.

The shelves are made from solid pine about 4 inches (100 millimetres) wide, the other dimensions depending on the space you have and the number of jars to be stored. The pieces cut to size are made into a frame with joints that are glued and screwed, and the hardboard back will help to keep the unit square. The individual shelves can rest on bearers screwed to the sides and can have lippings along their front edges projecting above the shelf to keep the jars in place. You can polish the shelf unit, staining it first if you wish, or you can finish it with a gloss paint – whichever goes best with your scheme.

Sliding table

Many kitchens and dining rooms are completely separate units, sometimes with a hatch between the two rooms with sliding or hinged doors. The hatch makes it possible to pass the food from the kitchen to the dining room and to return the dirty plates from the dining room to the kitchen. Here is an alternative to using a serving hatch. Make a built-in table between the kitchen and dining room which can be pushed to and fro. You can pull it out into the kitchen and set it for meals and also to clear it again afterwards. It makes a comfortable

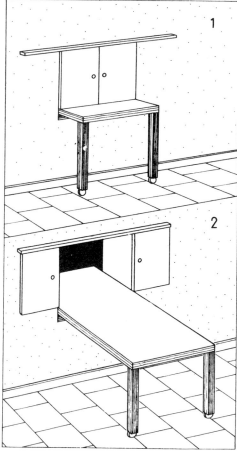

The hatch between the kitchen and dining room is less popular today. But a sliding table which can be pushed from the kitchen through to the dining room is very useful. Sliding doors cover the wall opening because hinged doors would not be as practical.

dining or work table for the dining room.

A table like this on casters is not necessarily expensive, but if you are going to install one it must be planned well in advance because serving hatches are usually positioned too high.

The table top should be 27½ inches (700 millimetres) above the floor. If the table top and supporting frame together are 2 inches (50 millimetres) thick, the height from the floor to the bottom of the opening should be no more than 25½ inches (650 millimetres) high.

One further prerequisite is that there is enough space in both the kitchen and dining room to take a table. Normally the table will be in the dining area and be pushed through into the kitchen only to be set and cleared. An ordinary dining-sized table will be too high – you will need to shorten the legs to accommodate the casters. It is best to have a sliding door to the hatch, for hinged doors would be likely to get in the way.

One other point is that you can't use a tablecloth on a table like this, but you can use place mats instead.

Wall shelves for the kitchen

Not every base unit will have a wall unit above it. If you have empty wall space above a worktop you can use it for open shelves. They are of course much cheaper than closed cupboards. They provide a lot of storage space for the shelf area is not interrupted by vertical partitions. One disadvantage is that on account of the cooking fumes and condensation, any thing placed on open shelves will get dirty more quickly than in a closed cupboard.

You can have wall shelves cut to size from chipboard or blockboard and paint them before putting them up. If you want natural wood use pine planks of the correct thickness. They are coated with a colourless varnish to show the grain of the wood. Staining is usually unnecessary, for pine will naturally go darker with age.

It is best to use brackets for putting up the shelves. Look for strong ones which are not only stable but look good as well. Fasten the brackets to the wall with wood

screws and wall plugs. Place the shelves on the brackets and screw into position. Shelves which are ¾ inch (19 millimetres) thick can span widths up to 39 inches (1000 millimetres). For longer shelves you will need brackets in between.

If you want to use the space right up to the ceiling area you can put three or four shelves one above the other. Possibly you could find room on the bottom shelf for accessories (e.g. small plastic drawers) in which you can store small items.

Anything that is seldom needed should go on the top shelf, but articles you need often should be within easy reach. You could screw hooks into the underside of the bottom shelf for cups, ladles, sieves and strainers, pan lids, etc.

These kitchen shelves are open, and are therefore accessible from either side, saving you time and energy.

BATHROOMS

Bathrooms are changing. In previous years they have tended to be poorly equipped, unpretentious rooms, but are now coming to be recognized as having a glamour of their own. They are no longer sober, purely functional rooms intended only for cleansing one's external parts.

Body care has become a time-consuming occupation, to which we pay a lot of attention. As well as care of the body, the mind, exhausted by work, should also find refreshment – a place for relaxation. The bathroom is used in the evening to cleanse oneself after the working day, and in the morning to help you start the day in the best possible way.

Bathrooms are larger nowadays, and have more elegant fittings. Ceramics have been joined by modern plastics in gleaming colours. Wet feet no longer have to stand on hard, cold tiles, but on soft, warm carpeting. Walls are more colourful and are no longer always covered in the traditional wall tiles. An important part is played by the atmosphere which you can create with lighting. In short, bathrooms are becoming so habitable that it almost makes it possible to live there.

This view of the changing role of the bathroom may seem rather utopian even today. Firstly bathrooms are still quite small and secondly not all homes have a bathroom even now. Added to which, as one might imagine, households with old-fashioned bathrooms by no means make full use of them. Nowadays when we economize on the size of the bathrooms it is easy to forget that once bathing was a most enjoyable social occasion. Admittedly one could contemplate much larger 'bathrooms' then – and these social bathers had no taboos which called for 'intimate' bathrooms. We know how the Ancient Romans behaved long ago with their large public baths, the therms. The more refined habits of the Roman upper classes who bathed in private have been handed down to us. The Roman attitude to bathing and the 'social' bathroom which served both them and their friends, is the dream of many of today's architects.

If you have enough room, you could install a bathroom similar to the one above. The whole area has been tiled, and there is a deep bath as well as a shower. The long radiator stops the area becoming cold.

Bathrooms need not be colourless and boring. Even cold, sober, old-fashioned bathrooms with high ceilings can become comfortable rooms with a little imagination. The photograph on the right shows made-to-measure bathroom fitments with a long unit for two basins, large mirror and roomy storage shelves. The wooden wall cladding gives a friendly atmosphere. Since the room has no window, there is generous lighting and good ventilation.

New walls for an old bathroom

In many old bathrooms the walls are painted in oil-based paint with a few tiles over the wash-basin. To improve a bathroom like this you will first have to consider making the tiled area larger (you will find instructions on doing this yourself on page 82).

But there are also other materials which you can use on bathroom walls. The suggestions found on these two pages will improve any old-fashioned bathroom. But even in new homes you can cover the walls with vinyl wallpaper or wood in various ways, with fabric or wooden tiles, with sheets of enamel or plastic. A brief definition of the various possibilities:

Fabric-covered board: Plywood or chipboard is covered with any furnishing

fabric of your choice. This is glued, nailed or stapled to the back of the board. The wall is covered with a framework of battens, to which the board is screwed using brass screws and washers. Before covering the boards you should protect them on both sides with a clear polyurethane varnish. When the fabric is in position on the boards it should be sprayed with a blind fabric stiffener.

Wooden planks: Here too you need a sub-frame of battening. To allow air to circulate behind the wall covering you will need to make air holes in the battens every 20 inches (500 millimetres). To make these, saw into the wood to about half its depth (making two cuts about 2 inches [50 millimetres] apart), and chisel out a hole. It is best to fix the timber into

In this example (top left) the bathroom walls are covered in vitreous enamel tiles. The two-colour pattern allows for large-scale effects, which work best on large walls.

Timber planks (top right) must be positioned so that air can circulate behind them. They are waxed or covered with a clear impregnating seal which allows the wood to breathe. The illustration shows western red cedar.

Fabric-covered walls are also possible in the bathroom (above). The fabric is tensioned over sheets of plywood or chipboard and then sprayed with a fabric blind stiffener before fitting onto the wall; this will make it water-resistant.

position with hooks. The wall covering should not reach right to the floor or ceiling, nor right to the edge of the bath or wash basin, but you should leave a gap of about 1 inch (25 millimetres). Before fitting either the battens or wooden cladding they should be painted with an impregnating seal (they should not be varnished).

Wooden shingles: They are normally used to cover roofs, but can also make a very attractive bathroom wall covering.

Horizontal battens form the sub-frame and the shingles are nailed to them with galvanized nails. They can be impregnated with a clear or tinted seal before fitting.

Plastic laminate: ¼-inch (6-millimetre) plastic laminate mounted on hardboard or chipboard panels is waterproof and easy to care for. It is fitted onto a batten sub-frame using the appropriate edge strips. Plastic laminate comes in various colours, patterns and textures.

This bright, checkered wall is made by using contrasting ceramic tiles. The towels and accessories are also in red and white, and numerous hooks provide space for anything that the occupants might need to hand, as well as adding to the decorative effect. Vinyl tiles could be used instead.

Creating space in a small bathroom

Dream bathrooms may be beautiful, but they usually remain a dream. Reality is usually completely different. Standard bathrooms are tiny, narrow and with no storage space. Where can you put all the jars and bottles, tubes and containers? A bathroom cabinet and shelf over the wash-basin will generally be inadequate for all cosmetic and bath requisites – not to mention larger objects like piles of towels. How can you make more storage space for your assortment of bath things? Here are a few suggestions:

Room over the bath: You can often use the wall above the narrow end of the bath. You can use ceiling-height shelf or cupboard units. If the bath tub goes right up to the wall (or if you have a shower and need freedom of movement), the units should be no more than 6 or 8 inches (150 or 200 millimetres) deep. Deeper cupboards of 12 to 14 inches (300 to 350 millimetres) give more storage space. You can choose the arrangement of the units according to your personal requirements from among drawers, open or drop-fronted compartments, clothes hamper, etc. Of course if the cupboard is near a shower the surface material will have to be resistant to water. The tiled pedestal between the bath and the wall should be left free, for this is a 'wet area'. If you prefer shelves, you should protect them with a plastic roller blind.

Room above and below the wash-basin: Usually a bathroom cabinet hangs above the wash-basin, but this does not always make best use of the space. You could swop a small cabinet for a large cupboard with a mirror on the front. There are also plastic wall units with built-in shelves, cupboard and mirrors which can be combined to cover any area size. Since the W.C. is usually alongside the wash-basin you can extend a wall unit like this over both fittings. They will replace both the bathroom cabinet and the shelf over the basin. Make sure that you don't make them too deep, otherwise you will bang your head while bending over the basin.

Beneath the wash-basin you could place a cupboard on casters with a top

If there is nowhere else, you might consider fitting storage units over the end of the bath (above left). They would have to be water-resistant and extremely firmly affixed to the wall. These will allow you to store towels, facecloths and even medicines if you can lock them up.

A cupboard covers the waste pipe and uses the space under the basin.

A plastic utensil holder (top) provides a lot of space for bathroom accessories. Here it occupies the space above the cistern, which otherwise wouldn't be used.

Wash-basins are usually in the centre of the wall. If you have to save space you could decide on a space-saving corner basin (above). There is a lot of storage space above and alongside the basin, though you must be sure that the shelf above the basin is not too wide or it will prevent easy access to the basin.

storage surface and either open or closed compartments for towels, bath caps, extra toilet rolls and other things. More storage room is provided by building a possibly larger closed cupboard (see page 196) around the basin. This will not, however, suit everyone for it can get in the way when you stand at the basin. The photograph on the right-hand page shows one example of a small cupboard under the wash-basin.

Room above the cistern: There is usually space right up to the ceiling above a low-level cistern. You can fill it with shelving the same depth as the cistern, which is hung free on the wall. Wall

tracks with matching brackets can be used to supply adjustable shelves.

If you are unable to find suitable shelves for the space over the cistern you can make them to size yourself (see page 196). Sometimes you can combine one of shelf units with a wall shelf extending over the wash-basin or to make use of an unused corner.

Room on the bathroom door: If your bathroom offers no other means of gaining storage space, there is always the bathroom door. You can't hang anything heavy on it, for most internal doors are incapable of supporting heavy weights. But even a light-weight door will take a

plastic or fabric utensil holder for small objects. It is most important that nothing can fall out of the pockets or shelves. The edges must be high enough to prevent this even if the door is banged to. Individual holders would be ideal, with one for each member of the family.

Room in corners: In bathrooms especially, corners are rarely or only partly used. The photograph above right shows what can be done with them. But you can only put the wash-basin in the corner if you have the plumbing installations altered correspondingly. There are also corner basins with cupboards below for storage.

Improving impractical bathrooms

Statistics clearly show that our bathrooms are too small. For this very reason it is important that they should have the right fitments and that even the smallest room should have the maximum comfort and safety. This applies equally to old-fashioned bathrooms which are to be renovated and new bathrooms with standard fitments.

Modernizing an old bathroom

The small diagram on the far right shows a standard bathroom from around the year 1930. Only the washing machine is a later addition. The two occupants, a young married couple, were not particularly happy with it. Not only did it look old-fashioned – it was also difficult to keep clean. They decided to change it completely and this was their plan of campaign:

All walls were to be retiled up to the ceiling – they would never have to paint them again.

The ceiling was to be covered with wood – here too the wish for an easily cared for bathroom was of prime importance.

The old-fashioned window with its many small panes and pelmet was also unpractical. A large window with a natural wood frame would be much easier to keep clean.

A monster geyser over the bath took up too much space and was to be replaced by an instant water heater, for which a new power cable had to be fitted.

The free-standing bath was totally unsuitable for a shower and both the inside and outside was old and ugly. Both a new bath and shower cabinet were planned.

A new wash-basin, W.C. and bidet were to be bought and installed along the left-hand wall. The water connections for these were already present.

The cabinet over the wash-basin and the old chest of drawers opposite had to be removed to make way for the shower cabinet on the right and the bidet on the left. It was therefore necessary to look for space-saving cupboard units which offered the equivalent storage space.

The old-fashioned W.C. was to be replaced by a modern one with a low-level cistern. In addition all the ceramic sanitary fitments were no longer to be white but green.

The washing machine was the greatest problem, for when the extra shower and bidet were added there was no longer room for it in this 9 ft 6 in by 6 ft 6 in (2.90 by 2.00 metre) bathroom. After a lot of thought it was moved to the cellar. This solution is not ideal but there was nothing else they could do. The small, square linoleum tiles on the floor were unattractive. Since neither occupant wanted carpet in the bathroom and the room was well heated they decided on white floor tiles.

The photograph at the top of the left-hand page shows that the couple were able to implement every aspect of the plan. A large mirror and a lamp were fitted above the large, new wash-basin on the left. Hot water is provided by a tank below the wash-basin. To the left of this (not illustrated) stands a roomy cupboard.

The bath and shower cabinet (right) have been combined into one continuous unit. The door and its frame have been gloss painted in the same moss green

General sketch of the construction over and around the wash-basin. The finished piece is illustrated on the right-hand page, below. Sizes depend on the size of the basin. You can have all sheets of glass, wood and plastic laminate cut to the correct size and fit them together according to the plan.

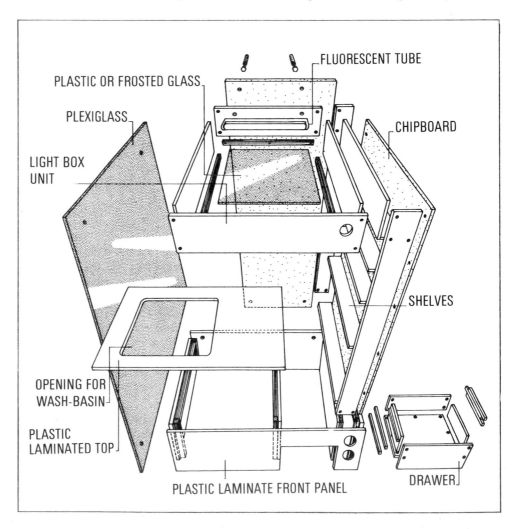

PLASTIC OR FROSTED GLASS

PLEXIGLASS

LIGHT BOX UNIT

FLUORESCENT TUBE

CHIPBOARD

SHELVES

OPENING FOR WASH-BASIN

PLASTIC LAMINATED TOP

PLASTIC LAMINATE FRONT PANEL

DRAWER

This brand-new bathroom with all modern fittings (left) was created from an old-fashioned, impractical bathroom – the diagram below shows it in its original state. Considerable alterations as well as new fitments were necessary to achieve this result. One example of this is that the bath and shower cabinet were combined into one unit on the right-hand wall.

This is what the bathroom originally looked like – old-fashioned and difficult to keep clean.

shade as the bath, etc. The convex white wall tiles extend up to the teak ceiling. The window frame and curtain pole are in the same wood. The window sill is tiled.

An elegant bathroom
In this case, the occupant of the apartment found the bathroom too boring. In addition, as in most bathrooms, there was hardly any storage space. He decided to add more colour and to construct a roomy unit around and over the wash-basin (see diagram on the left-hand page, and photograph near left).

The vanity table around the wash-basin, the front panel and its drawer, were made from plastic laminated board. A pane of plexiglass separates them from the bath. Inside, the right-hand side shelves were fitted to take all bathroom utensils. The boxed lighting provides an even, soft light from above. The towels hang on plain hooks and a shower curtain which keeps the bathroom dry when the shower is in use is not shown in the photograph. It hangs between the plexiglass and the wall.

Before conversion there was only a standard wash-basin with a bathroom cabinet above it in the middle of the wall. The rear wall of this piece of furniture contains a large mirror.

Safety and comfort

Relaxing in the bath tub is not everyone's ideal; many consider a shower much more refreshing. The main problem here is how to prevent the bathroom becoming flooded when you are having your shower, be it over the bath or in a shower cabinet, and how can you make the provision of hot water less problematical.

Shower or bath?

Few bathrooms have a shower cabinet closed off by a curtain or a sliding plastic door. A bath, and only a bath, is more usual. Sometimes showers are fitted over the bath, but only rarely will a bathroom have a bath and a separate shower cabinet.

Washing habits, on the other hand, by no means correspond to this fact. Some people claim that they need a shower to wake them up in the morning. Added to these are the many serious-minded people who choose a shower to save money (a view which is becoming more common in view of the current energy crisis). For a shower requires only one-third of the water needed to fill the bath – about 27 litres (6 Imperial gallons; 7 US gallons) as opposed to around 80 litres (17½ Imperial gallons; 21 US gallons). Opponents of bathing also point out that when you take a bath you are doing nothing more than wallowing in your own dirt – a view that not everyone would agree with by any means. But it is true of course that you can take a quick shower in less time than it takes to fill the bath. If there is a difference of opinion within the family and you have only a small bathroom you can compromise by installing a combined bath and shower: the bath needs the fittings necessary to enable it to be used as a shower cabinet. In other words, you need a screen to prevent water escaping from the bath, that is, from the improvised shower cabinet. This screen must be so constructed as not to restrict the possibilities of taking a bath.

There are many different types of screens for free-standing, corner or built-in shower cabinets and baths. Plastic curtains are the simplest. Rotating or sliding doors in glass or fibreglass and

folding doors made from vertical strips of plastic give better protection against spray or even flooding.

Anti-splash fittings

For shower units installed in a corner of the bathroom there are curtain rails of metal tubing curved into an 'L' shape, which are fastened to the wall with two clamps.

'U'-shaped rails for shower units in the centre of a wall are fitted in the same way. If a heavy shower curtain is used, the rail may sag slightly, so choose a rail with extra clamps at the point furthest from the wall.

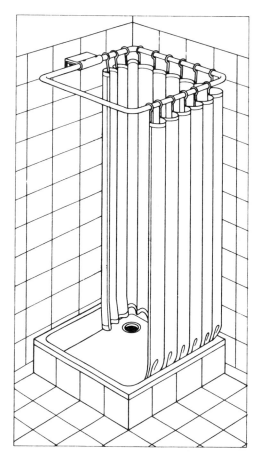

One of the many ways of hanging the shower curtain more simply and safely: The rectangular rail only needs to be fixed to the wall at one point, so you can draw, push or open the curtain at any point on the rail.

The diagram on the left shows another method. The square aluminium rail is here supported by only one bracket, so that the curtain can move freely in almost any direction. This fitting can also be installed over a bath.

Showers built into an alcove in the wall are most easily screened. In this case you can use a roller blind (see right). The plastic pole is fixed to the ceiling with two screws (supplied) and wall plugs. This blind is also suitable for baths; it must be fitted so that the blind unrolls perpendicularly to touch the inside edge of the bath. Then it will fit closely to the shape of the bath even when it is pulled down to just below the edge of the bath.

The simplest method for an alcove shower is a metal pole cut exactly to the width of the alcove and the corresponding ceiling fittings. Since this requires tools to fit it into position, a telescopic pole with steel springs and rubber feet has been brought onto the market. You simply push it together, place it in the correct position and release it. The springs hold it firm and you can take it down whenever necessary. A telescopic pole long enough for an alcove 60 inches (1520 millimetres) wide can be compressed to 36 inches (910 millimetres). It is not only useful in the bathroom, but could also be used to fit a curtain over the patio or balcony door, for example. It could also be used to curtain a shower over a bath, but the bath would have to be built into an alcove.

All types of folding and sliding doors can be used with built-in showers.

Shower curtains

Several of the methods described for built-in showers can also be used for a shower over the bath; curtains hung from a straight or curved rail, plastic roller blinds.

When you take a shower in a cabinet surrounded by curtains, suction can occur. This draws the plastic curtains towards the centre of the cabinet (the cold curtain will cling horribly to your body). To prevent this you should leave an air space of at least 12 inches (300 millimetres) above the curtain rail. This

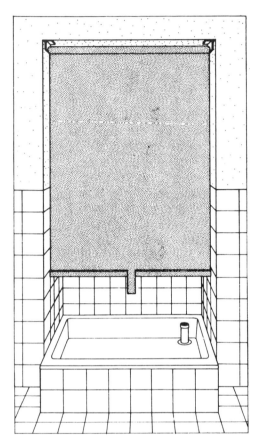

If the shower is built into a wall alcove you can use a roller blind to prevent spray. The blind consists of transparent, embossed plastic. It is also available in wider sizes for fitting over a bath.

If your shower is watertight, it can be installed in any available corner.

is unnecessary with heavy curtains for they will generally stay in position.

If you want a more solid (and more waterproof) method, you should opt for fixed built-in doors.

Water taps

Thermostats provide the greatest possible comfort and safety. You preset the required temperature on a scale and water runs into the basin, bath or shower at precisely that temperature. Many thermostats have shut-off mechanisms which prevent the temperature being set accidentally at more than 40°.

Taps like these are made not only for wash-basins but for all bathroom installa-

tions: for the bidet, for instance. Here, as in ordinary basins, you could use taps which aerate the water. These devices fitted into the nozzle of the tap mix air into the water flow, making it bubbly.

Mixer taps are becoming more and more widely accepted for the bath. Some of them have a useful attachment which automatically switches water from the shower through the tap nozzle.

In addition to the usual overhead showers there are body showers fitted to the side wall of the shower cabinet. Turbo-showers are still quite new; you can set these to give sharp jets of water which massage the skin; and foam showers which can be fitted as a later addition.

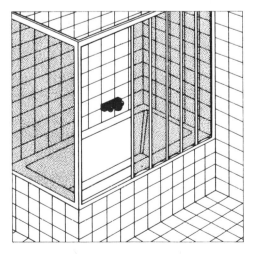

You can screen both shower cabinets and bath against spray with folding doors.

Practical built-in fittings

If you are looking for additional bathroom storage space, you may discover that quite small items are often more expensive than you thought. So reaching for your own saw, drill and screwdriver is particularly worthwhile for furniture for the bathroom. Here are a few suggestions.

Slatted folding table

The diagram below shows a folding table like those normally built to take a baby bath. But the table has other uses. It can serve as a useful storage and work area for both young and old. The amateur photographer who has to pursue his hobby in the bathroom can use it as a work table or as a place to put his enlarger.

The table illustrated consists of planed 1 by 1 inch (30 by 30 millimetre) battens. You will need about 19 pieces 27½ inches (700 millimetres) in length, five pieces of 28 inches (710 millimetres) and two pieces 12 inches (300 millimetres) long. The 27½-inch (700-millimetre) battens

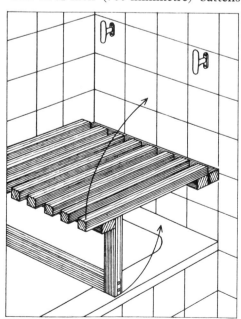

This shelf over the bath is made with planed battens. It can be used for a baby bath or for a basin for washing clothes by hand. After use it is folded against the wall where it is held by simple catches.

196

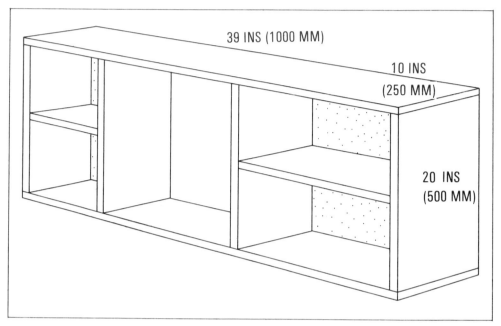

are screwed across two 28-inch (710-millimetre) pieces at ½-inch (10-millimetre) intervals – use a length of ½-inch (10-millimetre) beading to gauge the gaps. You should use brass screws throughout because they will not rust.

Make two more 28-inch (710-millimetre) lengths and the two 12-inch (300-millimetre) lengths into a rectangular frame and fasten it alongside one of the cross battens with brass hinges. The last piece of 28 inches (710 millimetres) is screwed to the wall with brass wood screws and wall plugs and joined to the folding table again with brass hinges. Now all you need is a simple bar to hold the table when it is not in use and folded away.

All wooden parts must be thoroughly covered with two coats of polyurethane finish seal, but you can also oil them. If you can get hold of hardwood battens cheaply you can use these – they are harder wearing than softwood. Here too you should seal the structure to protect the wood from moisture.

Blockboard bathroom shelves

Most standard bathrooms have only a plain shelf surmounted by a mirror over the basin. This does not provide much storage space. If you want to make better

Roomy bathroom shelf unit, built around the mirror above the washbasin. You can, of course, make the shelf unit first and then buy a mirror to fit it. The main body of the unit is made from ⅝-inch (16-millimetre) chipboard. A thin sheet of hardboard is used for the back. The chipboard shelves are here fixed, but you can also make them adjustable if you want. The unit is finally painted in one colour to match the rest of the colour scheme.

use of the available space you can buy a bathroom cabinet – or build a shelf unit yourself like the one described. The raw materials are ⅝-inch (16-millimetre) chipboard or blockboard. Ask your wood merchant to cut it into strips 8 to 10 inches (200 to 250 millimetres) wide. The length depends on the space available for the shelves. The base and top of the unit are the same length as the shelves.

The end and intermediate partition are set between the horizontal sections, so with ⅝-inch (16-millimetre) board their length should be 1¼ inch (32 millimetres) less than the overall height of the shelf unit.

All sections are glued and screwed together at right angles. A rear wall of hardboard will help you to get the cor-

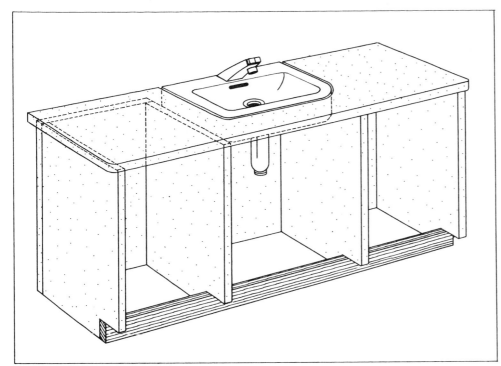

cupboard sections. Any shelves required should be supported by beading or small shelf brackets. You can use curtains to close the boxes but the cupboard will look better if you use sliding, hinged plain or louvred doors, bought ready made. These should be set back below the front edge of the top.

ners exact. If you are building the middle section around an existing mirror (all measurements will then depend on the size of the mirror) this compartment should not have a rear wall. If the mirror is fitted later (bought to fit the size of the shelves) this section can then have a rear wall and the mirror can be positioned from the front.

All front edges are covered with thin beading, about ¼ by ⅝ inch (5 by 16 millimetres), or strips of veneer. Then the whole structure is rubbed down with fine sandpaper. After priming, any ir-regularities and cracks should be filled. When dry, sand again until smooth. The bathroom shelves can be painted with two coats of gloss paint.

Built-in wash-basin unit
In almost every bathroom there is room for a built-in cupboard below the wash-basin – and often to either side of it as well. The side of the cupboard will depend on the available space. The under-frame is very easy to make but fitting the top is a job for the more experienced do-it-yourself enthusiast.

Let's begin with the frame. The cup-board needs a rear wall of hardboard. The ends and intermediate partition are in ¾-inch (19-millimetre) chipboard or blockboard. The partition should be pos-itioned 2 inches (50 millimetres) from the edge of the basin. They should be 2 inches (50 millimetres) lower than the edge of the basin and about 2 inches (50 millimetres) wider than the width (front to back) of the basin. This information should enable you to construct the out-side walls. At the bottom corner of the ends and partition saw out a section 2 inches (50 millimetres) deep and 4 inches (100 millimetres) high. When the cup-

A built-in wash-basin unit provides extra storage space in the bathroom. It is made from chipboard or blockboard with a hardboard back. The top can be covered in plastic laminate. Curtains or doors can be used to close the cupboard, and you can fit shelves or drawers depending on the type of storage required.

board is assembled a strip of chipboard or blockboard, 4 inches (100 millimetres) wide, is screwed on at this point and covered with plastic. The base of the cupboard is in ⅝-inch (16-millimetre) chipboard.

To improve stability you make two 'U'-shaped box units (see diagram). Joints are glued and nailed or screwed. The front edges should be protected by edge strips. The two box units are linked across the centre section by means of the hardboard back (you will need to cut out part of the middle section for the outlet pipe under the basin) and the front lower border strip. You can also screw it to the wall with wood screws and wall plugs.

The top fits flush to the wall and on the front and ends it overlaps the cupboard by about ¾ inch (19 millimetres). To help you make the cut out around the basin make a cardboard pattern: Place a piece of cardboard on the wash-basin and mark the edge of the basin exactly, cut out this section and check that the pattern fits the basin exactly. Then transfer the pattern onto the top of the cupboard, cut it out with a keyhole saw and then use a rasp, wood file or sandpaper for any minor adjustments. The space between the top and the basin should be as even as possible, it is filled later with caulking (see below). Cover the top with plastic laminate, then prime and paint the main

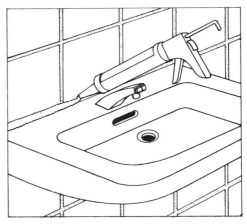

Gaps between the wall and fitments can be filled easily with elastic putty (silicon rubber caulk). This is applied from a tube or from a cartridge with an applicator gun.

Filling cracks with caulking
Since the advent of permanent elastic, self-vulcanizing filling putty (caulking), consisting usually of silicon rubber, it has become very much easier to fill cracks. Before filling, cracks must be made dry and clean and free from grease or dust.

Directions for use:

Tube: A tube is most practical if you need only a small amount of caulk. It is applied by turning a knob at the end which forces the caulk out through a cone-shaped needle.

Cartridge: Better than a tube for big jobs. The cartridge is placed in an ap-plicator gun, which is, however, more expensive.

Automatic cartridge: The putty is con-tained in a pressurized cartridge. When you open a valve gas forces the putty out. An easy-to-use method.

Minor repairs

What do you do if the wash-basin is blocked, if a tap drips or if the W.C. won't flush? It is a good thing to be able to deal with such things yourself – you will save money, but above all you will save your temper. For any plumber you phone will probably have more important and lucrative jobs on hand. And if he does manage to arrive before the whole bathroom is flooded, he will present you with a hefty bill – you are paying not only for his time and experience but often a call-out charge too.

Blocked wash-basins

Blocked sinks are usually caused by blocked water traps. Below the basin there is a device which prevents malodorous gases penetrating into the room. These water traps (siphons) can be unscrewed or opened – depending on the type.

If the water will no longer drain away from the basin, place a bucket under the water trap and open it. Then you can remove anything that is blocking the pipe. Finally it should be rinsed out thoroughly. When fitting it together again make sure that the washers are correctly positioned. There are two easier methods to help you to unblock the sink.

Hot soda solution: Pour in caustic soda solution or special cleaning chemicals. This will often help.

Plunger (diagram above left): It has a half sphere of rubber or plastic and is placed over the plug hole and pumped vigorously up and down. Cover the overflow outlet with a damp cloth to maintain the pumping pressure.

Emergency repairs to a W.C.

With normal and proper use it is impossible for a W.C. to become blocked. If this should happen it is almost always due to improper use of the W.C. When the block has been cleared you will know what has caused it, if not before.

First try flushing the W.C. a few times – this may wash away whatever is blocking it. Failing this, you can try a long wire, or a spiral cleaning rod works better. You may find that pouring chemicals into the bowl can bring surprisingly good results.

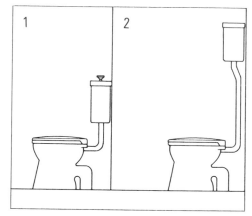

The normal low-level cistern (1) comes in plastic or ceramic in different sizes. The high-level cistern (2) is old-fashioned but efficient: it ensures adequate pressure at all times.

Faults in flush cisterns

High- or low-level flush cisterns of various capacities hold the amount of water necessary to flush the W.C. once and release it when a chain, knob or handle is pulled. The method of operation is the same in both cases:

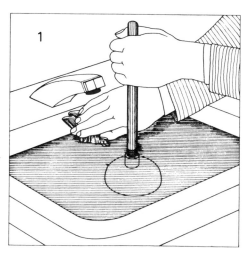

What do you do if the wash-basin waste pipe is blocked? A well tried method is the plunger illustrated here. It is pressed onto the plug hole and pumped up and down. The overflow should be covered to maintain pressure.

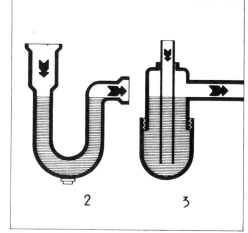

A water trap or siphon prevents unpleasant smells from the drains getting into the room. If it becomes blocked undo the screw (2) or the cap (3), removing any foreign material, rinse out the pipe and replace the screw or cap.

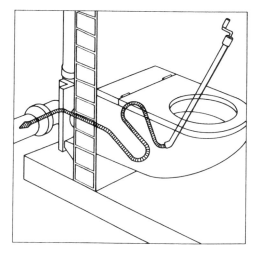

W.C.s can become blocked if you put things down them that are not intended to go down the toilet – from potato peelings to tea-leaves. You can free the blockage with a 'W.C. drill', a rotating cleaning rod.

Water runs into the cistern (metal, ceramic or plastic) through an inlet valve to a pre-set level. When the cistern is full a lever or ballcock shuts off the valve.

Pulling the chain, or similarly pressing the handle or knob, raises a bell-shaped object and uncovers the outlet pipe. Water rushes into the bowl – quite loudly but with an even pressure. During flushing the water level drops, the ball or handle activates the inlet valve again and the cycle is repeated.

Here are the most common cistern faults and how to remedy them:

Pulling the chain or pushing the knob or handle too hard displaces the bell. *Remedy:* open the cistern and carefully push the bell back into place.

Defective washer on the base of the bell. *Remedy:* turn off the water supply, take out the bell and change the washer.

The ballcock turns off the water supply too late or too soon. *Remedy:* loosen the adjusting screw on ball arm, adjust the arm and tighten screw.

Ball is no longer watertight. *Remedy:* buy a new ball, taking the old one with you as a guide – there are many different models.

First aid for a dripping tap

A dripping tap is the test of every aspiring do-it-yourself person. Taps in current use consist firstly of an underpart which includes the nozzle and is joined to the water pipe (and usually to the wash-basin too), and secondly of the movable top section, of which the knob is part.

Any repair to a dripping tap begins with cutting off the water supply. In modern premises the cockstop will most likely be below the basin. With combined cold and hot water taps you will have to find two stopcocks and turn them both off. But there should also be an individual stopcock to your own home.

A dripping tap usually indicates a worn washer in the tap. The washer above the pipe inlet is most prone to wear. This is at the lower end of the removable top section and is usually held in place by a small screw. Loosen this before changing the washer and finally screw it tight again.

When the tap has been in use for a long time the seating, into which the washer fits, may have scaled up and you will have difficulty in removing it. You can try to remove any sediment, but this must be done carefully and not with a sharp implement. If this does not help you will need a plumber with his wrench, unless you can borrow one. Modern mixer and thermostatic taps are more complicated than ordinary taps. Do not try to deal with these yourself.

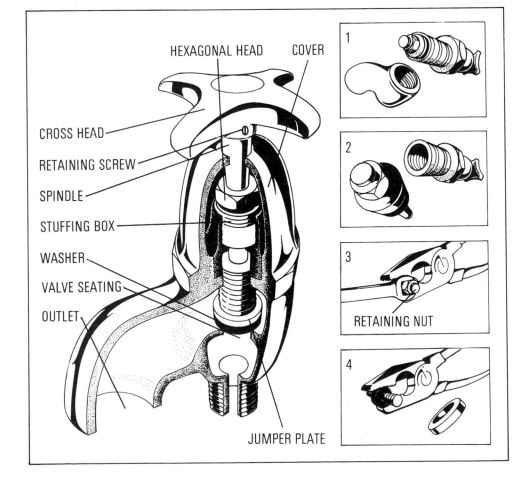

HEXAGONAL HEAD   COVER

CROSS HEAD

RETAINING SCREW

SPINDLE

STUFFING BOX

WASHER

VALVE SEATING

OUTLET

JUMPER PLATE

1

2

3   RETAINING NUT

4

Cross-section of a tap. If it drips it is usually because the bottom washer is worn. First, turn off the water supply at the main or from the supply tank. Now open the tap fully and unscrew the cover. Lift the cover and unscrew the hexagonal head (1) and lift away from tap body. The jumper can now be removed (2). Grip the edge of the jumper plate with pliers and remove the nut with a spanner (3). The old washer can now be removed (4). Reassemble the tap in the reverse order.

HALLS

From the nursery to the living room, back to the kitchen, from the kitchen to the bathroom – have you ever counted how many times a day you go through the hall? The hall is purely a passageway, but that is no reason why it should be inadequately furnished. For the hall is the first room that is seen on entering the home. This is equally true of yourself and your family as it is of strangers and visitors. You will wish to be welcomed warmly by this room and to be made to look forward to the other rooms in the house. Your guests and unknown visitors will always see the entrance hall as representing the whole home. The impression created by your hall will be transferred to the rest of your home – and naturally to you yourself.

When you consider how important a hall is, you may sometimes wonder why the architect was so unimaginative. Presumably there was no space left for this area – so it became a long, narrow corridor with doors leading off right and left into the other rooms. A long, narrow corridor, possibly with no outside light, with little inside light, boring walls, a white ceiling, with hard-wearing but dreary flooring – is this your hall?

You must be prepared to make the most of it, whatever it looks like. There are an astonishing number of ways of improving a comparatively narrow hall, a mini-hall, so that it is transformed into inviting introduction to the rest of your home. The following pages contain numerous examples. Begin by improving the lighting, for this alone can prove an effective remedy. Perhaps there is no window, or the glass panes in the door are neither decorative, nor do they essentially provide light for the hall. Consider whether you could fit a lighted ceiling or smaller area which will bathe the whole hall in soft light. Or try several separate lights on the ceiling to look something like a starry night sky.

Naturally you will need somewhere to put coats – your own, your children's and your guests'. Old-fashioned coat-stands are popular again. But you could also turn an old wardrobe into a cloak cupboard, make a shelf unit or combine several fitted units. Alongside the hanging space you will also need a storage surface. This may be a simple wall shelf or small cupboard, a trunk or chest of drawers.

If you have a little more space, you may like to fit a small seating area – for telephoning, for dealing with the mail, maybe even for a mini-desk where you can make out cheques or keep your accounts.

You can make good use of a high hall by building shelves. In this way you can make room for boxes and cases, beach mats and various other odds and ends. Only in a very large hall will it be possible to make a dining area. This should be separated from the entrance hall by fitted wardrobes or something similar.

A long and narrow hall is made to look very striking by the use of colour and spruce wood. A shelf for suitcases was built above the front door. Ceiling and wall mirrors make the room look larger.

A friendly entrance hall

Two of the many ways of freeing your hall from its Cinderella existence are shown in the photographs on these two pages – the one rustic and the other elegant. You should take a close look at them, for both have been worked out with flair to serve a double purpose. They can provide ideas for your own hall.

The log-cabin look (left): If you like the rustic life-style you can give your hall something of the log-cabin atmosphere. The wood wall cladding – here pine has been used – is a most effective way of adding country charm to a room. The wooden furniture emphasizes this atmosphere. In this case the wood has been neither stained nor varnished. Turned natural wood knobs serve as coat hooks. They are arranged in two rows to make full use of the wall.

Wall pockets in natural-coloured canvas for slippers, gloves, scarves, and other things you need on hand in the hall, echo the natural character of the furnishings. Only muted colours are used here:

the carpet tones with the light wood tones of the furniture, the other walls – like those of the neighbouring vestibule – are painted a soft green, which reappears in the stained wooden wall coverings.

The elegant look (below): The coat-stand can by no means be regarded as multi-purpose furniture. Coat-hooks unfold from it, like branches, and umbrella holders swing out from the trunk.

Plastic shelves provide storage space for the telephone and directories, note pad and calendar. A ceiling-height mirror allows you to look at your clothes from head to foot before you go out. The lamp swivels and the height can also be adjusted. A utensil holder (left behind the coat-stand) takes all the family's bits and pieces in its many pockets. Below it is a chest of drawers on casters for gloves, scarves, caps and similar articles; it has four drawers. Handbags and scarves hang on additional wall hooks. The wall decoration is rather reserved although the floor contrasts strikingly with it.

This hall is decorated to give a rustic, log-cabin atmosphere (left). The wall is clad in pine panelling. Natural-coloured wood furniture reinforces the log-cabin look.

This bright hall shows elegance and flair (right). The coat-stand is plastic. Storage space is provided by the shelves, utensil-holder and the small chest of drawers.

Made-to-measure cloakrooms

Hall furnishing systems made up of coat-hook, shelf, mirror and drawer units are available. These units can be placed side by side in a row and in many different combinations. In this way you can make a made-to-measure furnishing scheme for your own particular hall.

Other advantages of build-up systems are that they take up less room and so are suitable for very narrow rooms; they are also of uniform shape, and make for harmonious groupings. If you use these you can't go wrong when fitting out your hall.

Canvas cloakroom set: The wall units consists of 16 by 57 inch (400 by 1450 millimetre) panels covered in canvas which are fixed to the wall with brass fittings. The panels have either brass hooks and loops of tape or a mirror and canvas storage pocket.

Plastic wall units (far left): This system in gloss-finished plastic comprises units 20½ by 31½ inches (520 by 800 millimetres). In the illustration four are used, one incorporating a mirror, another shelves, a third with hooks for coats etc.,

and one plain. The one illustrated is red, but other colours are available.

Gloss-finish panelling (right-hand page): These panels with their horizontal emphasis, in white, brown or sand gloss finish, will turn your hall into a cosy, panelled den. Besides the wall panels in several widths and heights, there are mirror panels which match the panel sizes, together with a number of hanging units: hat shelves with clothes rails fitted under them, drawer units, shelves, an original umbrella holder and many more.

This system includes four different units which can be built into a stylish hall cloakroom. They are made of plastic, which is both attractive and hard-wearing.

These panels are available in a plastic or mirror finish. They are in two sections, the lower ones being used as coat hooks, if desired.

204

Upholstered cloakroom panels: The panels, which are 68 by 27½ inches (1720 by 700 millimetres) in size, are upholstered and covered in white or black canvas. They have a chrome-steel frame. A plastic shelf is fitted onto the panel so that when at the top it can be used as a hat shelf, or at the bottom (if you turn the panel round) as a handbag shelf. Since they are upholstered the panels can be used as bulletin boards.

Plastic-covered panels (below right): The panels in this system measure 7¾ by 78 inches (195 by 2000 millimetres) and

they come in blue, white or brown plastic, or with a mirror finish. The top sections of the panels can be pushed back to provide hangers on the lower sections – an original and elegant solution to the problem of cloakroom furnishings.

Steel panels: The wall units in this system, which measure 10½ by 75 inches (270 by 1900 millimetres), consist of sheet-steel lacquered either black or white. 'U'-shaped bracket of various widths can be fitted into the panels for hanging coats (with clothes rails or hooks) or for shelves.

Once again this elegant panelled cloakroom consists of build-up units. There are many different units: drawers and hat-shelves, mirror cupboards and shelves, umbrella-holders and more. The panels come in several widths and heights.

Furnishings for small halls

The hall is the room which receives least attention when it comes to furnishing. Also, most architects provide no sunlight and make it too long and narrow. Around its walls are one door after another, leaving hardly any wall area left for furniture. Confined halls like this are very difficult to furnish. These two pages will show through a few examples, how the right choice of furniture and the clever use of walls and alcoves can change a mini-hall 4 feet (1.25 metres) wide into an entrance hall that will take not only a cloakroom but also provide additional storage space for books, suitcases and linen.

Furniture for narrow halls should not be too deep, otherwise it will narrow down the hall even more. Items like that illustrated above right can be used as a chest of drawers. It is only 14½ inches (370 millimetres) deep and is surprisingly roomy. White furniture and light carpets give the room a friendly atmosphere.

Narrow halls are extremely high in relation to their width. By fitting a wide shelf above the doors you not only gain in storage space, but also improve the visual proportions of the hall.

Sometimes it is possible to convert the end wall in a narrow hall into a fitted bookcase. The illustration on the right-hand page shows shelving which is built around the door to reduce the amount of bookshelves need in the living room. A bookcase like this will make the room very cosy if painted a pleasant colour.

Often you can use the wall between two doors which are at right angles to one another for a shelf unit (photograph right). If you want closed-in shelving and there is no room for hinged doors, you could use decorative roller blinds instead.

The main features of this hall (above right) are the roomy drawers, coat-stand and pleasant light-coloured carpet. Picture frames are used around the bulletin board and mirror.

The wall between two doors at right angles is here used for a fitted wardrobe (right), which takes cleaning materials, linen, shoes, etc.

The door at the end of the hall has a roomy shelf unit built around it (right). The warm, dark brown shade of the paint makes the room more cosy.

Ceiling and wall lights

If you are worried about your small, dark hall, there is usually no point in just fixing up a few extra lights, even though that will provide more light than the standard ceiling or pendent light in the centre of the hall.

Light-coloured walls and ceilings and bright furniture can also improve the lighting. Finally, large mirrors will help a lot – providing the hall has sufficient light for them to reflect.

Basically you can only change the situation if you are extravagant with your hall lighting. Try one of the lighting methods shown on these two pages. Even a narrow corridor can be turned into an inviting entrance hall with bright but indirect lighting, with a whole starry sky of lights or perhaps with a lighted ceiling or wall.

Indirect light

Naturally you can light any hall directly by fluorescent tubes, but tubes fixed to the ceiling tend to look cold and functional rather than cosy and comfortable. Although you can get tinted tubes which give warm yellowy-red light suitable for living rooms, this unfiltered, unbroken light will not be suitable if you want a friendly light. Indirect lighting, on the other hand, provides a much more pleasant effect. You could build a timbered ceiling like the one described on page 32. But this is only to be recommended for very narrow halls as the timber has to be supported from one wall to the other. Larger halls, or those with alcoves and jutting-out walls can be better lit by strip lighting built around the walls below the ceiling.

To do this you have to fix a pelmet 8 to 12 inches (200 to 300 millimetres) below the ceiling. It can be made of chipboard or blockboard or wood, depending on the eventual finish you would like. Wood needs only to be sealed. You can cover chipboard or blockboard with the same paper that is used on the walls, or paint it to match either the walls or the ceiling.

The pelmet consists of strips of board or wood, about 4 inches (100 millimetres) wide, fastened to the wall with right-angled metal plates. Along the front

This ceiling light (below) consists of metal grilles used here as light fittings, but more commonly used as shoe scrapers, providing a light which is bright but doesn't dazzle. Plastic or aluminium grilles can also be used, if available.

Light panels on the ceiling and wall (above) will fill even a dark hall with a gleaming bright light. The pleasant colour combination gives a friendly atmosphere and the diffuse light gives the room almost an outdoor quality.

edge, fix a strip of board, or a 2 by 1 inch (50 by 20 millimetre) batten on end and then glue and nail or screw it.

The fluorescent tubes go behind this strip and are fixed into position all around the hall. They will be invisible from normal head height. The light does not shine directly onto the floor, but bathes the whole ceiling in a bright light.

'Starry sky' hall lighting

A lot of small lights – the number depends on the size of the hall – can give your entrance hall the effect of a starry sky. Since it will not look particularly effective if you simply fasten the lights to the ceiling it is best to build the lights into a wooden ceiling. You will find directions of how to make a ceiling like this on page 66. You will probably have to go to a special shop for lights that can be built into a false ceiling. Your electrician will certainly be able to tell you where to get them. Normal light fittings are not recommended – you won't be able to use them unless you have the special fixing units. The size of the holes you have cut in the wood or polystyrene ceiling will depend on the size of the lights. Call in an electrician to fit the additional installations. He will have to connect each light with the nearest junction and will make sure that you can operate them by the hall light switch.

Refracted light from a lattice

Metal grilles which can be used for ceiling lighting, as well as their more normal use as shoe scrapers, come in different sizes and in a variety of grille sizes. If you would like to build the ceiling light illustrated in the photograph on the left, you should use a grille with divisions of about 1¼ or 1½ inches (30 or 40 millimetres) square. They are generally made from galvanized iron, which will not look particularly attractive in your hall, so before putting the grille up it should be painted white. It is a good idea to use a spray gun for this. Order the grille to match the size of the ceiling. Make sure that you measure accurately, as it will be virtually impossible to correct later if it is the wrong size. Battens

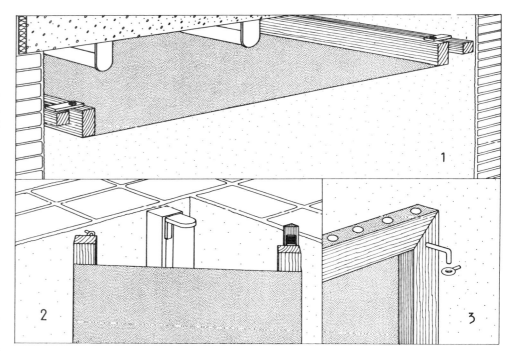

Two small metal plates (1) support the wall battens. For the vertical panel too you must first make a frame which is fixed with screw hooks and rings (on one side) and magnetic catches (on the other) (2). The hooks and rings are attached like this (3) – easily removed for cleaning.

screwed to the wall or metal right-angled plates are used to fix it into position. The metal grille is simply placed on them. Hang plain tungsten bulbs from the ceiling, with at least one for every square yard of ceiling.

Panel light for a hall corner

You can install vertical light panels in one (or several) corners of the room. They should be about 16 to 20 inches (400 to 500 millimetres) wide and their length will be the same as the height of the room. You can use plastic film or plain lining material to cover it. You can use screw hooks and rings to fasten the frame to the wall on one side, and magnet catches on the other (examples 2 and 3 in the diagram above). Behind it a fluorescent tube (or several, one beside the other) is mounted.

Plastic-covered light panel

You will find instructions on page 33 on how to make a ceiling light panel for the hall which is covered in muslin. The only difference here lies in the method used to hang the panel and the plastic film covering. The photograph above left shows a roomy hall which has light panels on the wall as well as the ceiling. For the ceiling lighting 3 by 1 inch (80 by 25 millimetre) planed battens are used for the frames – with the battens used on end.

1½ by 1½ inch (40 by 40 millimetre) battens will be sufficient for the wall panel. The frames are covered in a translucent plastic film. This can be fastened with drawing pins or staples.

To fix the panels into position you need to screw 1 by 1 inch (30 by 30 millimetre) battens to the wall. The panel frames are fitted onto them by means of flat metal plates (two to each side). These are screwed to the wooden frame so as to overlap the edge by about 1 inch (25 millimetres). Example 1 in the diagram below shows how the frames lie on the wall battens by means of the metal plates. Fluorescent tube or tungsten lights are installed behind, or above the light panels.

Useful articles to make yourself

It is always difficult to begin refurnishing. Often you will lack the ideas, and if not them then the money to fulfil them. The hall is usually left over 'until later', and often stands as it is for quite a long time.

Naturally it is pleasant to have a perfectly furnished hall, but even if you can't afford it at present there are a lot of inexpensive and original ways of attaining a stylish hall, which is not only functional and practical, but also friendly and inviting.

Furnishings for a narrow hall
The hall furnishings which we are about to discuss here have been designed for a comparatively small hall: 96 inches (2500 millimetres) long and 55 inches (1400 millimetres) wide, giving 36 square feet (3.5 square metres). There are many halls in one or two room apartments which are as small as this, if not smaller.

Two of the three doors (front door and two interior doors) open into the hall, to give more space in the room, so the wall area behind them cannot be used for furniture. The one wall which has no doors cannot be filled with furniture, for the narrow hall cannot be narrowed down any further. If you want to create storage space in a hall like this you will have to make very careful use of the wall space and also try to use the height of the hall where possible.

There was only one corner where a 'real' piece of furniture could go. Here you could have fitted a ceiling-height wardrobe or shelf unit, but a wardrobe would have made the hall look even smaller. So the occupants of the flat looked round for an old sideboard with two drawers and two doors. They found and bought one that was very cheap from a second-hand shop and happened to fit into the corner exactly.

The walls and the ceilings were painted partly white, partly bright blue. The interior doors were also the latter colour, as was the old sideboard. They used the lower cupboards for shoes, and the drawers held gloves, scarves and caps. An oval mirror with a richly carved gilt frame (also from a second-hand shop) was hung

above the sideboard. An old-fashioned lamp with a glass shade complete this corner of the room. A frosted glass dome was also hung on the ceiling for general lighting. There was no room left for a cloak cupboard. Two planed planks of wood 67 inches (1700 millimetres) long with coat hooks screwed to them were used instead. The planks were put up with wood screws and wall plugs. The natural colour and grain of the wood contrasted well with the blue wall. A roomy hanging shelf for cases, boxes and other bulky items was also built along one of the narrow sides of the hall. It is the same width as the hall (55 inches [1400 millimetres]), 32 inches (800 millimetres) deep and extends down as far as the door frames, thus giving a storage space 20 inches (500 millimetres) high. Like the coat hangers this too was left in its natural state. The ceiling above the shelf and the three side walls were painted blue so that it looks like a dark cave and is scarcely noticed, even though it is not curtained off. You will find instructions for building a shelf like this on page 213.

The floor was covered with fitted carpet. The carpet alone took up more than one-third of the amount budgeted for the hall – but they did not want to be without this for it made the hall look warmer and brighter. No professional help was needed when equipping the hall. The occupant of the apartment bought planks and board (for the coat hanger and hanging shelf) cut to size. They did their own wallpapering, painting, carpet laying, and putting up fittings.

There are various ways in which you can vary this 'economy' hall. One of these ways we are now going to discuss.

Spending a little more
Improvization is ideal if you want to save money, but naturally the mini-hall described above can be furnished slightly more lavishly, without you having to spend a lot of money.

Not only have we kept the ground plan the same, so that the room is the same shape as in the previous example, we

have also kept the facilities the same: it should provide room for coats, for a storage corner, and for cases, boxes and similar articles.

Once again a hanging shelf extending upwards from the door frames was built in on the narrow side of the hall. This was enclosed by two light doors consisting of a frame covered in plastic film. The same plastic was also stuck onto the wall where wet coats were to be hung – in this way they wouldn't damage the wall. The other walls in this area of the hall were painted a deep red, which went very well with the black-and-white chessboard patterned plastic. The door frames were also painted red but the doors were left white, as was the underside of the shelf.

Shelf supports – in the form of brackets – were fixed to the wall near the coats' area. These were painted black and each holds several white coat hangers. A deep wall shelf (for hats and ornaments) was screwed to the wall above the brackets and painted red to match the wall. The shelf is the same height as the hanging shelf. The storage area consists of simple cube-shaped units (with edges 14 inches [350 millimetres] in length) with various internal compartments which can be used in any combination. The floor was covered with a foam-backed vinyl floor covering which you can lay and cut yourself. This floor covering helps with sound-proofing and is easy to clean. Two spotlights were bought to light the hall; for the storage area and for the coats' area.

As the most expensive items were the box units, to make this furnishing scheme less expensive it would be possible to make the box units yourself or to replace them by a made-to-measure shelf unit. It is also possible to do without the doors to the hanging shelf – a curtain would be sufficient.

Built-in cloaks cupboard
If you have a little more space to play with than in the furnishing schemes described on the left-hand page, a cloaks cupboard made from prefabricated sections provides an excellent solution to

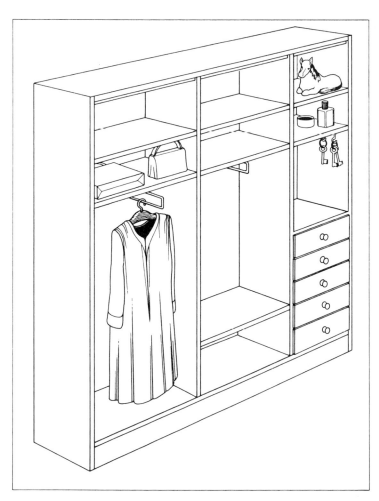

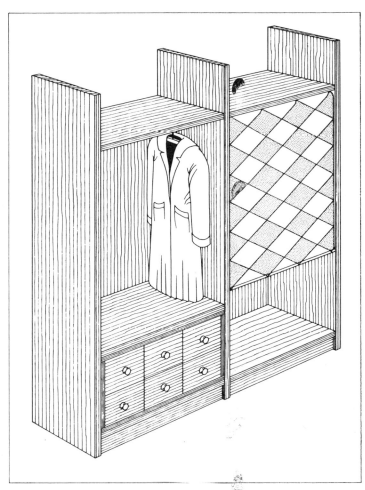

**Cloaks cupboard built from a range of components. All the
necessary boards, supports, doors, drawers, shelves,
clothes rails etc., can be supplied to fit your requirements.
They only need assembling and then staining, painting or
sealing as you prefer.**

**This country-look, fitted cloaks cupboard is also made from
components which can be combined in such a way as to fit
even into a very narrow hall. The separate components are
chosen from a manufacturer's list and assembled yourself:
side walls, drawers, shelves and clothes rails. The units are
made from plain spruce wood.**

storage problems in the hall without
involving astronomical expense. The two
diagrams on this page show hall
cupboards assembled from standard
units. The constituent parts (boards,
shelves, drawers, doors, clothes rail, etc.)
are selected from a manufacturer's list.

To ensure that it all fits properly in the
end, it is a good idea to make a diagram
of the wall section, against which the
cupboard will go, and to enter the
sections that you wish to order.

You can get finished units (stained,
matt finished, painted, etc.) which only

need to be assembled in accordance with
the manufacturer's instructions (the
example in the right-hand diagram is one
such model), or other models which you
can stain or paint as you wish after
assembly (left-hand diagram). These can
be cheaper than ready-made furniture.

211

Simple hall fittings

Is your hall too high? Then you can make it lower with a false ceiling. If it is too dark it is always possible to fit a window into one of the interior doors. Does it have sufficient storage space? If not, you can discover here how to build a hanging shelf yourself.

All the suggestions on these two pages require skilful use of saw and hammer.

Fitting a hall ceiling

With the dimensions normally found in new buildings, a narrow hall will often look higher than it actually is. Halls in old buildings are often high by design. In both cases you could put up a false ceiling which will make the hall lower. Constructions which are attached directly to the ceiling (including the so-called hanging ceiling) present quite a few technical difficulties – the different methods of fitting them are given on page 66. But often a continuous wooden or board ceiling is unnecessary. It is sufficient to improve the visual effect.

This can be done with a ceiling like the one illustrated on the left. It consists of planks arranged as slats stretching from wall to wall. You can see through it to the ceiling above. If you paint the ceiling and the section of the wall between the wood and the ceiling in a darker colour (often black) you will see only the wooden ceiling. This gives the impression of a lower ceiling than it actually is.

The spruce or pine planks used should be ¾ to 1 inch (19 to 25 millimetres) thick, about 6 inches (150 millimetres) wide and should be planed. They are fitted at intervals of about 6 to 8 inches (150 to 200 millimetres). The supporting structure consists of planed roof battens 2 by 1 inches (50 by 30 millimetres) which require cutout sections about ½ inch (10 millimetres) deep where the planks fit onto them.

The planks should be cut to the width of the hall – less ⅜ to ½ inch (8 to 10 millimetres) play so that the plaster will not be damaged when the planks are hung.

The planks must be cut away at both ends so that they can be fitted onto the battens. If the planks are 6 inches (150

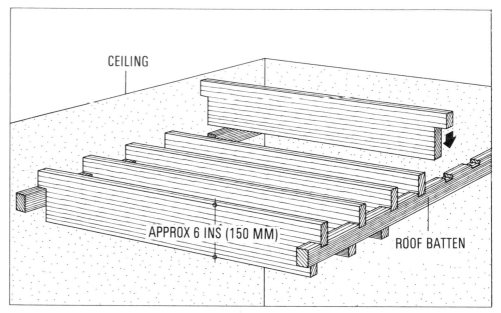

CEILING

APPROX 6 INS (150 MM)

ROOF BATTEN

Timber slats fitted from wall to wall are a simple way of reducing the height of a hall. It is suitable for halls up to 6 feet (2 metres) wide. It doesn't need to be attached to the ceiling. The softwood

planks run freely from wall to wall, resting on planed battens which are simply screwed to the side walls. You can paint the ceiling and walls above the timber in black.

millimetres) wide a strip 1 inch (30 millimetres) wide and 4 inches (100 millimetres) long must be cut away on each side (see diagram). The supporting battens can be left with their natural wood colour, or painted black like the ceiling. It is a good idea to treat the planks with an impregnating seal, but they could also be painted.

Fitting a door window

If your hall gets insufficient daylight and is therefore dark, you can fit a window into one of the interior doors. The following instructions apply only to a flat door – it is extremely difficult to fit a window yourself into older-style panelled doors.

Remove the door from the hinges and lay it across two trestles with the hinges underneath. Take off the door handles by removing the connecting rod or undoing the fastening screws. Take off the keyhole cover. The lock can be left in the door.

Then draw the required window opening onto the door. Always leave a border of 4½ inches (110 millimetres) at

the top and sides. Leave at least 12 inches (300 millimetres) below the window, otherwise the door is likely to fall apart.

If you are going to use a hand saw, you need to drill a ¾-inch (19-millimetre) hole in one of the corners to begin with. Begin with your keyhole saw at this point. Hold the saw completely vertical, otherwise your cut will not be very good.

If you have a hand-held circular saw, use the rip guide or fasten a straight edge onto the door (a batten clamped to the door, along the edge of which the saw can run). Simply push the saw down onto the door panel. It is better to use a hand saw for the corners.

Nowadays the inside of the door generally consists of corrugated board which you will see along the cut edges. But you need a smooth edge to your window frame and so you will have to stick on four pieces of wooden beading about 1¼ inches (32 millimetres) wide. Push back the corrugated board slightly before attaching the beading. If you do not have enough clamps to hold the beading until the glue has set you can carefully knock in ¾-inch (19-millimetre) lost-head nails around the edges.

Order a pane of glass to fit your cutout. It should be ¼ inch (6 millimetres) thick. You can use either transparent plate glass or frosted glass. You can buy both types with wire let into them.

Buy the frame for the glass ready made. It should have a groove of ½ inch (14 millimetres) to take the putty. When you have fitted the glass frame to one side of the door (preferably with brass screws), apply an even layer of putty into the groove, place the glass in position, apply more putty on top and then press on the glass frame for the other side of the door until it fits exactly. This too is held in place with brass screws. For doors in natural wood use strips of foam instead of putty.

Hanging suitcase shelf

The two diagrams on the right show how to build a hanging shelf by the 'sandwhich method': The shelf consists of several layers, making it more stable without being too heavy. It is made from ⅝-inch (16-millimetre) chipboard, strengthened by 2 by 1 inch (50 by 25 millimetres) roof battens which are then glued onto it.

The smooth underside consists of a sheet of hardboard, which is also glued to the battens. The shelf is supported by two battens screwed to the wall. The two outer battens in the middle of the shelf base must be set in slightly so that the finished shelf can slide easily onto the wall battens.

You can cover the front edge of the shelf with a strip of chipboard to conceal the joints between the batten, chipboard and hardboard.

The hanging shelf will span a width of up to 60 inches (1500 millimetres). It should be not more than 36 inches (1000 millimetres) deep, for this would make it too difficult to reach the back of the shelf. The lower edge of the shelf should be about 18 inches (500 millimetres) below the ceiling. In general it is made to fit in with the height of the door frames – and these can sometimes be used to provide additional support.

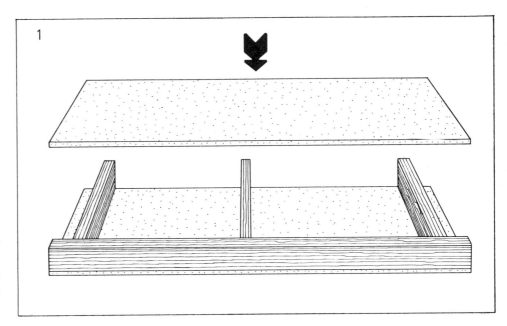

Here is a suggestion for a layered hanging shelf. The top is ⅝-inch (16-millimetre) chipboard, and the base is hardboard, and it is strengthened by battens. The outer battens are inset. The shelf should be painted afterwards to match the rest of the room.

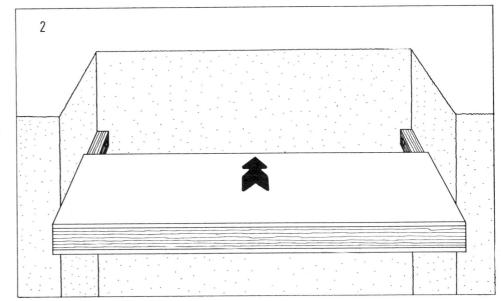

The 'sandwich'-method shelf is pushed onto battens screwed to the wall on each side, so it can be taken down whenever necessary.

Hall cupboards for shoes

There is one problem with which everyone is familiar: where to keep all the family's shoes? Apart from every day shoes, sandals and boots, you will also have special footwear such as gym and tennis shoes, slippers, ski boots, basketball, football and rugby boots.

Of course, you can buy shoe cupboards and racks for fitting inside a wardrobe, but most of these are too small to cope with the family's host of footwear. For extra shoe space, the hall is a good place to keep some of them. Often the shoe cupboard and shelves can be combined with storage for other things which are often in the way.

Shoe storage inside a door

This is a suggestion which is easy to put into practice, provided that you have a cupboard or box-room door where you can fix a simple shoe-holder to the inside. Using this method you can store at least a dozen shoes on one square yard of door area. The secret is a ladder-like framework with loops of cord into which you can stick or hang shoes. First a framework of 1 by 1 inch (25 by 25 millimetre) battens is fixed to the inside of the door as near to the edge as possible, but allowing room for the door to close properly – you will have to try this out. The upright sides of the frame

carry ⅜-inch (8 millimetre) hardwood rods or metal tubing at about 12-inch (300-millimetre) intervals (which is the normal shoe length plus a little more). You will have to drill holes for the rods or tubes before positioning the framework.

Knot loops of a thin clothes line onto these 'rungs'. The shoes are pushed down into the loops so that the heels rest on the rungs. It is important for the broom cupboard or box room to be well ventilated. If this is not the case, you will have to make ventilation holes or slits at both the top and bottom of the door. Do-it-yourself or hardware shops sell plastic grilles with which you can cover the air vents.

Louvred-door shoe cupboard

Is there an alcove in your hall which is at least 39 inches (1000 millimetres) wide and 12 inches (300 millimetres) deep? Or is there one of the narrow walls which doesn't happen to contain a door? If so, you could use the available space for a shoe cupboard with louvred doors, with ready-bought or home-made fittings inside.

Louvred doors come in various heights and widths ready made. If one of the standard-size doors does not come to the edges of the opening (i.e. if the doors are narrower than required – or lower) you will have to cover the space left with strips of chipboard or blockboard. Side panels should be built in first. It is easiest to fix them directly to the wall with metal corner plates, wood screws and wall plugs. The louvred doors are then hinged onto these side panels.

If the door size fits exactly, simply fix 2 by 1 inch (50 by 25 millimetre) battens onto the wall to which the doors can be fixed. Any panel needed between the door and the ceiling is fitted last of all when the doors are already in position.

This louvred shoe cupboard needs no inside walls, no base and no top. It is sufficient to paint the existing walls with washable paint or paper. Any accidental damage to the walls while fitting the doors must of course be repaired.

To store the shoes you can use a rail system with plastic stretchers, where the

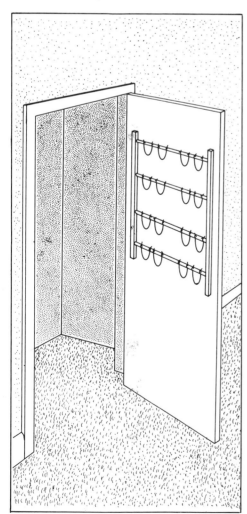

A simple and cheap method of storing shoes on the back of a cupboard door.

214

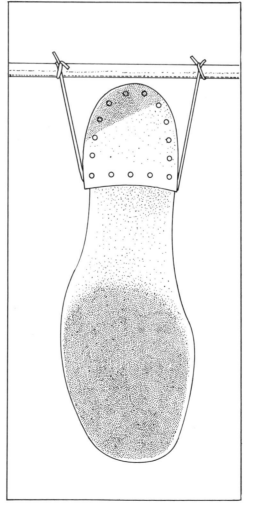

The shoes are hung in loops of string which are tied to the cross-rails.

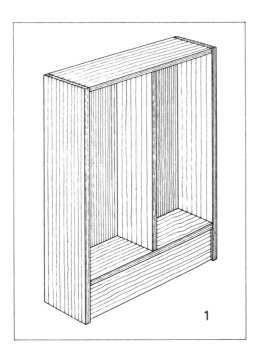

1

2

This is what the finished cupboard should look like. You can fit the shelves at any height you like. The back is made from hardboard. Two roller blinds are used to enclose this do-it-yourself, made-to-measure hall cupboard.

The first stage of construction for the hall shoe cupboard. The end panels are joined to the top and the base panel. Then the bottom shelf and middle partition are then fitted and screwed into exactly the right position.

upright rails are fixed directly onto the wall with wood screws and wall plugs. But there are other methods. You can fit strips of wood from wall to wall across which the shoes can be laid. The back strip should be about 4 inches (100 millimetres) from the back wall; the shoe heels hook over this. The front strip runs parallel to it, about 8 inches (200 millimetres) from it, and 2 inches (50 millimetres) lower. The front of the shoes rest on this one. The strips of wood do not need to be permanently fixed. It will be enough to support each batten in a notch right and left.

The gap between each pair of strips depends on the height of the shoes. You do not need to provide additional ventilation for this cupboard as the louvred doors allow air to circulate. When you have finished building the cupboard the doors should be varnished, and if you wish, stained first.

All-purpose hall cupboard

This all-purpose hall cupboard (diagram above right) can store shoes and linen as well as cleaning materials and any other items that you can't find room for anywhere else. If you want to build it, you will need to have had some experience in do-it-yourself – it is better for beginners to start with something simpler.

We cannot give exact measurements for the cupboard, for it will be individually built to fit your own requirements. In addition you have to take into account the sizes of the individual parts used, such as the shoe storage units. You could also fit wire baskets or plastic drawers and the size of these will determine the width and depth of the cupboard. Finally, instead of the usual chipboard or blockboard used here you could make it with veneered wood. This will save work with filling and

painting, but you will have to cover any exposed edges with matching strips.

But the method of construction remains the same: you need two side walls, a top and a piece to cover the base. The first shelf is fitted above this. Then the middle wall is fitted and a hardboard back. You should use ¾-inch (19-millimetre) chipboard or blockboard. When the back is fitted it is the turn of the rest of the shelves. Their positioning should be well planned if you don't intend to make them adjustable. The shoe compartment takes up most of the left-hand side of the cupboard. It is fitted with ready-bought shoe holders, or paired strips of wood (as in the previous example).

The right-hand side can provide space for linen. This should have a door which comes to 4 inches (100 millimetres) below the next shelf. You should also drill a row of ventilation holes along the lower edge of the door. The door can be a normal hinged door (with piano or cut-in hinges) or it can fold down – the latter will require a stay to keep the door horizontal when it is open. You can use a magnet catch to keep the door closed. You won't need a handle for you can easily get hold of the door through the opening at the top (through which you can also push in small items of washing, if you want to use the cupboard for dirty linen).

All front edges must be protected with hardwood or plastic edge strips. When the cupboard is completely assembled it must be sanded and sealed.

As an alternative to doors, the cupboard could be fitted with fabric roller blinds. The two pairs of roller mountings are screwed under the top of the cupboard, as close as possible to the side walls, bearing in mind that the roller has rods which have to go through the mountings and require a little room in order to turn more freely.

Cut the fabric long enough to pull down to the base covering. Don't hem the sides, but merely oversew them or cut them with pinking shears, otherwise the blind will not roll up properly. Make a wide hem at the bottom edge to take a batten.

215

DO-IT-YOURSELF

Everybody at some point in their life will most likely have need of some basic do-it-yourself knowledge, even if it is only to stop a tap from dripping, or to do your own wallpapering. It has become easier and simpler to make things yourself now that tools and materials are available which are geared to the special needs of someone working around the house, such as ready-cut chipboard or blockboard, ready-pasted papers or spray-on paints.

This basic course in do-it-yourself is intended for beginners who are faced with jobs which crop up again and again in the home and who cannot afford to, or do not wish to, bring in a professional whenever the smallest thing goes wrong, or when you want to make a small addition to your furniture. Do-it-yourself is not only money-saving, but can give you a great deal of satisfaction and fun as well.

The art of do-it-yourself does not, however, consist entirely of enjoyable work based upon given formulas. Every type of handicraft must be learnt, even do-it-yourself. As an introduction, therefore, here are a few basic rules which may help in overcoming initial difficulties.

Do not aspire too high – this applies to your tool collection as well as your plans. Even though you might have made a window-box it will be a long time before you can make a veneered bookcase.

Do not begin work until you have planned it thoroughly, for this will save time, money and materials. A plank cannot be made longer once you have cut it too short. A precise plan and list of necessary materials are indispensable to any job.

Try not to rush your work – if you hurry, something is likely to go wrong. Glue will need time to set, paints must be used according to instructions and so on – slip-shod work leads only to a frayed temper.

Do not try to economize on tools – poor quality tools or using the wrong tool for the job will be costly. If you use a chisel as a screwdriver or a woodsaw to saw metal, you will soon find the contents of your tool-box reduced to a sorry state.

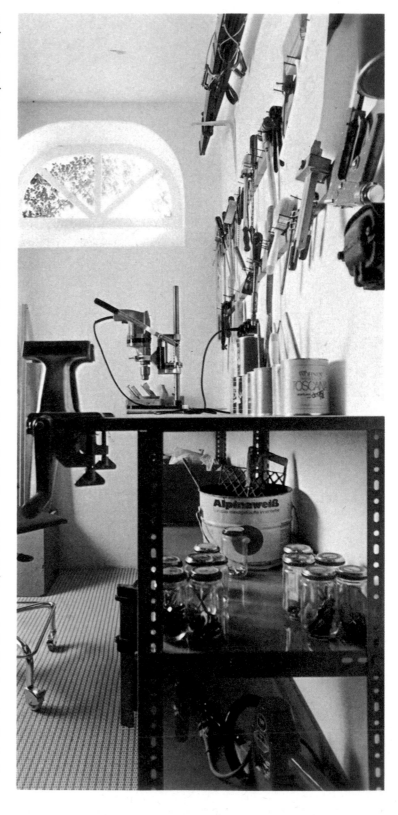

From tool-box to workshop

The term tool-box certainly cannot be applied to a spare drawer which contains, along with a few elastic bands, bits of string, instructions for the vacuum cleaner and a tube of dried-up glue, a battered hammer with a loose handle, a bent screwdriver and a rusty saw.

Starting with a tool-box
A tool-drawer is acceptable as a neat and handy place to store an initial collection of tools but it must not be allowed to become a collecting ground for all those things which 'might come in useful one day' and it must help keep the tools in order.

For this purpose small boxes or cartons can be used to divide it, or you can construct compartments with thin plywood. This is a simple way of storing smaller tools and materials (nails and screws, washers and wall plugs, for example).

A tool-box has the advantage over a drawer in that when necessary it can be carried to the work site so that all the necessary tools and small materials will be to hand without you constantly running to and fro. It is also worthwhile investing in a tool-box even if you have a small workshop with a tool collection so large that it cannot all be carried with you. In this case the tool-box can hold those tools and small items necessary for a particular job. A home-made tool-box is useful if you need a box large enough to be divided up to suit your own requirements. In all other cases it is better to buy a box.

You can buy practical tool-boxes of wood, metal or plastic with various compartments including removable ones for small items or insets to take specific tools. They range in scale from lock-up metal boxes with several compartments such as those used by an electrician or heating engineer, to open, plastic, basket-shaped boxes which have the advantage of being light to carry.

A growing collection
We begin with a drawer full of general tools. Gradually we acquire special equipment for particular jobs, usually an electric drill first, with a few attachments. The collection of materials and small items grows continuously. Where it was once possible to move your work place around and to saw, drill or nail in the kitchen or under the cellar stairs this method of working wherever the opportunity arises will eventually become unbearable. You will need to find a fixed place.

Once you find somewhere, perhaps in the cellar, loft, or garage the workshop can develop – the workshop which has grown out of a tool-drawer. Here you might have room for all the gear – from a work bench to a drilling table, from a flat bed saw to a bradawl. However, such ideal work places are rare and most do-it-yourself people make do with less.

The ideal work place
The demands of an ideal work place for the do-it-yourself man can be briefly described:

It must be able to be locked and not too small, so that materials can be stored with comfort alongside the work bench and tool cupboard.

It should be open to daylight and in addition with non-glare, shadow-free artificial lighting with several powerpoints (for a circular saw or soldering iron, for example).

It should have good ventilation to avoid damage to health from dust and fumes from strippers or paint.

It must have a dry, warm, resistant floor (unpolished wood, asphalt sheets, tiles, PVC or artificial stone over an insulating layer).

It should have the possibility of heating to an even temperature (18°C), with dry atmosphere and neither damp floors nor walls.

It should be sound-proofed to avoid work noises reverberating throughout the house. This can be difficult to achieve. A layer of felt under the legs of the work table, sound-proofing tiles on walls and ceiling can only help to a certain extent.

There must be water connections to a ceramic sink, with hot and cold water if possible, and a hose attachment to the tap.

A permanent workshop like the one shown on the opposite page is the ideal working situation. The wall above the bench has been used for tool storage. For those who cannot have a permanent workbench the 'Workmate' (above) is a good alternative. It is portable and available in various models.

Finding a suitable position
The ideals listed above are not always available in a new home. Where then can you put your workshop?

A do-it-yourself corner under a staircase or in a corner of the attic or cellar, means that you will have to use the space carefully (folding work bench, built-in cupboard or shelves).

A workshop in the garage has advantages particularly in summer and if heated it can be used throughout the year.

A workshop in a lock-up cellar is best. Here you will have room to spread out and maybe even install a planing bench. The tools which you need most often can be hung on the wall while other smaller items can be stored in plastic drawers, and hopefully there will be sufficient cupboard space for machinery.

Tools for the home workshop

A dozen or so tools will be enough to start with for do-it-yourself around the home, repairs and to make the occasional wood item. The tools which should find a place in your initial collection are listed below. Special tools for such jobs as wallpapering, painting or glazing are dealt with in the relevant sections.

Basic tools

Starting with the following basic tools you can gradually build up a more comprehensive collection. Quality is important when buying tools; it is not worth trying to economize.

The **hammer** of the type recommended to start your tool kit is known as a cross-pein hammer. It is indispensable for most types of work with the hands. The head should weigh about 8 oz (230 g) and should have a flat polished striking surface and a pein (the tapered end) of forged and hardened steel. Any hammer whose pein has become cracked and the edges of the striking surface rounded should be thrown away. The length of the handle depends on the weight of the head. The handle should be firmly joined to the head with a hardwood or metal wedge. When using a hammer always grip the handle near the base away from the head, for only when held in this manner is the tool in *balance* allowing the hammer to work effectively.

Pincers are used not only to remove nails and to bite through soft wire, they constitute a versatile tool to be used for holding, gripping and stretching. Pincers of forged steel, 6 to 7 inches (160 to 180 millimetres) in length, will be stronger than cast metal pincers whose edges soon become blunt and broken. Do not use the head of the pincers as a substitute for your hammer which may not be to hand, for once used as a hammer its other uses will be limited.

An **adjustable wrench** is an all-purpose tool for use with all types of plumbing, drainage and heating installations. The mouth opens to a width of 1¼ inches (32 millimetres) to allow the tightening and loosening of large screw joints in pipes (in a water-trap for example). For chrome joints place a rag between the nut and the wrench to avoid scratches.

Combination pliers are available with or without insulated handles. A 6-inch (150-millimetre) pair will suit most purposes. They have a flat and a rounded gripping area and two sets of cutters – an inner cutter for soft metals, and an outer cutter for hard wire.

A **multi-purpose saw** which often has interchangeable blades of toughened steel will saw not only soft- and hardwoods, but also plastic, rubber, asbestos and some metals. The blade should be tapered, allowing you to saw into corners freely. For more intricate sawing jobs it is worth having an additional small hacksaw with changeable blades. All types of saws should be stored away from other tools to avoid blunting the teeth.

A **bradawl** is a kind of awl with a pear-shaped wooden handle with a flattened or four-edged point. It is used to make pilot or starter holes in wood for small screws. It is also useful as a marking tool.

A **gimlet** is used to make screw or nail holes in wood, and it is best to buy several sizes. However, you will find it easier to drill with a small hand drill and it is worth investing in one of these if you do not intend buying an electric drill.

A **jumping tool** consists of a steel handle with a conical recess at one end in which finger-length fluted bits of various thicknesses are inserted. You will need to make holes for plugs in walls if your electric drill has no hammer facility. Like every drill, the jumping tool must be held quite straight. The end of the handle is struck with a hammer. After every two or three blows it must be turned a quarter turn, to clear the debris.

A **chisel** is meant exclusively for use in woodwork, where it is used to make holes, grooves and joints. A chisel with a bevel-edge blade of ½ or ¾ inch (18 to 20 millimetres) in width is an essential part of any tool kit. Other widths can be bought later. When working with a chisel it is best to use a large wooden hammer (mallet) where possible, rather than the normal steel hammer which will inevitably mark the handle.

A **screwdriver** is used exclusively for screwing in and removing screws. The blade of the screwdriver must fit the slot in the screw exactly. A good screwdriver will have a steel blade with a wood or plastic handle. It is advisable to buy several sizes.

A **scraper** will be needed for numerous decorating jobs. It is used to scrape off old paint and paper and also to apply and smooth down all types of fillers (plaster of Paris, putty, cellulose filler). The blade should be of pliable steel and the handle should lie well in the hand.

To complete your tool kit you will need a rule, two or three paintbrushes, a small can of light oil and a few sheets of sandpaper of different grades. If you will be working regularly with wood you will find that a simple plane (for smoothing edges) and a rasp or Surform (for rounding off edges and corners) would also be quite useful.

Storing tools correctly

Looking after your tools begins with careful storage. If you consider it too much effort just think for a moment what your tool kit has cost and how annoying it is when you cannot lay your hand on a particular tool at the right moment because they have been carelessly arranged.

The usual answer is to erect a shelf near the work table on which your tools can be arranged within sight and easy reach. It can be made of chipboard or blockboard. For a medium-sized tool kit it is also worthwhile constructing a sheet of peg-board nailed to a frame on which you can hang a great number of things. A shelf over the work table has the advantage that tools are kept away from dust; better still is a closed tool cupboard. You can build a tool shelf initially with a frame about 6 inches (150 millimetres) deep to which you can later add doors. The tools can also be protected with a sheet of polythene or even with a roller blind.

There are several possible ways of hanging tools – the most common are illustrated below. Screwdrivers, bradawls and awls can be stuck through screw-in rings or eyes. For such things as hammers, hacksaws and gimlets screw-in hooks are useful. Chisels can be stored upright in a small shelf in which slits have been made and are thus kept separate. Pincers, hammers and other heavy tools can also be hung separately on blocks of wood (see diagram). Another good solution is a magnetic sheet on which any light-metal tools can be hung freely.

Before beginning to hang the tools, carefully arrange your whole kit on a large table or on the floor and make a plan of how they are to be hung. This should take into account any additions you plan to make in the near future. Build the devices on which to hang your tools according to the plan and fix them into the storage area. Each tool will have its fixed place on the wall, which you can recognize at a glance by drawing round the tool with a marker pen, so you will be

The standard tools which are in regular use should have a fixed place within easy reach. Small screw-in rings or eyes (1) are recommended mainly for screwdrivers, a wooden shelf provided with slits (2) can take chisels, and such things as hammers and pincers can be held on screw-in hooks (3) or blocks of wood (4).

able to see immediately if a tool is missing.

If you buy a completely stocked tool cupboard it may not always contain what it promises. You would naturally check on the contents before you bought it. Beware of 'unrepeatable bargains' in this line. No one gives away good tools.

Electric drill

An electric drill is specially useful for everyday jobs around the house in two respects: You can drill holes with it, which is useful not only when assembling any construction of wood but also for inserting wall plugs. You can also use it for sanding, which will be appreciated by anyone who has had to sand a large item of furniture by hand. Of course, with the appropriate attachments a drill can do much more. But a circular saw attachment can only be of value if it is to be in regular use. If you generally buy wood ready-cut you can use a hand saw.

Milling and grinding attachments, buffs and polishers, a vertical drill stand and mitering attachments, knife sharpeners and hedge cutters and such things will not be found in an initial package, but you should choose a drill which is capable of taking them. A few points to watch when buying:

Performance: buy a machine that is capable of any job. It should have a hammer action facility, that is, it should be able to drill a hole even into the hardest concrete. It should be capable of taking any attachment without overloading the motor, in other words, it must be a multi-purpose machine.

Additional uses: the basic equipment must, when combined with attachments bought later, be capable of fulfilling as many functions as possible. The best attachments screw directly onto the neck of the drill as opposed to those which fit into the chuck.

Adaptability: the machine should adapt easily and quickly to its various functions. Time wasted in converting it is irritating. You will soon become disenchanted with the appliance if for three minutes sawing you have to spend 15 minutes converting it.

Hand-hold: machine and attachments should lie comfortably in the hand, so that you can use it safely and precisely without tiring.

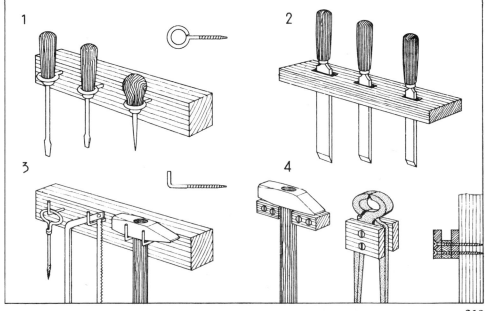

Using a saw, drill, hammer and screwdriver

If you already know how to do all these things you can skip these pages. But are you quite sure whether you should apply pressure to the saw or simply draw it through the wood as lightly as possible? Do you know how to drill a hole properly for a screw with a raised head, or what to do with a nail screw?

If you do not know the answers it would certainly be worthwhile for you to read through the following two pages.

Woodwork begins with the saw

Even those who have not the least intention of building the children's bedroom furniture or constructing a weekend house should know how to handle a saw. Our basic tool kit (page 218) includes a multi-purpose saw. Initially it can replace a joiner's crosscut saw, a padsaw, to which it is very similar, and a tenon saw which is indispensable, for example, for making mitred cuts for picture frames.

Generally speaking what is the best way to use a saw? Firstly, never saw at random, judging by eye alone, but along a carefully drawn (or scratched) cutting line. Here a steel tape, rule and set-square will be useful. Do not try to saw along the line for this would be too imprecise. The line is the edge of the piece of work and you should begin by sawing just beyond it. So you should saw as near to the line as possible without touching it. If you adhere strictly to this rule two planks cut to the same measurement should never be different in length.

The teeth of most saws are designed to work with a pushing movement. This means that wood is transformed into sawdust when the saw is pushed away from the body. The upward stroke is more or less ineffective. When using the saw you should concentrate on the downward strokes or quite soon the saw will begin to go askew. If that happens, turn the wood round and start a new cut from the other side. In any case, try to hold the saw perfectly upright and then it will be less likely to go out of true.

When sawing off the end of a plank or batten, it may happen that a piece of wood splits from the long edge just as you reach the end of the cut. This can be

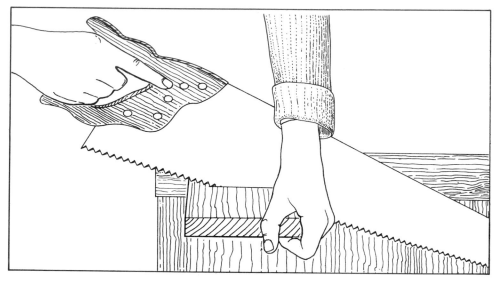

When sawing a plank or batten to length, a piece of wood may split from the long edge as you reach the end of the cut. This can be prevented by gripping the overhanging end and making the last few cuts very gently.

prevented quite easily by holding the free end of the wood and making the last few cuts very gently (see illustration above).

Points to watch when sawing

Firstly an explanation of terms: only a cut across the grain of the wood is known to the expert as sawing. A cut with the grain is called ripping. Cutting to length means sawing a piece from the end of a plank or batten (across the grain).

It is also useful to know how to avoid or correct some sawing faults:

Cutting out of true: if the saw moves continuously out of the required direction, hold the saw completely upright, saw more slowly and carefully, and test the sharpness of the blade.

If the saw overheats: have the saw sharpened and set. When sawing remember to apply light pressure only on the down strokes.

When the blade jams: have the saw sharpened and set. When making a long cut small wedges of wood may stick in the teeth and cause the blade to stick. Damaged teeth also cause jamming sometimes.

If plywood splinters: the teeth of the saw are too coarse. Do not saw upright but at a lower angle. Secure the underside of the cutting line with a strip of adhesive tape.

Drilling

There are no special instructions we can give for the simple gimlet. They are turned into the wood like a corkscrew. Should it stick, simply screw in the opposite direction and then it can be easily removed. Here are the most important basic rules for drilling with a twist bit in a hand or electric drill (you should buy a whole range of them): Mark the exact place to be drilled preferably with a bradawl or centre punch. Hold the drill at an angle (so that you can see the mark), then hold upright and drill.

For screws, drill a narrow hole the same length as the screw, then re-drill the top of the hole to the same diameter as the screw. For plywood timber, only drill slightly.

If the drill jams, continue drilling in the same direction and pull the bit out slightly. It is useless to drill in the opposite direction. When drilling right through wood the underside may split. This can be avoided by placing a piece of scrap wood under the one you are drilling. If you have to drill several holes to the same depth you need a depth gauge. You can make one by wrapping a small piece of adhesive tape around the bit.

The art of hammering in a nail
What we call a nail, experts call a wire-nail. Normally they will rust, but for use in a damp room you can get galvanized nails. Hardened steel nails are used for masonry and walls and are quite expen-sive. Nails are distinguished by length and shape of head and are usually sold loose by weight. Besides the common wire-nail with its medium-sized head used for all general jobs, the most impor-tant for do-it-yourself work are oval nails, the heads of which can be sunk into the wood, and which because of their shape do not split the wood. Tacks, which have wider heads, are generally used for up-holstering and carpets.

The correct procedure for nailing is as follows: Place the nail at an angle so that you can see it is placed onto the correct spot, then lift upright and hold firmly. With the head of the hammer (for very small nails use the cross-pein to start) hit the head of the nail carefully until it grips the wood and can no longer fall over. Then hit harder to drive the nail into the wood. Take care not to damage the wood with the last few strokes.

If the nail has to lie below the surface use a nail punch or thick nail to drive it 1/16 inch (2 millimetres) deeper into the wood, and fill the hole later. Thin pieces of wood or beading can often be split by a nail. To avoid this drill a small hole before nailing. To remove nails use pin-cers, but never directly onto the wood. Always place a thin piece of scrap wood under the head of the pincers to avoid denting the wood.

Screwing
Wood screws available differ in their raw material (steel, brass, light alloys, etc) in diameter (from 5/64 inch [1.3 millimetres] or No. 3) and in length (from 1/4 inch [5 millimetres]). There are also various head shapes.

Never use anything other than a screw-driver for screwing in or removing screws. The blade should exactly fit the slot in the screwhead if you are to avoid damage to the screw or screwdriver or both. Almost invariably the screw hole should be drilled in advance – see above section on drilling.

Normal wood screws do not always grip very firmly in chipboard. However, there is a special type of screw made for chipboard that has a larger thread.

If a screw is hard to turn, rub a little soap or candle wax onto its thread. This will help to lubricate the screw and also make removal easier.

It can be difficult to remove screws which are firmly embedded in wood. If they are rusty treat with a few drops of rust remover or diesel oil (heating oil), tap the screwhead sharply with a hammer and you will find that they will be easier to remove. If the head breaks off com-pletely your only course is to drill out the screw.

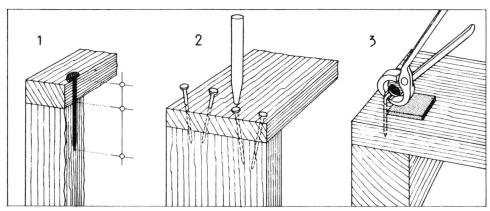

When joining two planks at right angles, one-third of the nail should lie in the upper plank and two-thirds in the lower (1). For crossply, nails will grip more firmly if knocked in at an angle (2). Use a nail punch to drive the nailhead into the wood. When pulling out nails place a piece of scrap wood under the pincers to avoid denting or scratching the wood surface.

The main types of screws (1). Left to right: round-headed screw, raised-head screw, countersunk screw. Holes for wood screws must be carefully drilled in advance (2). The smooth part of the screw shaft should not be too tight in the drill hole. The blade of the screwdriver shouldn't be wider or narrower than the slot (3), otherwise the slot and the screwdriver could be damaged.

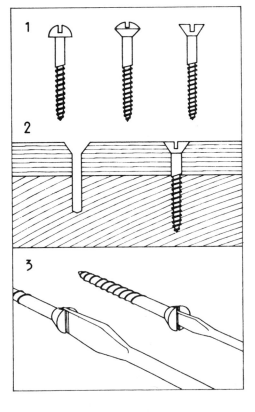

Wall fixings

It is very easy for anyone moving into a timber house to hang things on the wall. Nails, screws and hooks of any length and diameter will fit or screw easily into planks and beams. With plastered brick walls it is much more difficult. At best you can knock an ordinary wire-nail into a wall joint, but first you have to find the joint, and this can leave your wall looking as if it has been fired at with a shotgun! If you are unlucky and find that the joint is nowhere near where you need your nail, you must turn to a hardened steel masonry nail. With a little care it is possible to knock this into the wall, but it is ineffective against concrete or prefabricated concrete walls – the nail will only break.

What is a wall plug?

If the wall is too hard to take either a nail or a screw there is only one way of attaching anything to it: you must incorporate a piece of some softer material into the wall where you want to nail or screw. At one time to deal with such a case you had to knock a hole in the brick and plaster with a hammer and chisel, then plaster in a small piece of wood. You can still do this today but since it involves chiselling quite large holes in the wall it is impractical. Instead we normally use wall plugs. Today they are actually knocked, rather than plastered, into a hole drilled in the wall. They are so designed that when a screw is driven in they expand to grip the sides of the drill hole and become immovable.

Plugs for brick and concrete

Although there are many variations of wall plug, the most common types are listed below:

Fibre wall plugs are suitable for small- and medium-sized fixings. They will take all types of wood screw.

Plastic and nylon plugs are available as strips which can be cut to length, or as plain or finned plugs. The fins stop the plug rotating while inserting the screw. They have the advantage of one plug taking three sizes of screw.

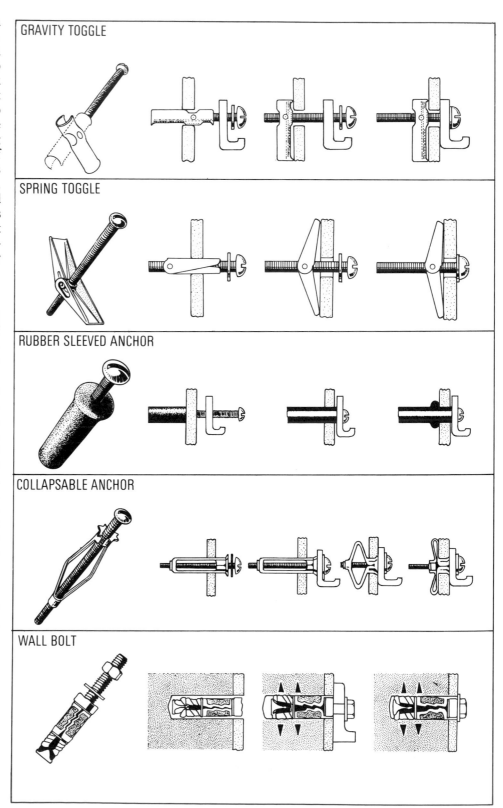

GRAVITY TOGGLE

SPRING TOGGLE

RUBBER SLEEVED ANCHOR

COLLAPSABLE ANCHOR

WALL BOLT

Metal plugs are made from white bronze and are used in places where there will be high temperatures, such as a fire grate.

Compound filler is a mixture of asbestos and filler powder. This is moistened with a little water and moulded into a conical shape and pushed into the hole. Then you make a starter hole in the compound and insert the screw when set. It is particularly useful for oversize and irregularly shaped holes.

Wall bolts are for large and heavy fixing jobs. To fit them, drill a hole in the wall to the same size as the shaft and tighten the nut on the end.

Fixings for cavity walls

These are designed to take light loads on hollow partition walls and ceilings.

Spring toggles are designed for ceilings. They have a bolt attached to two spring-loaded toggles, which are pushed through the hole. As the toggles clear the hole they spring out and the bolt is tightened. The toggle is lost if the bolt is removed.

Gravity toggles operate in a similar way to spring toggles but are designed for walls. They consist of a bolt attached to a single toggle which falls into a vertical position after it has been inserted through the hole. Again, the toggle is lost if the bolt is removed.

Collapsable anchors are made of plastic and use conventional wood screws or metal with a bolt threaded through the end. They consist of strips between the base and a flange at the top, which collapse behind the wall as the screw is tightened.

Rubber-sleeved anchors work in the same way as collapsable anchors but have a bolt threaded into a rubber sleeve with a flange on the top. After pushing into the hole, the rubber sleeve compresses behind the wall as the bolt is tightened. They produce an air- and watertight hole. Both these types of fixing are not lost if the bolt is removed.

Drilling the hole

You cannot use a plug without first making a hole in the wall. It should be deep enough to take the plug comfortably – never more than a little deeper – and the same diameter.

It is easy to control the exact drilling depth: stick a strip of adhesive tape round the bit to correspond exactly with the required depth. When drilling, the hole will be of the required depth when the tape comes up against the wall.

On no account should the plug have too much play in the hole, for then it can no longer be guaranteed to hold firm. If you drill the hole too large the only thing you can do is to use a bigger plug, but this will no longer be the right size for the screw. A useful tip is to stick a smaller plastic plug inside the larger one and turn through 90° (a quarter turn).

To make the hole by hand use a jumping tool, also known as a masonry drill (see page 218). Place the point of the bit perpendicular to the wall on the required spot. Use a fairly heavy hammer but take care with the first blows that the plaster does not crumble or crack.

When the bit has gone some way into the wall you can hit harder. After every second or third blow turn the bit slightly until you reach the required depth. Turning should prevent the bit jamming in the wall.

Electric hammer drill

Making holes with a jumping tool can be quite difficult, especially for holes in solid ceilings when you have to work above your head. Here an electric hammer drill will be valuable. Most modern electric drills have an in-built hammering action (older machines take a hammering attachment). This action revolves while shattering the stone by means of short, rapid blows. For normal drilling jobs and cavity walls the hammer action is switched off.

Do not use conventional twist bits for hammering, but only carbide-tipped masonry bits. For hammer drilling the bit should have the same diameter as the plug. Since masonry bits are expensive you should stick to two or three standard sizes for bits and plugs – around 3/16 inch (4 millimetres) or No. 8, to ¼ inch (6 millimetres) or No. 12 in diameter. Hammer drills usually have two lower speeds; the slower speed is used for masonry. The drill should be pressed firmly against the wall or ceiling. When drilling a wall, catch the falling dust in a paper bag attached to the wall under the drill hole. Do not use the hammering action on ceramic tiles, but switch to hammer when you reach the brick beneath the tiles.

Drilling mishaps

The most common problem is for the plaster around the drill hole to break away. You can repair any damage with filler once the plug is in, which is not too time-consuming.

If the drill hole hits a wall joint the plug may not grip firmly. If it is impossible to move your hole to firmer brickwork the best solution is to choose a longer plug and screw or use a compound filler plug.

When drilling concrete walls or ceilings, you may hit a steel girder. Do not drill further for you may endanger the load-capacity of the structural support. Instead, drill a new hole a few inches away.

Drilling could be fatal if you were to hit an electric cable in the wall, although most modern electric drills are double insulated. If there is no simpler way of tracing the route of the cable you can hire or buy a metal detector, which will also show water or gas pipes (and of course, steel girders). A lamp will light or a noise will be heard if the machine passes over a critical spot.

Sometimes when fastening a large structure to the wall it is difficult to drill the necessary holes to coincide exactly with fastening holes in the object you want to hang up. Here you should use the process known as 'drilling through'. Hold the structure (a curtain rail, for example) firmly in the correct position and drill through the existing holes into the wall. Then you will be able to push through the plugs and screw them into the correct place.

Adhesives and cements for use in the home

The term glue covers many different things. Everyone knows that you don't use wallpaper paste to stick wood, that you can't use ordinary glue to stick glass and metal and that you can't stick ceramic tiles to the wall with floor-tile adhesive. There is a type of glue for every job, though often one may be suitable for a variety of jobs.

Adhesives

The possibilities of modern adhesives are almost limitless. Many old methods of joining have disappeared since the plastics industry has been able to provide one special glue after another.

Today there is hardly any substance which cannot be glued firmly and lastingly. So it is worth considering every time you have to make a join whether you could use adhesive instead of nails, screws, rivets, etc.

Basically every join is made up of the two materials which are to be stuck together and a thin film of adhesive which binds them. This film makes a bond by means of cohesion (the force of attraction of the molecules). Joining something to an adhesive surface is known as adhesion (the clinging together of two bodies). The better the adhesive clings to the sticking surface, the closer the contact between the molecules of the surface and the adhesive, and therefore

the greater will be the adhesion and firmer the bond.

A well-glued bond should be virtually inseparable. If not, the adhesive is usually blamed. But the fault almost always lies in the choice of the wrong glue or lack of the correct preparation of the surfaces.

Tips for gluing

The places which are to be glued must be well prepared, not only by cutting them so that they fit exactly (be it a plug into a hole, or edges and surfaces which are to fit side by side), but also by cleansing them of dust, grease, paint and any other sediment. If you are re-gluing, any old glue or adhesive must be completely cleaned away. Both surfaces should be roughened with coarse sandpaper to provide a 'key' for the glue.

White PVA glue is applied to small surfaces, such as beading, with a brush and to larger surfaces with a glue comb (serrated spreader) or glue roller.

The glued sections are brought together immediately and must be held together under an even pressure for 20 to 60 minutes depending on the type of wood, its dampness and the room temperature. To hold them together you will need one or more clamps. These are unnecessary where the sections are nailed or screwed as well as glued.

Wallpaper paste

Starch paste (flour paste) used to be used for wallpapering but now it has been replaced almost exclusively by cellular paste. Cellular pastes are dissolved in cold water as given in the instructions and must be left to stand for about 20 minutes before use. The quantity of water used depends on the weight of the paper.

Paste should be kept in a non-rust bucket. It can be kept for short periods in a closed container. It can be used only for wallpapering, sticking paper and for covering distemper (so that the colour does not come off when anything touches it).

PVA glue

For interior joinery white PVA glue is mostly used today and is bought ready for use in tubes or bottles. It is a by-product of polyvinylacetate (the same base as clear multi-purpose glue).

White PVA glue can be used for all bonding of wood, including veneering, and also for mounting photographs onto a wooden sheet and for sticking leather, felt and textiles to wood.

White PVA glue is easy to apply (with a paintbrush or glue spreader), can be thinned with water and is almost colourless when dry. Only with very absorbent surfaces will you need to apply the glue to both surfaces, usually it is enough to apply it to one surface only.

The join will need cramping (or temporary nailing or screwing together) for between 20 and 60 minutes – depending on the type of wood, its dampness and room temperature.

White PVA glue should not be allowed to come into contact with metal implements or tools, for they may become discoloured.

Any tools used must be cleaned with cold water immediately after use. Once the glue has dried in the tube it can no longer be diluted with water.

Traditional warm and cold wood glues are no longer widely used today. The main type is animal glue, also known as bone glue, Scotch glue, fish glue, hide glue, warm glue or joiner's glue and is usually made from bones. It is sold in

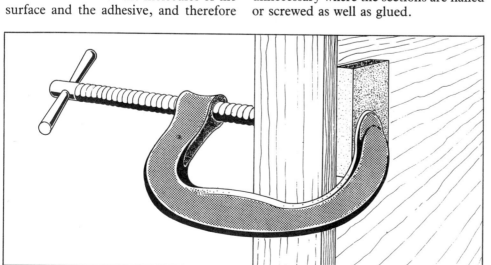

When cramping a glued joint, always use a piece of scrap wood between the jaws and the wood to prevent damaging the surface and also to spread the load.

slabs or as pearls which must be left to stand in cold water for 8 to 12 hours and are then warmed until runny by standing the container in hot water. If you want to re-glue with PVA glue or another adhesive, an animal glue join that has become loose, you must first remove any remaining glue completely with hot water.

Multi-purpose glue

The story of modern synthetic glues began with the development of multi-purpose glues, a dilution of the plastic polyvinylacetate which is clear and brittle in its natural state, in an organic solvent (acetic acid, alcohol, ketone). Softening agents are generally added to reduce its brittleness.

As the glue sets the solvents evaporate. Not all clear adhesives in tubes, plastic bottles or spray bottles have the same consistency – there are more runny and more solid glues, smoothly flowing or viscous types. Good glue should be fluid, colourless, waterproof, withstand light and ageing, and be insensitive to acids, caustic solutions, benzine and oil. It sticks quickly but remains elastic when dry. Its main uses are for paper, card, wood, leather, textiles. It is not recommended for large areas because it is difficult to spread. For easy joints apply to one surface only, for difficult joints apply to both, allow to dry, apply another thin coat and press together.

A variety of multi-purpose glue is hard glue which is used mainly in model building where it is used to glue delicate parts quickly and lastingly. This special glue dries quickly and becomes very hard. Hard glue is waterproof and clear when dry. It can also be used to join celluloid, plexiglass and Astralon. Around the home it is most used for quick repairs, for example to picture frames or wobbly table legs.

Contact adhesive

Like multi-purpose and hard glues, contact adhesives belong to the family of solvent glues. The most important raw material used is synthetic rubber. They are generally recommended for bonds which must stick without being kept under pressure for a long time.

Contact adhesive is lightly applied to both surfaces (with a brush or spreader), which are left to dry for about ten minutes and then carefully positioned and pressed together. A short, strong pressure is enough to produce an almost physical join immediately, which is however immediately completed by a chemical join (intermeshing of the molecules) and in the end the join is absolutely firm.

The advantage with contact adhesives is that you can proceed with your work without allowing time for cramping or drying. There is one disadvantage – the components must be carefully positioned before pressing together; subsequent sliding or other corrections are impossible. Contact adhesive is recommended mainly for sticking plastic laminate sheets onto wood, for veneering and for attaching edge strips (see page 232). But it can be used equally well for sticking things to stone, concrete, hard PVC and for flexible materials such as leather, felt, foam, etc. The addition of special hardening agents improves its strength and heat resistance. Any surplus adhesive can be removed with a special thinner.

A further development from contact adhesives are adhesive thixotropic jellies which, unlike the normal contact adhesives, do not either dry up or form a thread. The jelly-like paste is easy to use even in the home. For example it will not run on an upright surface and therefore won't drip onto the floor.

Summary: special glues

The number of special glues for specific jobs is extremely large. The most important of them are:

Epoxy glues consist of two components, a hard glue and a hardening agent which have to be mixed in given quantities just before use. They will bond all kinds of metals, glass, ceramic, porcelain, marble, concrete and wood to a similar surface or to one of the others. For example you can use them to stick cable clips or coat hooks to concrete, hinges to chipboard or shelf brackets to tiles.

Plastic glue is used to stick plastics to one another or to other materials. When buying it you should state the purpose for which it will be used – not every plastic glue will stick every type of plastic.

Hard foam glues are used exclusively to stick pieces and sheets of polystyrene to one another and to other materials. You can use this glue for example to stick polystyrene sheets to walls and ceilings.

Tiling adhesive is used to stick ceramic, plastic or metal tiles to plaster or wooden surfaces. For hints on its use see page 182.

Cement, fillers and caulking

These are closely linked with adhesives for they have to adhere firmly to a surface, in a cavity or groove. Alongside the familiar putty the most important for home use are:

Plastic wood is paint thickly mixed with a filling material of a paste-like consistency. It is used to level out the surface of a piece of work (e.g. knot holes and splits in wood, sheets of chipboard). Before application the wood must be primed and afterwards it can be sanded and painted.

Wood cement, consisting of fine sawdust and a binding agent, is used to even out splits, holes, scratches etc., in wood which is not to be painted, but which is to keep its natural surface. It is available in all common wood colours. When dry the filler can be drilled, cut, sawn and sanded.

Fluid enamel of an acrylic material and filler is available in all the usual colours and is used to repair enamel. For damaged metal parts you can get fluid metal which is a plastic paste and metal powder.

Elastic fillers, mostly with a silicon rubber base, are used to seal 'movable' joints (extension joints) for example between the bath and wall tiles, on windows and doors and on brickwork. Hints on use are given on page 197.

Planks and boards: wood as raw material

Wood, especially panelling, used to be very popular as an interior decoration, and is now becoming popular again. Wood is no longer used primarily for roofs and walls, but is used as a creative element by architects and builders. It brings a little of nature into the house to complement our more sophisticated shapes and surfaces. In addition a variety of techniques have been developed for producing wood as a raw material; for example easy-to-work chipboard, hardboard, plywood, blockboard and fibre boards, so that wood, with its rich traditions, is now frequently in use as a modern material.

The structure of wood

Wood is a growing, living material. It does not consist of one single element, but is made up of distinguishable structural parts. Also its properties vary according to the direction in which it is cut, be it with the grain or through the age rings. Two pieces which have been cut from the same trunk are therefore not at all similar.

Everyone must at some time have seen the age rings on a tree trunk that has been sawn up. Even in a tree with very regular growth they will not be regular. One can observe ring-shaped stripes, some light and some dark coloured. Where the rings are light in colour, the wood is more porous, where dark you will find that it is more solid.

This appearance is due to different rates of growth in different seasons. In the early part of the year, large, thin-walled cells form to give the light spring wood, in autumn a late wood with small cells is formed which is more solid. The closer the rings the better is the quality for softwood. With hardwood, however, wide rings are best.

In the course of time the cells formed in springtime dry up, are filled with deposits and solidify. It is these cells that make up heartwood, while the outer layers of the trunk consist of sapwood which, being rich in water, is not as good. The pith or heart of the tree is found right at the very centre of the age rings.

Warping of wood

In its natural state every wood 'works', that is, it expands, retracts, grows crooked or twisted as dictated by the amount of water contained in the wood fibres. Fresh wood contains up to 70% water, dry wood only 10% to 20%. During drying the volume decreases and inexpert drying will produce splitting. Dried wood will absorb water and thus increasing its volume will expand.

The tensions in the wood structure which this inevitably produces cause warping. Suddenly the plank is no longer completely straight but takes on a slightly furrowed shape. The further from the pith the plank was cut, the more it will tend to warp, and indeed the plank will bend away from the centre of the trunk. Expressed in specialist terms, the *outside* of a plank (seen from the pith), referred to as the left side, becomes hollow during warping (concave); the *inside* (again seen from the pith), referred to as the right side, becomes round (convex) during warping.

You must take measures to prevent warping when you cut the wood for a particular purpose. Even glue, nails, screws and sophisticated joining techniques cannot prevent warping, can indeed at best only lessen its effect.

Using the correct methods of construction one can ensure that the tensions which are produced by warping are eliminated:

When nailing together a flat surface (for a table, for example) arrange each plank so that the right side is uppermost.

When gluing planks together alternate them, that is, place left and right sides uppermost alternately.

When nailing or gluing large pieces to each other place left sides together, that is with the right sides of the planks outermost.

Wood for use at home

Softwoods such as spruce and pine, both conifers, are best for use in a home workshop. Hardwoods have become very expensive, and are used mostly by the experienced cabinet-maker. They also appear as veneers (thin slices of wood which are glued to boards), to provide a top surface for a piece of furniture, for example, or as veneered boards and panels.

Ready-cut soft timber is available in so many varieties that you should normally have no difficulty in finding what you want at a wood merchant or do-it-yourself shop. If you want something special it is better to go to a joiner's shop where you will normally find a selection of woods from which the joiner will be able to cut a piece to your requirements. Here follows a rough description of the different types of cut wood that are available:

Planks: Sold in widths ranging from ¾ inch (19 millimetres) to about 12 inches (300 millimetres). The scale of thickness starts at ¼ inch (6 millimetres) and goes up to a thickness of 1½ inches (36 millimetres) – the latter end of the scale. There are also fluted and tongued planks, latticed planks, and planks of exotic woods used for encasing and covering.

Beading and battening: Available as squared beading in every conceivable size starting from ⅛ inch (3 millimetres). Battening is needed above all in the size suitable for roof battens (generally 2 by 1 inch [50 by 30 millimetres]). Wood for picture frames is not standardized, you will have to look for a suitable pattern in a picture framers.

Building timber: Common sizes will be available from a wood merchant. It is not worth going in for special formats if you have to cut them yourself.

Plywood and blockboard

Plywood consists of at least three sheets of veneer of varying thicknesses, glued together with the grain going in different directions. It is available in thicknesses ranging from ¹⁄₁₆ to 1 inch (3 to 25 millimetres); the thicker sheets have correspondingly more layers (always an odd number).

The cross-bonding of plywood effectively counters the strains caused by the bulging and twisting of the timber. Plywood rivals hardboard (see below) for use in backing wardrobes and shelf units.

Today you can also buy plywood whose layers are welded together with synthetic resin. They are not only suitable for indoor use, but also for items which will be exposed to the weather (for garden chairs, for example, or boat-building). But this excellent waterproof quality is rather expensive.

Plywood is also available with a plastic or wood veneer – this saves veneering it yourself.

Blockboard is constructed in a similar way to plywood (see diagram below). The central core consists of strips of softwood bonded together; the covering layers top and bottom are a hardwood veneer which is glued across them. Two different types are in general use.

Blockboard is available in thicknesses ranging from ½ to 1¾ inches (13 to 45 millimetres) and is also available with a decorative wood veneer.

Laminboard is similar to blockboard, except it is constructed with a core of narrow strips of wood. This reduces the chance of the pattern of the strips showing through the veneer facing.

Chipboard and hardboard
With chipboard the natural wood grain is no longer recognizable. It consists of wood shavings with synthetic resin used as a binding agent, and has a smooth surface suitable for all kinds of coating. Like wood though you can saw and plane it, drill and nail it, sand and fill it. You can also get chipboard with a tempered, textured, layered or veneered top surface.

The chipboard most in use in the home tends to be of a thickness between ⅜ and 1 inch (6 and 25 millimetres), though even thicker boards are available. It is usually sold in sheets 8 feet by 4 feet (2400 by 1200 millimetres). In specialist shops you will be able to buy pieces cut to the correct size.

For uprights (dividing walls, furniture walls, shelf supports) you can use chipboard up to the standard sheet size without hesitation. However, with horizontal pieces which have to bear some weight greater caution is required as they can easily sag. For a bookshelf, for example, chipboard ½-inch (14-millimetres) thick should span a distance no more than 18 inches (500 millimetres). Otherwise it may well sag in the course of time and turning it over does little good. For a shelf span of 36 inches (900 millimetres) you need ¾-inch (19-millimetre) or better still 1-inch (25-millimetre) board. Battening which is glued to or under the shelf can also prevent sagging.

Chipboard is the ideal material for the home workshop – not only for furniture and built-in cupboards but also for converting the attic, for example. If the cut edges of chipboard have to be visible, they should be covered with an edge strip (see page 232).

Hardboard is similar in form to chipboard, but is made with finer shavings and under greater pressure. One side has a smooth surface, the other a rough, slightly corrugated or grained surface. The rough side is best for gluing as it provides a good 'key' (see page 224).

Hardboard withstands knocks and pressure. Its main uses are for covering furniture and walls, panels and rear walls of cupboards. The most appropriate for the home workshop is hardboard ¼ inch (6 millimetres) thick. If you need something thicker it is better to use plywood or blockboard. The most common board size is 8 feet by 4 feet (2400 by 1200 millimetres). Before use boards of all kinds should be left to stand in the home workshop for two or three days to become acclimatized to prevent them twisting after fixing.

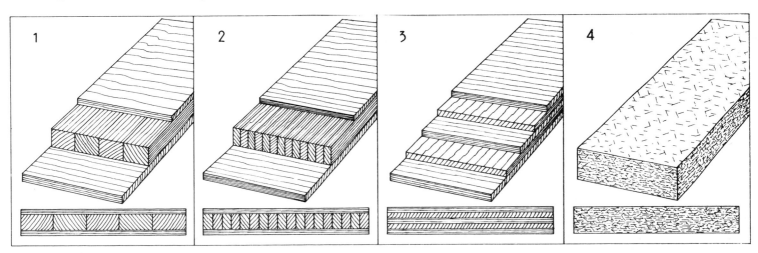

Timber boards are a popular material for the home workshop not least because they are cheaper than solid wood. (1) Blockboard has a central core made up of strips of softwood 1 inch (25 millimetres) wide. (2) Laminboard is better since the narrower strips in the central core are less likely to show their pattern on the surface. (3) Plywood is available in thicknesses up to 1 inch (25 millimetres) and consists of at least three layers of veneer. (4) Chipboard or particle board is made from wood shavings and synthetic resin; the grain of the wood is no longer recognizable.

Wood joints for beginners

The question of how sections of wood should be joined most neatly and effectively has concerned carpenters and joiners for generations. Nowadays we have very efficient glues and adhesives which were of course not available to the craftsmen of earlier times. But if a joint is badly cut its effectiveness will be reduced.

Half-lap joints

Half-lap joints are used above all for battening and beading, for corners as well as cross joints. Using this method you can build the frame for a wardrobe door, for example (eventually covered with plywood), or the frame for bookshelves.

At the point where the joint is to be made you must remove half the thickness of the wood on both pieces. When marking the wood it is best to mark it out rather smaller than necessary – you can always take a bit more out later, but if you cut too much away you won't be able to put it back. The method of work is as follows.

End or corner joint: Using a tenon saw, saw across the batten to half its depth. Now saw vertically down until you meet the first cut. Repeat the process on the other batten. Then glue both battens at the point where the wood has been cut away, checking for square. You can reinforce the joint with screws, although you will need to drill pilot holes in the wood first.

Cross joint: Saw to the left and right of the section to be cut away, and to make your work easier make a few extra cuts between these two (see diagram below), then chisel away the waste. The joint must fit exactly. As above glue the joint and screw it together. You can also use this method to join round pieces of timber.

Lap joints

Above all lap joints should ensure that corners made by joining two planks or boards together will look neat. Secondly they will give greater stability, which is especially important if you are working with chipboard – because nails or screws alone will not hold it particularly firmly and will not give you a good join.

Diagram 1 in the illustration below right shows a corner joint linking a plank and a sheet of chipboard. The rebate in the plank can be made with a plane or circular saw. The edge of the chipboard will then be covered by the plank. This is the kind of technique that can be used to attach a plywood or hardboard back wall in a wardrobe so that the edge cannot be seen. The depth of the rebate will depend on the thickness of the back panel.

It is easier to make a glued corner joint. Here a piece of planking or board (2) or a batten (3) can be used to form a rebate. The screw holes in the board and also the supporting batten must be predrilled.

You may want to try another possible way of making corner joints with chipboard which is to use plastic corner blocks. These consist of two pieces of plastic which are bolted together. Each piece of plastic is then screwed to a piece of chipboard.

Pin joints

Pin joints are used mainly for the construction of simple tables and armchairs. They are used to join a narrow piece of beading to a thicker one or to a plank (see diagram above), generally at right angles. Begin by drilling a hole in the larger piece of wood, a plank for example, (using a twist or wood bit 1 to 1¼ inches [25 to 30 millimetres] in diameter). The end of the thinner batten must now be made to fit this hole. This is easiest done using a sharp knife. When you have done this saw two-thirds of the way into the prepared point across the direction of the grain of the plank which you have drilled. Coat the point with glue, push it into the drill hole and then tap it home. Then

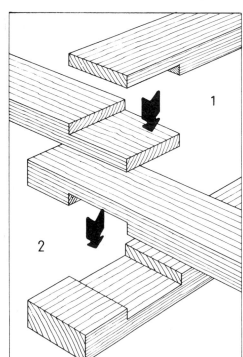

A half-lap joint is a simple technique used for battens and beading, for corner (1) and cross joints (2). At the point of the joint half the thickness of

wood must be removed on each piece. Notches are sawn into the batten (3), then the wood is chiselled away layer by layer (4).

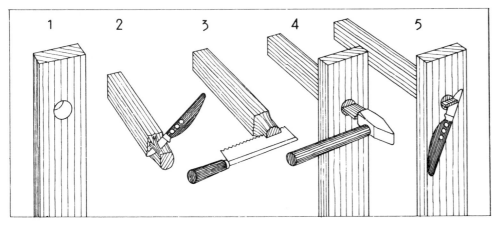

Pin joints are used for making tables and chairs. A drill hole is bored (1) and a plug cut to fit it (2) with a wedge slit made in it (3). The plug is glued and fitted into the hole and a wooden wedge is hammered into the slit (4). Any excess wood and wedge is finally cut off flush (5).

glue a wooden wedge into the sawn slit. When the glue is dry cut off the excess portion of the pin and wedge with a saw. To finish the joint, use either sandpaper or a plane.

Dowel joints

Little can go wrong with dowel joints if you know how to measure and mark exactly. You must also remember when you are drilling (preferably with a twist bit) that you will have to hold the drill upright.

The simplest are the corner joints (1 and 2 in the diagram below) for both holes can be drilled at the same time. The plank and post joint (3) is more difficult. For this mark exactly the drill holes on one section and knock small pins into the centre of the mark. Then pinch off the heads. Press the two sections together, fitting them together exactly. In so doing the drill-hole marks are transferred from one section to the other by the pins.

You can buy the dowels ready to use (round rods of ramin). You will have to cut them to length and then sharpen the ends slightly. Before hammering them into the drill holes you should first coat them with glue – and also coat the edges of the wooden sections. The dowel will then fit so tightly into the drill hole that you should find that no additional fastening is necessary.

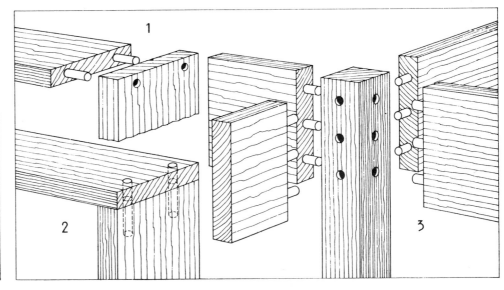

The rebated corner lap joint (1) involves most work, for the rebate must be planed out. The glued lap (2) or batten (3) is easier and holds just as well.

The diagrams illustrate the uses of dowel joints. In examples 1 and 2 the holes are drilled at one go. This has the advantage of avoiding bad fit. How you match the drill holes for the third example is explained in the text. You can buy dowels in various diameters from handicraft shops.

229

More advanced joints

If you can master the techniques for joining wood and chipboard which are shown here, you will be able to make more professional-looking articles.

Corner joints

One day you will find that making corner joints by simply placing two boards or planks together and nailing or gluing them is not enough. The diagram shows a more sophisticated and more difficult method: gluing in tongues of hardwood or plywood, 3/16 to 1/4 inch (3 to 5 millimetres) thick depending on the thickness of the boards to be joined. The wood will also need a groove corresponding to the thickness of the tongue.

Use a plough plane to plane out the groove or use a 'wobble' attachment on a circular saw (this makes the saw swing from side to side so that it does not cut a narrow slit in the wood but grooves of varying widths). Alternatively make several passes with the saw.

The diagram below shows corner joints for frames. The plain mitred corners which are glued together hold least well, the mitres with glued hardwood tongues hold best. A good method is to use metal corner or triangular plates which are screwed on. If the corner joints are to be visible you can recess the corner plates.

Mortise and tenon joints

This joint is useful among other things for making tables and chairs, frames and structures from battening, etc.

The tenon can be cut with a tenon saw. The mortise is chiselled out – this becomes easier if a drill is used first. The main uses for these joints are as end joints which can extend to the whole width of the timber (1) or can be concealed (2); with centre joints too (like rungs of a ladder) you can choose either the open or concealed joint (3).

Dovetail joints

This joint holds particularly well; it will withstand both pressure and tension for

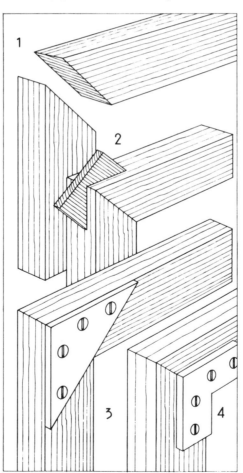

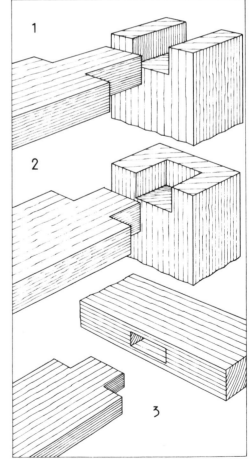

Two corner joints for planks or blockboard. The tongue (of hardwood or plywood about 3/16 to 1/4 inch [3 to 5 millimetres] thick) are glued into grooves made with a plough plane. A groove made with a circular hand saw with a 'wobble' device is better.

230

Mitred wooden frame pieces merely glued together (1) do not hold particularly well. A tongue glued into the outside of the corner improves the joint; excess tongue is finally cut away (2). Simplest of all are metal right angles or triangles (3,4).

Mortise and tenon joints require precise chisel work. The diagrams show a through corner joint (1) and a concealed joint (2) as well as a central joint (3) which can be made either through or concealed depending on the finish that you require.

the two sections grip one another like interlaced fingers. The diagram below right explains the method of work for dovetailing. The dovetails on one section are completed first and then the second section is marked using this first set of dovetails as a guide. Pins of equal width are sawn and chiselled out in both pieces of timber. Even here it is safer to do one section first and to mark the second from it. Before gluing, test that they fit together so that mistakes can be rectified.

Housing joints

Building furniture concerns more than just making corner joints. How do you put in shelves in shelf units and cupboards in a workmanlike fashion so that they also contribute to stability?

The diagram on the right illustrates the main way of doing this. We can distinguish between the through housing (easily sawn out with a tenon saw guided by beading attached to the wood) and the stopped housing which is chiselled out.

The through housing will be visible in the finished product, the stopped housing, however, will not be. The simplest housing joint (1) has no tongue, and looks slightly clumsy. A well-shaped narrow housing with a tongue on one side (2) is neater and holds better.

Housing joints are used for building shelf units and cupboards. The easiest of these joints is a housing to fit the full depth of the shelf (1). Often the shelf can be cut to a narrower tongue with a correspondingly narrower housing (2). In both cases you can use either a through housing joint which will be visible (3) or a stopped housing which will be concealed (4).

(1) Cut the tails with a fine-toothed tenon saw. (2) Remove the bulk of the waste with a coping saw or chisel. (3) Clean up between the tails with a bevel-edged chisel. (4) Mark out the tails with a fine scriber using the tails as a template. (5) Saw down the pins with a tenon saw and remove the waste with a coping saw. The finished joint should fit firmly together.

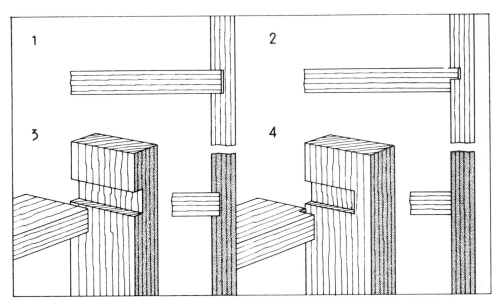

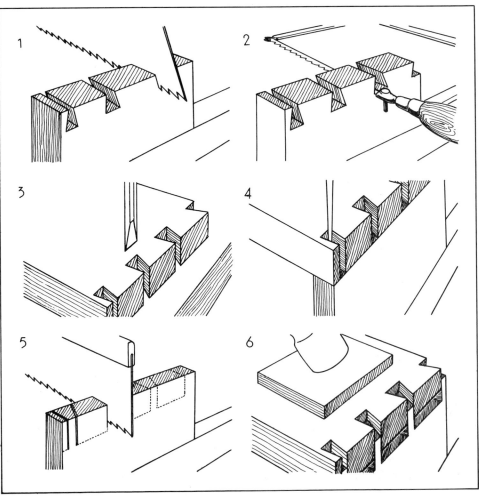

231

Covering boards and planks

The top surface of anything made from chipboard or blockboard or from timber can be improved in widely varying ways. Natural wood surfaces (solid wood or veneer) should be treated in such a way that they retain the natural surface markings (see page 234). Cheaper surfaces are covered by a coat of paint (page 236).

In both cases the rough piece of work must be carefully sanded, boards may also need some filler and then an edge strip. Finally you can also stick a sheet of plastic to the surface or cover it with laminated plastic. These techniques will be discussed here.

Abrasives

Even a thick layer of paint can only partly conceal irregularities, cracks, joints and nail holes in the surface wood of a piece of work. So before reaching for your paint brush or roller, all visible surfaces must be a) carefully sanded and b) levelled out with filler where necessary (and then sanded again). The most important tool for this is abrasive paper, often called sandpaper or glasspaper. It is sold in several grades each of which has a number. Always choose the grade required for particular purpose:

Rough: 30–60, for preliminary sanding of unplaned surfaces, for removing old paint and rust;

Medium: 80–100, for preliminary sanding of flat surfaces (doors for example), for sanding down paintwork before re-painting;

Fine: 120–180, for fine sanding of timber and boards, also for sanding down after filling or undercoating;

Very fine: 220–320, for finely sanding paint, matt finishes and coverings on wood and metal.

The numbers refer to the size of grit used; the higher the number the finer the paper. 'Wet and dry' paper is available for rubbing down paintwork between coats. It is used with water to prevent the paper clogging.

Sanding and filling

When sanding by hand it is difficult to keep an even pressure on the wood surface. It is better to wrap the sandpaper around a sanding block, made yourself from a piece of wood, or a bought cork one. If you have to sand rounded surfaces you can wrap the sandpaper round a firm plastic sponge. You can also buy pieces of foam blocks with an abrasive coating; one side is coarse the other medium. These blocks can be washed in water to remove dust.

Natural wood surfaces should only be sanded against the grain in very rough work, otherwise always work with the grain. For an extra-smooth surface, damp the wood and let it dry. The wood cells which have been crushed by sawing, planing, etc. will open out when damp, the grain will stand out and will sand down very well. This procedure is not recommended for chipboard.

If you often have large surfaces to sand it is worthwhile buying a sanding attachment for your electric drill, or a purpose-built orbital sander.

You can take away any protrusions on the surface of the timber or board by sanding, but it can do nothing to correct dents and depressions in the surface. These must be evened out with filler. If you are intending to keep the natural wood surface use plastic wood in the shade closest to that of the wood that you can find. If the wood is to be painted use a paint filler.

The filler is best applied with a thin-bladed filling knife. It must be pressed firmly into cavities and cracks and smoothed flat. Deeper holes must be filled using several layers, allowing each layer to dry before adding another. If in doubt it is best to apply too much filler rather than too little. Excess filler can be sanded away when it is completely dry. After sanding you will be able to see and feel where it is necessary to apply more filler.

Dealing with edges

In your home workshop it is best to use either chipboard or blockboard. Their chief disadvantage lies in the fact that the sawn edges are unattractive. When you work with chipboard, separate shavings are pulled out of the binding resin thus leaving the edges of the board rough and porous. With blockboard you will only get a smooth surface if it is cut parallel with the internal blocks. When cutting across the grain of the blocks, slits of varying size may appear between the blocks which you will not want to be seen.

The simplest solution in both cases is to carefully conceal all irregularities on the edges with paint filler, preferably in several applications. But you should only do this with chipboard if the edges are not to be subject to strain, otherwise the filler can break off. The time spent in filling will then be wasted and the paint ruined. Visible edges of chipboard and blockboard (when cut across the grain) should where possible be concealed by an

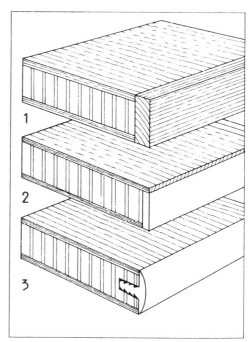

Dealing with the edges of chipboard and blockboard: (1) Edge strip made from a solid wood beading. (2) Edge strip of plastic laminate. (3) PVC edge strip with flange for which a groove must be cut. There are also edge strips in light metal available both with and without flanges.

edge strip. The simplest type will be adequate in most cases. This consists of a strip of hardwood about ¼ inch (5 millimetres) thick and the same width as the board which is first glued to the edge and then fastened with small countersunk nails.

Where the edge strip and the board surfaces meet you will need to sand thoroughly and then, once it is painted, you will not be able to tell that an edge strip has been used. You can also use a plane to even out the edges. Any gaps between the edge strip and the board must be filled. In many cases it is possible to glue on a wider strip than necessary to give the impression of a thicker board. This can also be done even when the board is to be positioned below eye level, for example with work surfaces, table tops and low shelves.

Edge strips

There are other ways of covering the edges of boards:

Plastic laminate strips: If the piece of work is to be covered with plastic laminate you can also apply edge strips of the same material. The strip is cut slightly wider than necessary and when stuck in position any excess can be sanded away or planed with a small plane specially designed for the job.

PVC edge strip: Most have a flange (see diagram) and you will need to make a groove in the board edge to take this. The edge strip is stuck with contact adhesive. Continuous PVC edge strips are useful above all in protecting the edges of tables.

Light metal edges: Like PVC edges they have a flange which requires a groove cut into the edge of the board. It is fixed with contact adhesive.

There are also PVC and metal edge strips with a slightly raised edge along one side used, for example, for covering the edges of kitchen work surfaces or for the edges of bathroom shelves (they prevent articles falling off so easily).

Adhesive plastic

If you are going to cover surfaces (and edges) with adhesive plastic you can eliminate or cut down on sanding and filling. Only large depressions or protrusions which might show through the plastic need to be filled or sanded. Cut the plastic sheet so that it will extend to at least 4 inches (100 millimetres) into the underside of the surface you are covering (along shelf edges for example).

After removing the backing paper stick the plastic down. The under surface must be completely clean, dust-free, grease-free and oil-free. Very porous surfaces that are to be covered should be coated in advance with sealer.

You may not always succeed in fitting two widths of plastic exactly together. In such a case stick on the widths with an overlap of about 1 inch (25 millimetres) and cut through both layers exactly in the middle of the overlap with a steel ruler and sharp knife. Remove the two excess strips and press down the edges firmly so that they form a butt joint. If a gap appears later at this particular point it is usually because you have stuck it down under tension.

Sticking plastic laminates

Plastic laminates are fixed with contact adhesive. When buying a sheet of laminate have it cut slightly larger to allow spare at the edges. It is best for covering chipboard and blockboard. Solid wood should only be covered if used for a small item.

Plastic laminate is easy to cut yourself.

Score with the corner of a chisel and break along the scored line over a steel ruler. Thicker sheets should be cut with a fine-toothed saw (but this procedure will blunt it), or with a circular saw for which you can get special blades for cutting plastic.

The plastic laminate and the surface to be covered are coated with contact adhesive (using a comb spreader). Allow both surfaces to dry for 10 to 15 minutes.

Position smaller pieces carefully at an angle and then press onto the surface. They should fit exactly at the first go, for you will not be able to move them. Press down the surface with a rubber roller, rubber hammer or an ordinary hammer with a piece of wood under it. Then sand the edges with sandpaper or even them up with a plane.

For larger pieces lay three or four pieces of battening across the surface to be covered after you have glued it. You can position the laminate exactly on the battens. First remove the middle batten and press down the laminate in the centre. Then follow suit with the other battens until the whole sheet is stuck down. It must now be pressed or hammered down and the edges sanded or planed.

Thin boards and all kinds of timber should also be covered on the underside to avoid warping. This is also true of veneering which is done as follows. Cut veneer with a very sharp knife. If veneering large surfaces, stick the strips of veneer together on the upper surface with adhesive tape which is later removed.

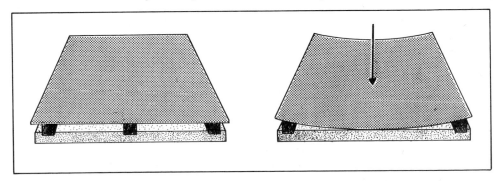

Lay the plastic laminate in position on thin battens. Remove the centre batten **and press down the laminate. Now remove the remaining battens.**

Wood surfaces

It is always best to use a covering layer (such as paint) on the top surface of the wood (or of wooden boards), where, although smooth and clean, it is unattractive. More about this on page 236.

Beautiful and impressive wood surfaces should not, however, be hidden beneath paint but should be treated in such a way as to keep and emphasize the figure of the wood. There are a host of procedures you can use to do this and these are dealt with on these two pages.

Preparing the wood surface

When choosing your wood and while working on it bear in mind that you will want to display the wood surface. This will only look effective if you choose matching, similarly structured wood and veneer and keep it as clean as possible while working on it. For pieces which are to be painted, on the other hand, you can cover mistakes (gaps in joints, nail holes, hammer dents) to a limited extent with filler. It is also difficult to remove spots of glue, grease or oil. All the procedures for finishing the wood bring out its natural beauty, but they can also show up mistakes.

The most important preparatory work lies in damping, cleaning and sanding the wood. Damping down expands the fibres of the wood cells so that they can be sanded without difficulty. Cleaning should remove fingermarks, grease, dirt and, if necessary, traces of glue.

Rinse with clear water then leave to dry overnight and sand with fine sandpaper with the grain. Carefully remove the dust. Then even out any cracks and holes with wood filler. After sanding and dusting again you are ready to coat it. You can give it a matt, semi-matt or gloss finish. Many of these coating materials are pigmented and therefore make it simple to colour the wood. You can also stain (colour) it first and then use a clear top coat.

Staining

Stains can deepen the colour of a wood or completely change it without covering its natural grain. Stains are available in the usual wood colours and also in unnatural colours such as yellow, orange, red, blue or green which can change the colour of the wood. Stained surfaces in general need a protective coating because the stain itself does nothing to protect the wood.

There are two types of stain readily available – water-based and spirit-based. Both types can be bought ready-mixed or in powder form. The water type has the disadvantage that it raises the grain. To counteract this, dampen the wood surface and allow it to dry, then sand it smooth. The surface is then ready to be stained. Stains of the same type can be mixed to produce other colours. Powder stains can be mixed to any degree of intensity by adding more powder or liquid to make it respectively stronger or weaker. If you want quite a deep colour, it is better to apply two or three weak coats than one strong coat.

You can choose a matching shade of stain from the colour chart in the shop. Since the particular colouring and tannic acid content of woods can vary, do carry out a test staining (on a piece of wood or the back of the piece of work), otherwise you may have an unpleasant surprise. You can only get a true impression of the final colour effect when the test stain is dry and has been varnished.

Apply the stain to small areas with a brush, and to large ones with a well-charged sponge in the direction of the grain. When the whole surface is wet go over it again with the brush or sponge across the grain, then working with the grain remove any excess stain with the squeezed-out brush or sponge. Uprights are stained from top to bottom.

It is best to leave the surface to dry overnight before applying the protective coat. Dry stained surfaces should not be sanded again. You can use a fairly stiff brush to remove any threads lifted during staining.

Finishes

There is a wide range of finishes available for finishing wood. Each has its own advantages and disadvantages.

Bee's wax: This is a traditional finish which is cheap and easy to apply – although hard work. It gives a soft sheen, and allows the open texture of the grain to be seen. It is suitable for most woods, particularly oak, although it will make light-coloured timbers look dirty. The disadvantage of a wax finish is its lack of durability, but it can be easily renovated with a fresh coat.

Apply wax with a cloth, a stiff brush, or wire wool working it well into the grain. Two or three coats should be applied leaving an interval of a few days between each application. Finish with a soft brush, finally buffing with a clean cloth.

Oiled finishes: These give a similar dull sheen finish as with wax. The finish is water-resistant and improves with age. It is particularly well suited to teak, but rosewood, mahogany and oak all take the finish well.

Mix equal parts of linseed oil and pure turpentine and rub well into the wood with a brush or cloth. After an hour wipe off the surplus with a dry cloth. Repeat the application a couple of days later and finish by hard rubbing with a soft cloth. A little wax will give the finish more sheen.

Teak oil is similar to linseed oil, but contains drying agents. It is applied in the same way, but with shorter periods between application and finish.

Polyurethane lacquer: This is a tough, durable finish available in matt, silk and gloss, all of which can be bought in exterior and interior grades. It can also be obtained in different wood colours and vivid translucent greens, reds, oranges, etc. However, they do not have the same intensity as wood stains and several coats must be applied to obtain a deep colour. Surfaces should be clean, dry and dust-free before application.

It should be applied with a brush or wad of lint-free cloth. The first coat should be thinned slightly with white spirit to prime the surface. Each coat should be rubbed down lightly when dry with fine sandpaper or wire wool. Repeat after 24 hours. Two or three coats are

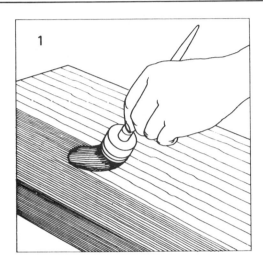

Wood stain is applied with a brush in long, even strokes. Any excess stain must be removed with the brush. Work with the grain of the wood.

Larger surfaces can be stained better with a sponge. The sponge is filled and applied by pressure on the sponge in the direction of the grain.

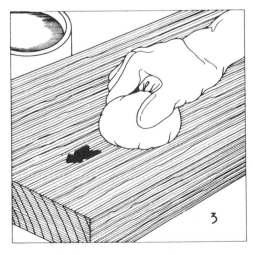

Matt finish is applied with a ball covered in stockinet. The movement of the ball should follow the grain. Before matt finishing, the wood surface should be treated with a porous or hard base coat.

enough for most surfaces, but floors and exterior surfaces should have four or five.

Plastic finishes: These are ideal for table tops or work surfaces where extreme heat will be encountered. They come in two packs which must be mixed together. Two or three coats are necessary. The finish can be burnished to a high gloss or rubbed with wire wool to obtain a matt finish.

French polish: This is the classic finish used by the cabinet-maker for fine furniture. It works itself deep into the wood to bring out the beauty of the grain and is best suited to quality, close-grained hardwoods. Although it makes an excellent finish, it marks easily. This polish consists of shellac dissolved in methylated spirit and is applied by pouring a little onto a wad of cotton wool covered with a lint-free cloth, known as a rubber. The rubber is worked across the wood in a slow figure of eight movement (a little linseed oil on the surface of the rubber will act as a lubricant) and recharged when necessary. When a smooth, even finish has been built up, the surface must be 'spirited off' after two day's drying time. Make a new rubber, and just dampen it with methylated spirit. This is rubbed lightly along the grain to remove the linseed oil and rubber marks until a fine finish has been achieved. French polish can also be applied by brush.

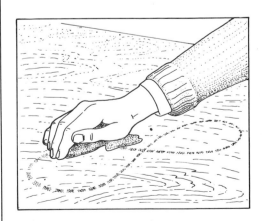

French polish is applied with a rubber, in a figure-of-eight movement.

Painting wood and metal

Gloss paint will hide many faults in the work surface or give a brand new look to a piece covered with unsightly old paint. Paint can do a lot – but you should not use it unless there are valid reasons for not simply applying a protective coating (page 234) to the wood surface. Painting techniques for metal are basically the same as those used on wood.

Paints for home use

Oil-based emulsions and glosses which had vegetable oils (like linseed) as a binding agent, are no longer in use in this plastic age. Three main types of paint are useful for home use:

Oil-type paint with synthetic resins (alkyds) as a binding agent and a highly volatile solvent, can be used on both wood and metal, for walls and similar surfaces. It is available in different finishes, matt, silk finish and high gloss. Apply it in several coats: priming with wood primer, painting with undercoat then two coats of topcoat. After the undercoat it should be filled and sanded.

There are also one-coat paints for household use, which cover well and are quick drying. These thick (thixotropic) paints are smooth, non-drip and will not run on an upright surface.

Acrylic paint also consists of a plastic, not in this case dissolved in a solvent, but broken down into very fine particles contained in water. Consequently it can be thinned with water and can be applied to damp surfaces or wood which has not completely dried out (unlike oil-based paint which requires a completely dry surface).

Acrylic paint is suitable for both inside and outside use on wood. It needs no primer – you simply apply more coats of paint until it covers sufficiently. Acrylic paint is also recommended for use on metal, plaster and stone. The paint surface is less smooth than that of oil-based paint which makes it very elastic and permeable to steam. As a result patches of paint should not fall away. When it needs a new coat of paint no preparation is needed, all you have to do is repaint it.

Cellulose paint has nitrocellulose (a converted natural substance) as a binder and a highly volatile solvent. It dries very quickly and can be used equally well for spraying or painting. It should not be applied on top of old oil-based paint.

On the other hand you can apply oil paint to an undercoat of cellulose paint. It is used mainly as a sealer to insulate absorbent surfaces. It is used chiefly for metal but also for wood and plaster.

Brushes and rollers

Do not begin painting until the surface has been thoroughly prepared. It must be free from dirt, rust, damp and grease.

Brushes: The bristles should never be used horizontally but at an angle to the surface. Dip the brush into the paint so that it covers only one quarter of the length of the bristles and wipe off excess paint on the edge of the tin. First paint all the corners, edges and parts which are difficult to reach, then go on to the flat surfaces.

Any runs or drips should be removed with a clean brush. Do not paint them in with a full brush – this will give too thick

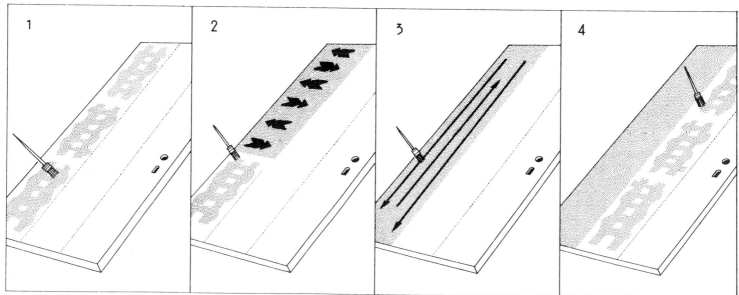

When painting a door, it is a good idea to work in stages: (1) Roughly divide the door into three from top to bottom with two brush strokes. (2) Paint one stripe using crossways strokes and working from top to bottom; overlap brush strokes by about 1 inch (25 millimetres). (3) Smooth over the whole area working from top to bottom. (4) Treat the other stripes in the same way, overlapping with the completed stripe by about 1 inch (25 millimetres). Stand the door upright until dry. Sand down lightly before adding a second coat of paint.

an application of paint. When painting large areas begin bottom left.

Rollers: Do not use a lamb-skin roller for paint but a short-pile synthetic roller. It is used in the same way as the lamb-skin roller (page 240). Any corners that the roller will not reach can be filled in with a brush. The paint must be poured into a large, flat container before use.

Repainting wood
Surfaces covered with old paint must be thoroughly prepared. There are three possible ways of dealing with this depending on the state of the old paintwork.

Undamaged: Wash down the paint with liquid ammonia solution, rinse and allow to dry, lightly sand, apply one or two coats of gloss.

Damaged: Remove any loose paint, wash down with liquid ammonia solution and sand down. Cover any bare wood with wood primer and fill if necessary, then apply undercoat. If necessary sand down again thoroughly. Apply two or three coats of oil or acrylic paint.

Badly damaged: Strip old paintwork (see page 239) to the bare wood. If a caustic stripper is used wash the surface thoroughly and allow to dry. This is unnecessary with solvent strippers (clean down with white spirit). Sand thoroughly, apply wood primer, fill and sand again. Undercoat, sand and fill again, apply two coats of oil or three of acrylic paint (as for new wood).

Painting radiators
Radiator paint must be specially durable to withstand high temperatures and changes in temperature without flaking off, softening or quickly yellowing. With new radiators remove any rust with a wire brush and sandpaper and treat any grease with a degreasing agent. Then prime with an anti-rust primer and apply two coats of paint. Heating pipes are treated in the same way. Any brass fittings should not be painted. Usually radiators leave the maker ready primed.

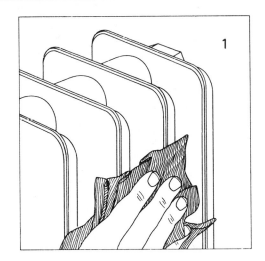

If the radiator paint is sound there is no need to remove it. Wash the radiator with liquid ammonia solution, rinse with water and allow it to dry.

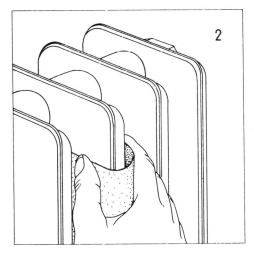

Then rub down the radiator with sandpaper – the inner surfaces too. This will roughen the old paint so that the new paint will take better. Clean away any dust.

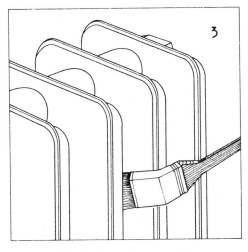

For painting use a brush with a bent head. The radiator will generally need two coats of paint.

Painting with spray cans and guns

The basic principle of paint spraying is quite simple: the paint is pressurized and pushed through a nozzle. It is sprayed in tiny droplets which are blown onto the painting surface where they combine into a film of paint.

There are two techniques: sprays cans and spray guns. In the can pressurized gas provides the necessary pressure. In the spray gun this is provided by a pump. Both methods can be used for household painting jobs. A spray can is suitable for occasional use but it is only worth buying a spray gun if you often want to paint large areas.

Painting or spraying

The range of spray paints is increasing all the time. For the handiman there are on the one hand special oil paints, and on the other a large range of colours in spray paint for cars. We can ask the same questions of both. Does spray paint really make the work easier? And is it worth its higher price compared to ordinary paint?

You cannot buy a can of paint and then cheerfully start spraying at once. When you have mastered the first principles of spraying (see below) you can in fact work more easily and also get better results than with ordinary paint.

Certainly ordinary paint is more economical, but it cannot be stored very long. Paint left over in a tin forms a skin which cannot be stirred into the paint but must be removed, thereby causing considerable waste. This will not happen with spray paint. It will always remain fresh in the spray can. For ordinary painting you will need a brush which has to be cleaned with brush cleaner or a solvent. If you do not do this the brush will be unfit for use. If you are to compare prices accurately you must also include the cost of the brush, cleaner and solvent. But spray paint also has disadvantages. Firstly, in spraying, a substantial quantity of paint is lost. It lands on the floor or on the masking around the work surface. The work surface must be prepared more thoroughly than with ordinary paint for spray paint is more fluid and does not always cover irregularities. Also you cannot mix spray paints but must take

238

the colours available (which is why the colour choice for spray paints has become so great).

Preparations for spraying

The painting surface itself is prepared in the same way as for ordinary painting. New wood is sanded, undercoated, filled and sanded again. Old paint in good condition should be washed down with liquid ammonia solution and rubbed down with fine sandpaper. Damaged paint should be removed where it is flaking – these spots must be primed and undercoated and thoroughly sanded. Undamaged places are treated as for paint in good condition. Badly damaged paint should be stripped – see diagrams on the right-hand page. Now for the preparations for spraying:

Buying the paint: It is annoying to have to break off painting because the paint runs out. Later the paint surface will show where you began again. So it is better to buy one can too many.

Cleanliness: Spray paint is quite quick-drying, so there is not much time for dust to settle on the surface. Nevertheless you should choose a place to work that is free from draughts. Rough cement floors (in the cellar, for example) should be sprinkled with water before you start work so that your movements when spraying do not stir up dust.

Masking: Floors, walls, furniture and other fittings which are not to be sprayed should be well covered with newspaper or sheets of plastic before you begin work. These covers should be held together with adhesive tape.

Spraying chamber: For small pieces of work it is worth making a chamber from a large cardboard box or brown paper box. The work is hung in the box and rotated so that you can easily paint each side of it.

Masks: Buy a mask with renewable filters from the chemist to prevent your nostrils becoming quickly coated with

paint (through inhaling particles of paint). For spraying jobs that will take quite a long time, you should also cover your hair.

Rules for spraying

Don't set about your spraying wildly but follow these rules:

Shaking the can: Always follow the maker's instructions which recommend thoroughly shaking the can before use – this applies particularly to cans which have been standing in one place for a long time.

Work at a distance: Never hold the spray can nearer than 10 inches (250 millimetres) from the painting surface, otherwise the paint will produce an orange peel effect. Don't hold it more than 15 inches (350 millimetres) away or part of the paint will land where you didn't intend it to. Hold the can perpendicular to the painting surface.

Thin coats: Do not apply the paint thickly all at one go or it will run. Move the can in a zig-zag to and fro over the surface, depressing the knob a few inches from the surface and releasing it a few inches further away. Do not lean on the painted surface!

Cleaning the nozzle: After spraying turn the can upside down and press down the knob for a moment. Only gas will come through which will blow the nozzle clean.

Working with a spray gun

Professionals (in a car paintshop, for example) work with an air-pressure spray gun. These are too expensive for household use so it is better to ask for an air-free spray gun which is used without a compressor. A small high-pressure piston pump sucks up the paint and sprays it in droplets through a nozzle which can be adjusted as required (for a wider or narrower jet).

Normal paint must be thinned with the appropriate solvent. You can test the consistency with a testing beaker (viscosimeter). Paint which is too thick will either not spray at all or spray too thickly. If it is too thin it won't cover the surface properly, and will also tend to run on upright surfaces.

The gun should not be swung about in a carefree manner, but moved to and fro at a constant distance from the painting surface (6 to 12 inches [150 to 300 millimetres] depending on the nozzle). The same instructions apply as for the spray can.

Stripping damaged paint

You should not apply any kind of paint, including spray paint, on top of damaged paint. The new coat of paint will not hold. In this case the old paint must be stripped completely.

One can distinguish between strippers (paste strippers) with an alkaline base and stripping fluids with a solvent base. In both cases they are applied to the surface that is to be stripped. After allowing a few minutes for it to take effect (the exact time will depend on the thickness and state of the old paint – note the manufacturer's instructions!), the old paint can be removed with a scraper. In some cases, where the paint is particularly old and thick, you may have to repeat the procedure several times for it to have any effect.

Alkaline strippers have the disadvantages of poor results with polyurethane paint, of discolouring the wood and needing rinsing with water after use – the diagrams on the right explain what to do step by step. For less demanding jobs, for example if the surface is to be repainted, an alkaline stripper will be good enough.

Stripping fluids with a solvent base are simpler and cleaner to use. They should not be rinsed down with water, but can be worked on again as soon as the solvent has evaporated. It can if you wish be wiped over with white spirit (recommended if you want first-class results). Old paint which is in a reasonably good condition need not be stripped, it is sufficient just to wash it down with a liquid ammonia solution and then sand down.

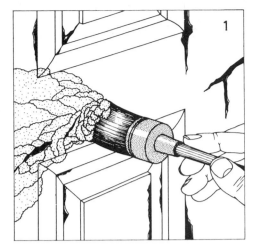

Alkaline base stripper (paste stripper) is applied to the damaged paint with an old brush and left to work on it according to the manufacturer's instructions.

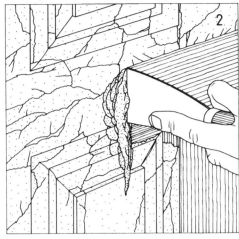

After a few minutes (depending on the thickness and condition of the paint) you can remove the old paint with a scraper. Sometimes a second coat of stripper is necessary.

When all the old paint has been removed, wash down the wood several times with warm water. Then leave to dry overnight.

It is easiest to rub down flat surfaces with sandpaper wrapped around a hard foam block. For crevices and corners it is best to hold the folded sandpaper between your fingers.

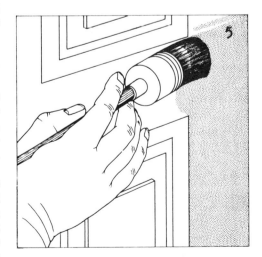

As with new wood the surface is coated with wood primer and then with undercoat. Any holes can be previously filled with plastic wood.

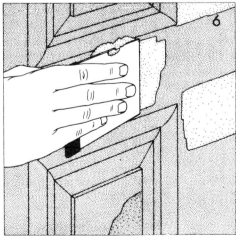

After the undercoat, cracks and uneven patches can be evened out with paint filler. After sanding down once more the surface is given two coats of paint.

Painting walls and ceilings

Walls and ceilings used to be distempered, usually with lime-based distemper and less often with chalk-based. Nowadays a washable emulsion paint is almost always used and is applied with a lambskin roller.

What is emulsion paint?

The binding agent is a plastic in a fine, stable and even distribution in water (emulsion or suspension). After use the water evaporates leaving a continuous yet breathing film of plastic on the wall or ceiling. Consequently emulsion paint can be thinned with water (or wiped up with a damp cloth), but when dry it is no longer soluble in water. Splashes and spots can only be removed with a nitric solution or emulsion remover.

You can paint over emulsion paint again and again, so it is suitable for rooms which get a lot of use and which have to be redecorated regularly, for kitchens, bathrooms, halls and stairs, for example.

Unlike distemper, it is not possible to prepare this paint yourself. Emulsion paint is sold in cans and can be thinned if necessary – according to the instructions. Since there is a great number of special mixtures, state the exact purpose for which it will be used when you buy it. The shop will have a colour chart to help you choose the correct shade.

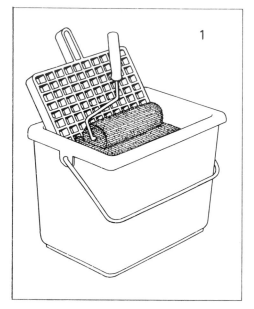

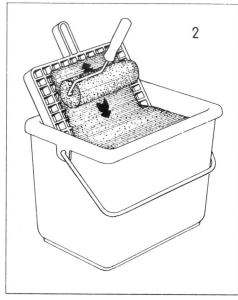

Nowadays a lamb-skin roller is used for painting walls and ceilings. Dip it carefully in the paint so that it is covered completely (1). Then roll it up and down the grille a few times to spread the paint evenly (2) – otherwise you will get blotches on the wall.

The technique for painting with a roller: First roll in a long sweep from bottom to top – with an even, not too firm pressure (1). Spread the paint on the wall zig-zagging the roller across it (2). Do not tackle too large an area at one go. Finally smooth out the paint with long, even strokes from top to bottom (3). The whole area should now be evenly covered.

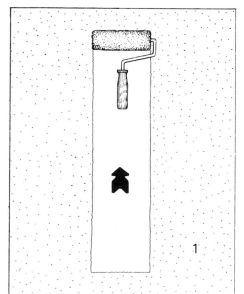

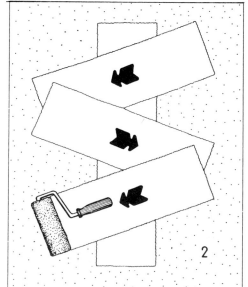

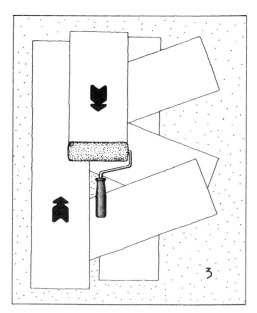

Preparing the surface

You can paint over old emulsion paint or chalk distemper without any problems. Old lime distemper or wipeable, but not washable, emulsion paint must be completely washed off, otherwise the emulsion paint will not hold. Firmly fixed wallpapers can also be used as a base for emulsion paint. Damaged or loose paper should be removed so that you can paint directly onto the wall.

Any damaged sections of the wall (cracks, holes, crumbling plaster) should be filled. You will find instructions on dealing with larger cracks on page 251. Very absorbent plaster must be primed – you can get special primers for this. Any spots of rust or grease must be covered to prevent them showing through later. Your paint shop will have the necessary covering material. Only when the wall is perfectly smooth and even can you begin painting. If you want to test the state of the wall hold a strong light at a sharp angle to the wall. This will show up any irregularities.

Using a lamb-skin roller

Lamb-skin rollers have the great advantage that if used correctly they will not splash (unlike old-fashioned ceiling brushes). Using it correctly means: After dipping the roller in the paint, roll it thoroughly to and fro on the grille which goes with it, so that it is evenly coated with paint. Do not coat the roller in too much paint, otherwise the surface will not be smooth. When rolling ceilings or walls do not work too fast, but take your time.

The lamb-skin roller gives a surface which is slightly rough in appearance rather than absolutely smooth. Most rollers are 10 inches (250 millimetres) wide, although small edging rollers are available.

The diagrams below left show how the paint is applied: First the roller is dipped in the paint, then rolled up and down on the wall. This leaves a thick coat of paint which you spread by zig-zagging to and fro. Finally use long, even strokes up and down to give a good covering film of paint. Using a roller leaves no sign of where you began work or of brush marks. Use a brush only to paint areas which the roller cannot reach.

Begin with the ceiling

It is advisable to paint the ceiling first. This will avoid splashing a finished wall. Apply the paint first towards the light, then spread crossways and finally roll again towards the light.

It is best to paint in stages, covering an area of about 4 square feet (½ square metre) at a time. This will make your work easier and safer for you will not have to stretch so far. It will also avoid rolling the paint out too thinly.

If you paint the edges in advance with a brush, don't paint only the edges of the ceiling; do the edges of the walls as well. After the ceiling it is the turn of the walls. Here too do not cover too large an area at a time. Work basically from top to bottom.

Emulsion paint usually gives such a good cover that one coat will be enough. If a second coat is necessary – on new walls, for example – thin the paint slightly for the undercoat.

Special emulsion paint can also be used on exterior frontages, on asbestos cement or concrete. Do not use ceiling and wall paint.

Highly resilient paints

If your walls are painted with normal emulsion paint (which can be washed when necessary) you will need no other paint. Only ceramic or plastic tiles are more hard-wearing. If individual surfaces only are to be washable (or if you want to gloss the whole room when decorating) there are several other possibilities:

Emulsion paint on bare plaster: Clean any dusty walls with a brush, thin exterior emulsion paint with 20% water and use to undercoat, cover with high-gloss emulsion paint (with roller).

Emulsion paint on oil-based paint: Wash down old paintwork with liquid ammonia solution. Apply one or two coats high-gloss emulsion paint (if using two coats, the undercoat should be thinned). Use a wide brush.

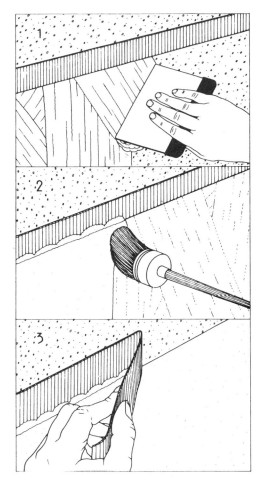

Walls which get rough treatment should be gloss painted. Mark the height of the wall base with a strip of masking tape, fill and sand to give a smooth painting surface (1). Coat with primer and then paint (2). Remove the tape before the wall dries (3) or it will damage the paint.

Oil paint on bare plaster: Prime (with priming oil) and fill all surfaces and when dry sand thoroughly. Prime large areas of filler. Apply paint.

Giving a paint edge: This can be done, if you want it, with masking tape (diagram above). The tape must be removed before the paint is completely dry, otherwise part of the paint surfaces will be pulled away with it. You can also use a piece of flat beading to make an edge which is removed when you have finished.

241

Preparing for wallpapering

Walls and ceilings need redecorating every four years at least – by then they will have a very lived-in appearance. We begin here by discussing the highly important preparatory work and the wallpapering of ceilings. Points to watch when papering walls are included in the two following pages.

Preparing ceiling and walls

Papering is similar to painting, in so far as a papered surface can never be better than the work surface allows. Here are the various possibilities:

New walls: Newly plastered walls may have to be left for six months before papering, depending on the plaster. Any cracks or holes should be filled and the surface sized.

Painted walls: Old lime distemper must be washed off, emulsion paint must be sized – in both cases the walls should be sized before papering.

Papered walls: You can paper on top of old wallpaper if it is firm to the wall but you should sand down the joins (where the separate pieces of wallpaper overlap). Damaged or loose paper must be stripped, using warm soapy water and a scraper.

It is easier if you use wallpaper stripper – after application the old wallpaper can be conveniently pulled off in strips. Level out any cracks or holes in walls or ceiling with filler. Sand when dry. For large-scale damage to plaster see page 251.

Hints on buying paper

Once you have established what kind of paper you want (plain, patterned, quality) don't immediately set off to the wallpaper shop without reckoning how much you will need. This is based on the perimeter of the room (= sum of the lengths of each wall, including chimney breasts and alcoves) and the height of the room. For example: For a room with a floor area of 12 by 15 feet (4 by 5 metres), the perimeter is 54 feet (18 metres). Rolls of wallpaper are around 21 inches (500

242

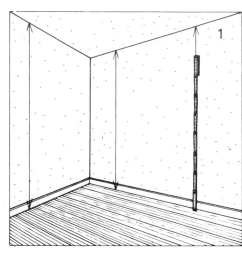

(1) **Don't cut the paper exactly until it's on the wall. When getting the widths ready measure the wall height in several places to ascertain the height measurement.**

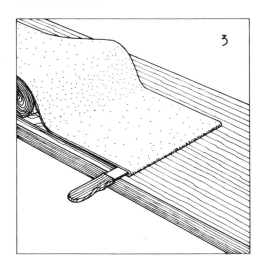

(3) **Lie the widths of paper exactly together – a pasting table is the best place for this. Turn the paper back and fold it along the marked line.**

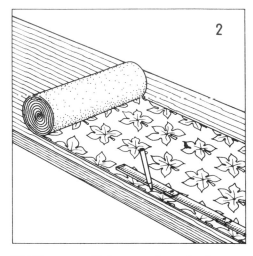

(2) **Measure off the same length of wallpaper as the wall height with an additional 6 inches (150 millimetres) or so. With patterned papers you will have to match it up.**

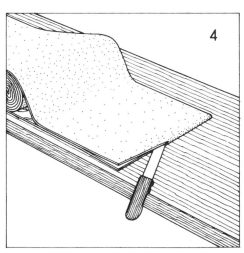

(4) **Cut the wallpaper along the fold line with a knife. The next strip of wallpaper is cut the same way. Place the strips one on top of the other, reverse side up, ready for pasting.**

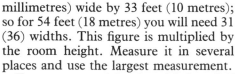

millimetres) wide by 33 feet (10 metres); so for 54 feet (18 metres) you will need 31 (36) widths. This figure is multiplied by the room height. Measure it in several places and use the largest measurement.

For an assumed height of 8 feet (2.5 metres) you will need widths of paper with a total length of 31 by 8 (36 × 2.50)

= 248 feet (90 metres). Subtract from this door and window areas. Add 10% of the total length to allow for cutting and corrections. Let us assume that the amount deducted for windows and that added on for cutting are the same, then you will still need 248 feet (90 metres) total length.

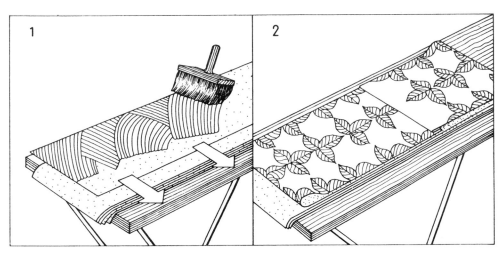

When you have cut all the widths of paper begin pasting. Depending on your work rate always paste three to five widths at one go. Take care that no paste gets on to the front of the paper. Fold each sheet when pasted with a narrow fold at the top and a wide one at the bottom. Then fold both these folds together. Leave the paste to soak in for a few minutes.

This number now has to be divided by the length of the roll. Normal rolls of wallpaper are about 33 feet (10 metres) long so divide 248 by 33 (90 by 10) = 8 (9) rolls of paper must be bought. This calculation is valid only for plain or small-patterned papers. Papers with large patterns need more adding on to allow for matching. The paper must be laid so that the pattern continues from one width to another. Therefore you can't simply cut width from the roll without taking the repetition of the pattern into account. Depending on the height of the wall this will mean that you are wasting more paper than usual and this must be allowed for in your calculations.

Wallpapering equipment

Basically you can manage with a few tables placed side by side, scissors, paste-brush (ceiling brush) and an old clothes brush for brushing down each width of paper. With the 'correct' tools the work will be easier. If you don't want to buy them you can perhaps hire them from a hire shop or even borrow from friends. These include:

Pasting table about 6 feet (3 metres) long and up to 24 inches (600 millimetres) wide, and 30 inches (800 millimetres) in height (so that you can work sitting down), preferably one which folds away.

Paste brush for pasting the lengths of wallpaper, also a plastic bucket to hold the paste (not a metal container!).

Papering brush, a brush which isn't too hard for smoothing on the paper.

Edge roller, a small hardwood roller used to roll the paper flat where the edges butt together.

Stepladder to stand on when papering walls and ceilings, or better still two low pairs of steps with a strong plank placed across them.

Other tools include 12-inch (300-millimetres) scissors for trimming, pencil to mark hanging lines, screwdriver for taking down plugs and switches.

Do-it-yourself wallpapers are almost exclusively sold ready for use nowadays, that is, with the edges already cut. With old wallpapers the plain edges (selvedge edge) had to be trimmed off.

The diagram on the left shows how to cut the paper, the two diagrams on the left show how to paste and fold it.

Papering the ceiling

Begin work by papering the ceiling (provided this is not going to be merely painted). The paste must be put on thicker than when papering walls for it has to support the weight of the paper. After pasting fold the paper in a concertina fashion and allow it to soak. It is best to have someone to help you – the extended broom used as a prop will help if necessary. The joins should run towards the light.

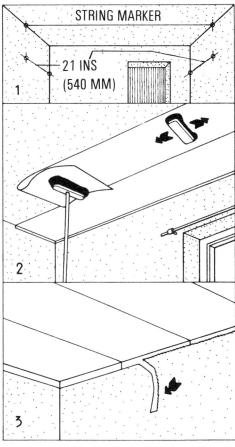

When papering the ceiling mark the starting line for the first width of paper with a string (1). If you have no one to help you an extended broom can be used to support the paper (2). The edges which overlap onto the wall should be trimmed off (3) – this will give a better join with the paper on the wall.

Wallpapering

The walls are prepared, dry and smooth, and you have bought the correct amount of wallpaper and cut it to room height. It is ideal papering weather: about 18°C with humidity as high as possible – hothouse weather. Don't do your wall-papering in the height of summer when it is very hot – and in winter don't overheat the room you are going to paper, otherwise the paper won't go on flat. If it dries too quickly it may split and bubble.

Preparation

Place the cut paper face down and neatly stacked on the pasting table. The paste has been made in accordance with the manufacturer's instructions and has stood for the recommended time. Before you can begin pasting you must decide on the position of the first piece. Although the walls are even remember that the corners may not be exactly perpendicular. So never begin papering in a corner, but about half a width away from it. Establish the position of the starting line with a plumb line (a piece of string with a heavy nail tied to it will do) or use a spirit-level. Basically you should work from the window outwards, so put the first piece up near the window. In this way the light will shine into the seams and completely illuminate them. Normally the paper should go onto the wall the same way that it comes off the roll. So the first piece from the roll should always go at the bottom, near the skirting board. Experts prefer to alternate plain papers, that is they turn every other piece around and stick it with the bottom edge at the top. This gives a more even colour.

The diagram top left on the previous page shows how to paste the paper. In general you paste the furthest half on the stack of paper, then pull the sheet to-wards you and paste the nearest half. Now fold over paste to paste a hands-width strip, the hand grip, at the bottom end. Fold the top end over a good quarter of the length of the sheet. Then fold the sheet over again so that the hand grip overlaps the edge of the top fold. Leave the pasted, folded sheet to soak for a time. While it is doing so stretch the paper a little to give a smooth surface later. While drying it will retract again.

It is impossible to give an exact time for soaking. It depends on the weight of the paper and the thickness of the paste. After soaking, the paper should feel evenly soft and supple.

It is usual to paste three or more sheets and then begin by putting up the first sheet which by now should be well soaked.

If you don't put the paper up as quickly as you estimated the pasted sheets can become too soft which will lead to tearing. So in the beginning at least don't be too ambitious.

Technique of papering

To paper the wall pick up the soaked sheet carefully and first unfold the top. Then climb onto your steps or platform, hold the paper against the wall and straighten it up; top edge to the ceiling corner, side edge along the plumb line. If both lines match, carefully press down the top edge first and then (where un-folded) the middle of the sheet. If the paper is not quite straight the paste will allow you to slide it gently into position. When the top half is in place unfold the lower fold and stick down the same way.

The diagrams on the right-hand page show how in general you should handle the bottom edge. However, if you have detachable skirting boards take the paper as far as the floor and finally put the skirting board back. Finally you should smooth the whole width with a brush or roller and smooth the seams with a seam roller.

Wallpaper repairs: A piece of left-over paper is placed on the wall and covered with a cardboard stencil. Cut around its edges through both old and new paper at one go.

Now you can carefully remove the damaged paper – it is best to use a knife or scraper. Clean any bits of wallpaper or paste away with the scraper from the wall surface.

Paste the patch, place it carefully and press down so that it fits exactly. Repairs of this kind are only worthwhile if the paper has not faded, otherwise the patch will be particularly obvious.

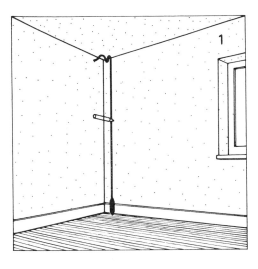

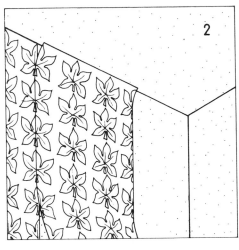

(1) Walls are not always straight so never begin papering in a corner. Begin slightly away from a corner determining the starting line for the first width with a plumb line.

(2) Hold the width of wallpaper in front of the wall and position it exactly along the top and side edge. Then press it down. You will need particular care with patterned papers.

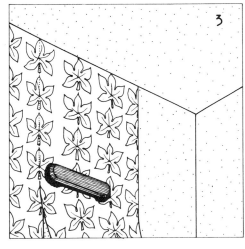

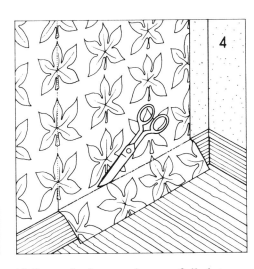

(3) Now you can smooth down the piece with a brush or roller working from top to bottom. It should be completely smooth with no bubbles.

(4) Press the lower edge carefully into the skirting board with scissors, taking care not to damage or rip the soft paper.

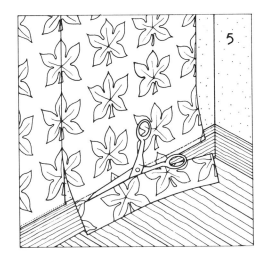

(5) The paper should overlap the skirting board slightly. Cut off the strip near the mark with the scissors.

(6) When the whole strip is firmly on the wall you must deal with the seam. This is done with a seam roller with which you press down the whole length of the seam.

Minor problems

Most problems arise when some obstacle has to be bypassed. These can be overcome:

Pipes: You can cover them with odd bits of paper if they are firmly embedded against the wall, and put up complete sheets on either side of them. Pipes which stand away from the wall should be painted in a colour that matches the paper.

Switches and plugs: Remove covers before papering, while remembering to take out the fuses first. Paper over the area then simply press your finger over the installation point and carefully tear out a small circle. You can put covers back later.

Corners: Never try to take a complete sheet round a corner, overlap the corner by ½ or 1 inch (15 or 25 millimetres) at the most and start the next sheet in the corner. Otherwise you will have problems in matching.

Light fittings: With patterned papers you will have to cut the paper exactly. With woodchip and other plain papers you can cut a spare piece of paper the size of your palm so that it fits exactly and stick it on. When applying the whole sheet around the light an approximate cut will do.

Holes in the paper

The simplest way to deal with this is merely to hang a picture or stand a cupboard in front of the hole. Since this is not always possible you may have to patch it. This is only worthwhile if the paper is unfaded and is still the same colour as the other pieces which you have carefully stored away.

With woodchip paper a piece that is the size of the hole will do. Tear the edges carefully. The diagrams on the far left show how to deal with patterned wallpaper. If you want to get really good results you will of course have to stick on a whole new sheet or even repaper the whole wall.

Covering and upholstering furniture

From the day upholsterers began using foam to make furniture softer and more comfortable, upholstering has become much simpler. Foam can generally be used with no difficulty if you know a few tricks, and covering it with fabric is no problem for anybody who is good with a needle.

Foam for upholstering

One must distinguish between rubber and plastic foam, but both are suitable for household upholstering. You can buy ready-cut pieces of the required thickness and quality in do-it-yourself shops, foam shops or by mail order. The main characteristics of the two different types of foam are:

Latex foam (foam rubber): Made from natural rubber sap (latex). Available in sizes up to mattress size and in thickness from ½ inch (10 millimetres) upwards. Thicker foam has a smooth top surface and on the underside has tube-shaped recesses. Soft and medium soft foam is mainly recommended for upholstering (see also page 154). Latex foam is not resilient to oil, petrol or light and so should always be covered. Use rubber glue or cement (puncture-repair kit glue) or even all-purpose glue to stick it.

Polyurethane foam (plastic, polyether foam): Available in sizes up to mattress size and in thicknesses from ¼ inch (5 millimetres) upwards. Resilient to oil, petrol and light but should nevertheless be covered to avoid discolouration and tearing. Use plastic glue or all-purpose glue to stick it.

Nowadays foam mattresses often use combinations of foam in varying grades of softness (stuck together).

Working with foam

Apart from the choice of adhesive the basic principles are the same for both kinds of foam. You can cut foam easily with damp scissors up to a thickness of about 1½ inches (40 millimetres). For thicker pieces use a sharp carving knife or a special foam knife (see diagram below). Knives too will cut better when damp. The knife should be moved gently through the foam without pressure.

If the piece of foam is not large enough for the work you have in mind you can stick on a second piece of the same thickness and material. When gluing cover both edges completely with adhesive, leave it to dry slightly so that it no longer sticks to your finger when you touch it and then press the two pieces together with a light pressure. If the foam edges contain recesses stick a thin piece around them to give a smooth edge. It is also possible, but not particularly necessary for normal use, to strengthen joins with a textile or plastic adhesive strip.

Mattresses and loose cushions for chairs, stools, benches and complete landscaped seating schemes (if irregular in shape) can be cut to the exact size by use of a paper stencil. You can later use the stencil to cut out the covering fabric. Sew a zip into the cover on two or three sides so that you can remove it for washing or cleaning. For particularly good results cover the foam with widths of upholstery wadding or a sheet of very soft foam before covering.

Upholstering a chair or stool

The diagrams above right show how it is done. Cut a piece of foam the size of the seat and stick a plastic adhesive strip around the edges. Then place the cover over it and tensioning it nail it down. If you want to take a little more trouble with your work, there is a better way: When you have cut out the cover, fasten it to the work table with drawing pins. Stick the foam firmly to the seat of the chair or stool with adhesive tape.

Then place the cushioned stool or chair on the spread-out covering material and

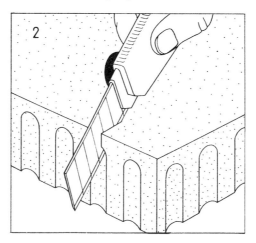

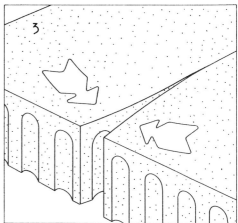

(1) **Thin pieces of foam can be cut with scissors – it is best to damp them. Before cutting draw a line with a marker pen. Be careful to cut absolutely perpendicular!**

(2) **Thicker foam is cut with a sharp knife – the sharper the better. With the cutting tool in the diagram you merely break off part of the blade when it has become blunt.**

(3) **Foam upholstery material is easy to glue. Cover the edges with the appropriate glue and simply press them together. In this way you can use up any small left-over pieces.**

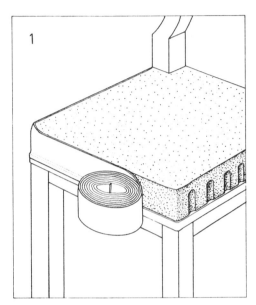

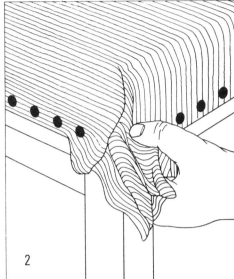

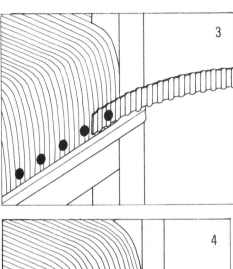

(1) **Foam upholstery:** Cut the foam to size and place on the chair. Fix it at the edges with a wide strip of adhesive.
(2) **Place the covering material over it and nail it to the chair frame with small upholstery tacks. Fold the corners under and nail them carefully.**

(3) **You can use tacks which will be visible, but you could also cover the nails with braid. Nail the end of the braid firmly into a corner.**
(4) **Then turn the braid back and glue it neatly. The end should be at the back of the chair where it should be nailed.**

press it down so that the foam is compressed into half its thickness (use screw clamps for this). Now you should fold in the covering material and nail it in place. When you take off the clamps the covering material will be tensioned and will fit smoothly.

New cover for an armchair

Remove the old cover carefully and use it as a guide so that you can cut out the new cover correctly. Recovering begins with the cover for the seat (diagrams left). This can be either tacked to the lining material or nailed to the wooden chair frame.

Generally piping is used between the sides and top of the seat cover – this looks better but above all will be stronger. Sew the side pieces to the top with a curved upholstery needle, the underside should be sewn or turned under and nailed (according to the construction of the chair). Treat the back and arm rests similarly.

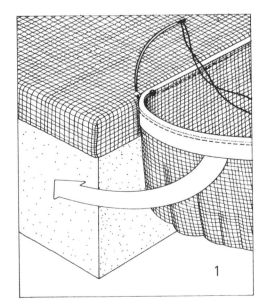

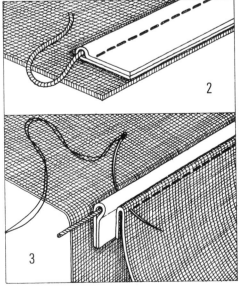

When re-covering armchairs begin with the seat cover. Then sew the side sections to this with piping between them. The piping usually consists of upholstery fabric in a different colour.

A thick piece of wool or a piece of string is then threaded through the fold (2). It is simplest to use a curved needle for upholstery when sewing all the sections together (3).

247

Adjusting doors and windows

Windows and doors are in constant motion and anything that moves will become worn. Thus it follows that windows and doors should be treated carefully. However, it is not particularly difficult to fit a normal windowpane, nor is draught-proofing (see page 82). With doors, with the exception of redecorating, you should confine yourself to regular oiling and occasional adjustments to the catch plate if the door won't close properly.

Using a glass cutter

Professionals work with a diamond-cutter – a basic glass-cutter with a tempered steel wheel is sufficient for household use. The pane of glass that you want to cut should be placed on an even surface which is not too hard (cover the work bench with thick cardboard). If it is not absolutely flat the pressure of cutting may split it.

Hold the glass-cutter perpendicular to the cutting edge but at a slight angle to the glass. When determining the cutting edge bear in mind that the glass-cutter won't cut directly along the edge but a little way away from it. It is best to try it out first on a spare piece of glass. Run the glass-cutter across the glass with one continuous stroke, applying sufficient pressure to score the glass with an even grinding noise. Don't press too hard on the glass at the start and end of the cutting line otherwise bits of the glass could break away.

Finally break the pane along the cutting line. If you tap along the back of the cutting line with the glass-cutter or a hammer, this will make the cut deeper. You should then have no difficulty in breaking the glass cleanly over a sharp edge. Sometimes you will be able to make the break just by tapping it lightly with a hammer.

Often you will not be able to break a narrow strip of glass off cleanly. This should be dealt with using the notch on the glass-cutter. If necessary you will have to break away the strip piece by piece. The diagram below shows what this involves.

Fitting a window pane

To fit a window pane begin by removing the window casement. Lay it on the work bench or across two trestles and first remove the glass, nails and putty. Wear a pair of old gloves to avoid cutting yourself on the glass. Any stubborn bits of putty will need an old chisel or scraper. Rub down with sandpaper. If the paintwork needs renewing the putty rebate should be reprimed. Don't paint the window frame until you have reglazed and the putty has hardened.

The new pane of glass should not fit too tightly or it could soon break. Cut it so as to allow a space of about $1/16$ inch (2 millimetres) all round it. If you have the

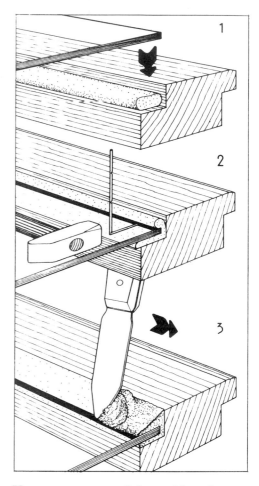

How to cut panes of glass with a glass-cutter (below): Position the cutter perpendicular to the cutting edge (1). Gently tap the cut on the back (2) and break the glass over a straight edge (3). Narrow strips are broken off piece by piece with the glass-cutter.

Putting in a window pane with putty (above). Line the rebate with putty and carefully press the new pane down (1). Then knock in glazing nails at intervals of 6 inches (2). Putty the corner between the glass and the frame and use a putty knife to get it smooth and even (3).

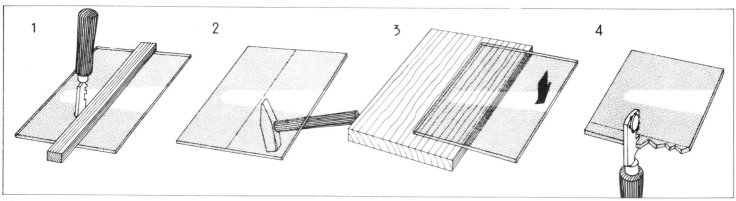

glass cut by a glazier give him the exact measurement of the opening – he will allow for space.

Before using the putty, knead it together to even out its texture and get rid of any lumps. If it is too oily spread it out on some newspaper to draw out some oil, or add a little linseed oil if it is too dry.

Now lay a layer of putty around the whole rebate. Work the putty into rolls the thickness of a pencil, place in the rebate and press down gently. Now place the window onto it and press down firmly until it rests on a bed of putty about 1/16 inch (2 millimetres) thick. The putty which is squeezed through to the underside is later scraped away with a putty knife.

The next stage is to knock in headless nails called sprigs. Do not use nails with heads instead. Now fill the angle between the glass and the putty groove with putty. Use a putty knife to get an even, sloping surface. Finally you can powder the window with whitening to remove traces of putty from the glass with a ball of putty.

Glass panes in doors (see page 212) can also be fixed into a thin layer of putty but where this is done, it is important that they are then surrounded by beading.

Panes of insulating glass (double glazing), on the other hand, are housed in special units – this is best done by a specialist.

Adjusting the door

A normal lock for an interior door should fulfil two functions:

Holding the door fast: This is done by means of a catch, which is moved by turning the door handle. It keeps the door closed and protects from the wind, but it provides no security as it can be easily opened and closed by anybody.

Locking the door: This is provided by the bolt. Since it can only be moved with a key it gives protection against unlawful entry.

The counterpart of the catch and bolt is the catch-plate in the door frame. It should normally be fitted so that when

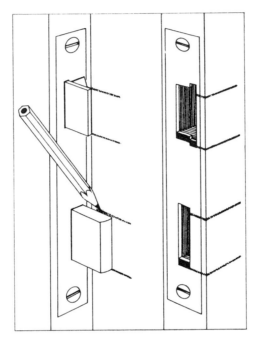

When an interior door has sunk you can lower the catch-plate, or (as illustrated) file it down. With the door pushed to (left), carefully mark where you need to file. It is easier to file if you remove the catch-plate.

the door is locked it can only be dismantled by use of force (by breaking down the door).

If the door will not close properly it could be because the mechanism of the lock needs oiling or greasing so that the latch sticks inside the end-plate of the lock, the shield. If you oil the inside of the keyhole, the catch and bolt, you can quickly cure the problem. Oiling will, however, make no impression on a lock which is generally difficult to move. It must be removed, immersed in diesel oil (heating oil) and then treated with a non-acid grease. It should then work for years with no trouble.

If the door has sunk, which tends to happen mostly with old panelled doors, the only thing you can do is to set the catch-plate lower in the frame, or to file it to fit.

The diagram above shows how it should be filed. First, with the door pushed to, mark the actual position of the

catch and bolt on the door frame and continue the mark onto the catch-plate using a joiner's corner-plate. It is best to remove the plate at this point, normally there will only be two screws to undo, then file the latch and bolt housings removing any obstructing metal as precisely as possible.

Draught-proofing doors

If the door lets in a draught you can stick on strips of foam, but this would only be a temporary measure. Sometimes it is worth repositioning the catch-plate to stop the door rattling in the wind, but you would have to chisel out part of the door frame.

You can also get a draught under the door – this has been very common since we have stopped using door sills. A strip of foam or felt will not be much help here.

Draught-proofers are better. They are screwed on or let into the bottom edge of the door.

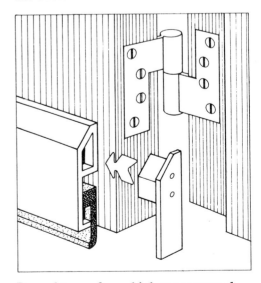

Draught-proofers which are mounted on the door banish under-door draughts. The one illustrated can be fixed in a matter of minutes. The main body of the draught-proofer and its end section can be matched with the floor.

Minor repairs to furniture and walls

Very few people enjoy household repairs, but since you can't call someone in every time a cupboard door sticks, or a drawer squeaks or a crack in the wall needs filling it is better to be your own odd-job man and to do your own wedging, sanding and filling. Not only will it save you time, it is also cheaper.

Repositioning cupboard doors

If you have a cupboard door that sticks persistently (usually found in large wardrobes) it is generally due to careless positioning. Very few floors are exactly even, so furniture will usually need supporting. All you have to do is find out which corner or side needs supporting with a small piece of plywood, wooden wedge, small piece of beading or thin bits of cardboard to allow the necessary movement of the door. Although there are quite a few reasons why doors might stick, the diagrams below show two of the most common cases:

Loose screws in hinges: Screw them in firmly. If this is not possible because the screw holes have become enlarged, fill them with wadding and all-purpose glue (or with wood glue and wood shavings; or dual-surface glue).

Bent hinges: These must be taken off, straightened and refitted (or changed completely).

If the whole wardrobe has gone out of true, perhaps it has been over-filled. If supporting the cupboard won't help all you can do is to plane or sand the doors where they are sticking.

Drawers which stick

Drawers may stick because the wood has become damp. This can be cured by taking them out and leaving them to dry out in a warm, dry place. If they then move freely you have found the cause of the problem. Alternatively, you could move furniture slightly away from the wall or move it to a drier position. If necessary plane or sand the drawers where they stick. Waxing the runners will only provide a temporary solution to the problem.

Sometimes sticking is due to the way the drawer has worn. The drawer itself, the side grooves on which it slides, or the runners become worn in the course of time. To correct this you will have to reinforce them carefully with beading, plywood or strips of plastic laminate. Sometimes drawers stick for the same reason as doors, because the piece of furniture is not positioned quite straight. Then you will need to support it to cure the problem.

Creaking floorboards

Wooden floors are just like wooden staircases (see page 50), when they are old they begin to creak. The wood has dried out over the years and the joints have become loose. The boards rub against one another and on the joists.

It usually does no good to knock the old nails in again with a hammer or even with a nail punch. They can no longer hold the boards fast. You will have to knock in new nails, or (better still) use long screws. The nail- or screwheads should be countersunk.

A radical solution is to completely cover the old floor with chipboard. This not only gets rid of the creaking but also makes a smooth surface for fitted carpet. The chipboard should be nailed or screwed down and should be at least ¾ inch (19 millimetres) thick.

Cracks in stone floors

Cracks in stone floors, in a cellar or utility room say, will get deeper if they are not repaired immediately. Eventually whole pieces of the floor will break away.

Clean out the crack removing any loose material, and any dust. Then thoroughly coat the hole with an adhesive agent. For the filler mix one part cement and three parts fine sand with a little water – it is better that the mortar should be too dry rather than too fluid. Fill the hole with the mortar. Fill small cracks using a scraper, but for larger holes you should use a piece of board. When dry you can rub down the surface with coarse sandpaper.

As soon as possible the floor should be coated with special concrete paint. This will protect the floor and prevent it cracking so easily.

If a cupboard door jams it is almost always due to an uneven floor and to the positioning of the cupboard. If your doors jam like this you need to support the left-hand side.

Here we see the opposite case. The doors will not jam if you support the right-hand side of the cupboard. Use thin plywood or wooden wedges to support it.

Wall and ceiling cracks

These are by no means confined to crumbling old housing, quite the contrary; they are even found in new houses usually when the plaster has not been allowed to dry out long enough. The reason can also often be attributed to seams where construction boards and walls meet. The method of repair (see diagram below) is similar for each.

First thoroughly scrape out the crack with a small chisel, an old screwdriver or a scraper and enlarge it slightly. Then dust it down with a paint brush or the smallest nozzle of the vacuum cleaner.

If you are going to use plaster as a filler you will have to damp the hole thoroughly. This is unnecessary with ordinary cellulose filler. For very deep holes you will have to apply several layers, allowing each to dry before proceeding with the next. The surface of the plaster or filler should be smoothed over with a scraper for small areas and a board or trowel for large. When dry, sand down.

Cracks which continue to break should be covered with strips of gauze. These are covered with filler and will hold firm. When the wall is painted or papered the crack will be invisible. Gauze can also be used to cover cracks between plaster or insulating boards or joins between new partition walls and the original room wall. 'Movable' gaps such as that between the bath and the wall should be filled with an elastic putty.

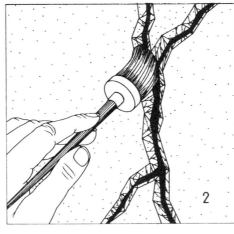

(1) **Cracks in a plastered wall: Scrape away all loose plaster with a chisel or old screwdriver. It can't be stuck back with filler.**

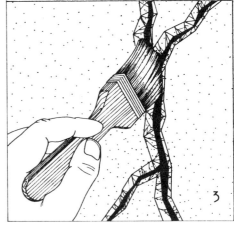

(2) **Thoroughly clean away any grit or dust with a dry brush so that the filler will hold and not break away again.**

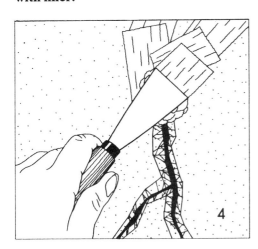

(3) **If you are going to fill with plaster the edges must be thoroughly dampened to give a smooth join. It is unnecessary with ordinary fillers.**

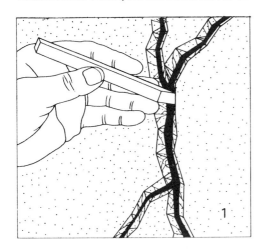

(4) **The hole is filled with plaster mixed according to the instructions or more simply with filler. With very deep holes you will need several layers.**

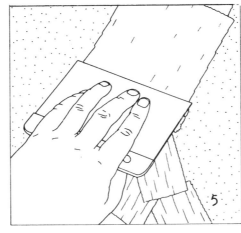

(5) **Smooth the top with a scraper or trowel like a bricklayer's trowel (board with a handle). Dip it in water from time to time during use.**

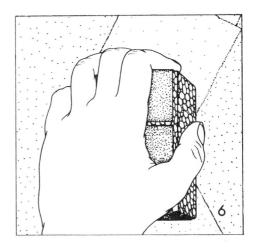

(6) **When the filler is completely dry smooth it down with sandpaper and a sanding block. If it is going to be wallpapered, it should be sized first.**

INDEX